SOCIAL SCIENCE

Table of Contents

vi

Foreword

The purpose of our Committee of the American Bar Association in translating this prize-winning book and putting it into the hands of our high school and college teachers is to give them an effective teaching tool. We do this with a caveat. This social science textbook is a communist document carefully designed to convince all high school students in the Soviet Union that their social and governmental system is the best in the world and bound in the end to triumph over ours. Indeed, a whole chapter is devoted to capitalism and its decline, in which is sketched our certain downfall and the inevitable victory of socialism—of communism.

It is hard for some Americans to realize that every student in the Soviet Union has dinned and drummed into his ears at every stage of his education the scientific superiority of his system over ours. Those responsible for education in the Soviet Union (the Communist Party) are not content to live and let live, to truly coexist in open competition.

The truth of the matter is their system cannot stand open competition and comparison with ours. That is why there is a Berlin Wall and nonexistent free emigration and travel from the Soviet Union. Every time there's a crack in the wall, the people of the "perfect socialist society" vote with their feet and go west.

If we are, as this book describes (See Chapter 3—Imperialism—Capitalism's Final Stage), in our death throes, there are a lot of people on the communist side of the wall who'd like to join us—if they could. There is and would be very little reverse flow. It seems to us, if readers of this book will keep that one fact of life in mind (freedom to leave our society and no freedom to leave the worker's paradise), they will not be misled by the propaganda they read and will have a very good yardstick to compare and contrast our system with theirs.

William C. Mott, *Chairman*

American Bar Association
Standing Committee
on Education About Communism
and Its Contrast With Liberty Under Law

American Bar Association

Standing Committee on Education About Communism

Preface: The Nature of Social Science Teaching in the Soviet Union

Soviet space achievements in the 1950s aroused Western interest in the communist educational system. Caught by surprise, the American public wanted to know what caused the apparent technological superiority that enabled the Soviet Union to launch the first *sputnik*.

Original Western indifference often was replaced by equally uncritical overestimation of Soviet capabilities. Exhaustive studies have been made of Soviet teaching and research in the fields of natural sciences and technology to determine, first, the number of available scientific personnel and, second, the quality and organization of Soviet educational and research institutions.

Uneasy about the Soviet technological thrust, produced and maintained by the immense power of a totalitarian party-state, many have wondered about the motivation of the Soviet effort to overtake and surpass (*dognat'i peregnat'*) and ultimately replace the "capitalist" (free-enterprise) system in a worldwide contest.

One way to clarify the problem of communist motivation—for many in the noncommunist world, still "a riddle wrapped in a mystery inside an enigma"—is to analyze Soviet educational programs in the field of social science.

It has been suggested that it was the German schoolteacher and social-science (history) textbook that conditioned most of the population to accept extreme nationalism and the belief in German racial superiority, leading ultimately to the national socialist, totalitarian form of government. This world outlook (*Weltanschauung*), which produced Hitler's *Mein Kampf*, was not taken seriously enough by non-Germans as well as many Germans, and the consequences are well known.

Admittedly, Nazi and communist world outlooks are vastly different. Their common totalitarian character, however, is reflected in the efforts of both their leaderships to enforce universal acceptance, within their orbit of control, of basic doctrinal tenets about society and its development, and about the nature and role of man in the world. The educational system is serving the USSR, as it served Germany under national socialism, as chief instrument of compulsory indoctrination according to Party policy. The Nazi world-view has become of only historical interest. Governments motivated by the communist world-view, however, at the present time control approximately 26 percent of the world territory and 36 percent of the population.

A great effort is being made by those governments to give the rising generation in their countries a thorough formation in the communist world outlook. A study of the content of this political-ideological education may help to discover the underlying cause of their obviously dynamic behavior.

The USSR serves as the best case for study, for other governments under communist control are generally emulating the Soviet prototype. More than fifty years of communist rule in the Soviet Union has created the most elaborate and efficient educational system of political-ideological indoctrination.

It begins with the social science course for the graduating class of secondary schools, a single, comprehensive course on the fundamentals of the Marxist-Leninist doctrine.

"*Obshchestvovedeniye*," as it is called in the curriculum, was introduced as a separate subject in 1963. (Formerly it was taught as part of a course on the "History and Constitution of the USSR.") In 1961 the XXII Congress of the Communist Party of the Soviet Union (CPSU) approved the new Party program in which "the education of the entire population in the spirit of scientific communism" was stated as one of the most Party important objectives. It was necessary to commission a textbook for the course, the first edition of which appeared in 1963. Seventy hour-long periods per year (two hours weekly) are devoted to it, according to a review article in *Sovetskaya pedagogika* (*Soviet Pedagogy*, February 1963, no. 2, pp. 3-9).

The translation presented here is of the eighth edition, dated 1970.[a]

A comparison of this latest edition with the original reveals, first of all, the basic continuity of doctrinal content of Marxist-Leninist social science. There are changes, however, that reflect the leadership situation within the CPSU. In 1963, Nikita S. Khrushchev was still in control of the Party and state apparatus as First Secretary of the CPSU Central Committee and Chairman of the Council of Ministers. His picture and short biography as a "Leninist type leader," together with quotes from his speeches, are included as parts of the textbook. Also, the 1963 text, is interspersed with rather exuberant statements about the achievements of socialism in its economic confrontation with capitalism, which, as we know, have not since been confirmed by socialist performance.

By contrast, the 1970 edition does not even mention the name of the present CPSU Secretary General, Leonid I. Brezhnev, who obviously achieved ascendancy within the Politbureau after the text was printed. Also, its tone reflects the more sober attitude of Khrushchev's successors regarding the real "correlation of forces [economic, political, military]" between the capitalist and socialist systems.

This does not suggest any change of mind on the part of the communist leadership to actively cooperate with those historic forces which will ultimately lead to the revolutionary replacement of the decaying capitalist system by the progressive socialist and, finally, communist system. The textbook leaves no doubt about the resolve of the CPSU apparatus to pursue the identical aim in a more realistic way, which makes them even more formidable opponents.

---

[a]G. Kh. Shakhnazarov, the writer in charge of the group that produced all eight editions, has since been given the important position of Executive Secretary of *Problems of Peace and Socialism*, the monthly of the International Communist Movement published in Prague in twenty-three languages.

One shift in doctrinal emphasis in the 1970 edition should be noted: importance of CPSU ties with other "fraternal parties" and the cooperative effort of the entire world communist movement are stressed. The Main Document adopted by the International Conference of Communist and Workers' Parties at Moscow in June 1969 is quoted in the text in order to buttress the argument of irreversibility of the historic revolutionary process and the belief in communism's final victory on the global scale.

A glance at the fuller picture of political-ideological indoctrination as it is continued and broadened at the level of Soviet institutions of higher and specialized education and, in addition, in the unique Party educational system reserved for future *apparatchiks* may be of interest.

The population under communist control—the indoctrination target—may be divided into two basic groups: Party members (6 percent) and non-Party people (*bezpartiynyye*, 94 percent). Both groups receive higher education in the state school system, where regardless of the field of the student's specialization, heavy social-science study continues to be mandatory. It covers all the components of the doctrine: Marxist-Leninist philosophy (dialectical and historical materialism) and political economy. The history of the CPSU is also required. In a 1963-64 revision of the university curriculum, an additional obligatory subject, "Fundamentals of Scientific Communism," was introduced for students in their final year. Requiring seventy hours per year, by decreasing time alloted to the other Marxist-Leninist disciplines, this new subject defines "the general sociopolitical and ideological laws governing the preparation, emergence, and development of the communist system, as well as their specific manifestation in different countries."[b]

Obviously not satisfied with the results of state-school political education and concerned about the ideological indifference of Soviet young people, the USSR Ministry of Higher and Specialized Education issued (May 27, 1971) a detailed five-year indoctrination plan, coinciding with the economic Five-Year Plan (1971-75), together with instructions on "Scientific Research into the Problems of Communist Education of University and College Students." A single educational plan for the entire USSR directed towards ideological student indoctrination has never existed before.

Despite this impressive effort to mold all Soviet youth into conscious "builders of the new society," we should not overestimate the practical results, which are considered, as is well known, far from successful by the CPSU itself. The very fact that the Soviet government finds it necessary frequently to reorganize and enlarge its instruction on Marxism-Leninism suggests poor response from the average Soviet pupil. This should not lead us to the opposite extreme of disregarding the importance of at least passive submission to the Marxist-Leninist world-view by large numbers of the people, who have no access to free information.

On the other hand, it is well to recall that there are persons in the USSR as

[b]See *Voprosy filosofii (Problems of Philosophy)*, 1965, No. 5, p. 143.

well as in other communist-controlled countries who, even if few in number, accept the Marxist-Leninist world outlook by conviction and actively promote it as members of the apparatus of their respective communist parties. These *apparatchiks*, the hard core (3-4 percent) of CP membership, are professional revolutionaries in the true Leninist sense.

They qualify for responsible Party or government work by attending the Higher Party Schools, a separate educational system for formation of Party cadres. These schools are exclusive, not well publicized, with stringent entrance requirements. They are the Higher Party School at the CPSU Central Committee, Moscow (a postgraduate school for training top-level cadres), the Union Republic and Inter-Regional Higher Party Schools (with a two- or four-year study course), and the Higher Party Correspondence School at the CPSU Central Committee (requiring a minimum of secondary education).[c]

Thus, the entire Soviet educational system, both Party and state, serves as an instrument of ideological-political indoctrination. The Soviet authorities do not conceal their aim. They consider it only natural that the state organs are at the service of the Party's overall goal:

The foundations of a scientific world outlook are laid in school. To give all pupils thorough and sound knowledge and, by closely linking this knowledge with work and sociopolitical activities, to instill in every pupil a dialectical-materialist outlook and correct views on life and his responsibilities to society— this is a particularly important task for the school today, when the education of the new man has entered its highest, its communist stage.[d]

Every Soviet citizen is obliged to acquire the basic knowledge of the Marxist-Leninist world outlook in his final year of secondary school by learning the *Social Science course* translated here. In the words of its authors, it is intended "to acquaint students only with the essence of the Marxist-Leninist theory about society and to bring out the importance of the revolutionary theory as an instrument of knowledge of the world and of its transformation."[e]

Charles T. Baroch, J.D., Ph.D.

Scholar-in-residence
American Bar Association

---

[c]*Kommunist (The Communist)*, March 1971, No. 4, p. 128.

[d]*Sovetskaya pedagogika (Soviet Pedagogy)*, February 1963, No. 2, p. 3.

[e]See review article, "The Social Science Textbook," *Prepodavaniye istorii v shkole (History Teaching in School)*, 1963, No. 1. While this statement was made in connection with the first edition, it of course also applies to this revised eighth edition, which, incidentally, has had a printing of one million five hundred thousand copies in the Soviet Union.

OBSHCHESTVO-VEDENIYE

**UCHEBNIK DLYA
VYPUSKNOGO KLASSA
SREDNEY SHKOLY
I SREDNIKH
SPETSIAL'NYKH
UCHEBNYKH ZAVEDENIY**

Izdaniye vos'moye

Izdatel'stvo Politicheskoy Literatury
Moskva. 1970.

Uchebnik podgotovlen avtorskim kollektivom:
Shakhnazarov, G. Kh. (rukovoditel'),
Boborykin, A.D., Krasin, Yu. A.,
Sukhodeyev, V. V., Pisarzhevskiy, O. N.

Perevedeno s russkogo na angliyskiy.
Pod redaktsiyey Karla i Yekateriny Barokh.

Kniga pechatayetsya po zadaniyu
*Postoyannogo komiteta dlya izucheniya
kommunizma v sravnenii so svobodnym i
pravovym obshchestvom,* AMERIKANSKOY
ASSOTSIATSII ADVOKATOV.

Amerikanskoye izdatel'stvo:

Lexington Books
D.C. Heath and Company
Lexington, Massachusetts
Toronto   London

SOCIAL SCIENCE

TEXTBOOK FOR THE GRADUATING CLASS OF SECONDARY SCHOOLS AND SECONDARY SPECIALIZED EDUCATIONAL INSTITUTIONS

8th edition

State Publishing House for Political
Literature (Moscow: 1970)

Prepared by a group of authors:
G. Kh. Shakhnazarov (Editor-in-Chief),
A.D. Boborykin, Yu. A. Krasin,
V. V. Sukhodeyev, and O. N. Pisarzhevskiy.

Translated from the Russian.
Edited by Charles and Catherine Baroch.

This book is published under the sponsorship
of the American Bar Association, *Standing
Committee on Education About Communism and
Its Contrast With Liberty Under Law.*

Lexington Books
D.C. Heath and Company
Lexington, Massachusetts
Toronto   London

SOCIAL SCIENCE

Introduction

The Party's goal is to educate the entire population in the spirit of scientific communism, thus assuring that the toilers fully understand the world's development—its process and prospects—evaluate the domestic and international scene correctly, and make a conscious effort to construct their lives in the communist manner. There must be intimate connection of communist ideas and communist actions in every individual person's conduct and in the activity of every organization and collective. From *The Program of the Communist Party of the Soviet Union*.

At the threshold of adulthood we give earnest thought to the conduct of our lives. We seek the meaning of events around us and our place in society. We must understand, first of all, the epoch in which we are destined to live and act in order to avoid wandering in the dark, in order to live with clearly defined purpose, confident in our strength.

The twentieth century, which has changed mankind's life quickly and profoundly, has received, as a result, a great variety of titles. It was called the century of electricity when electric power was put at the service of technology and everyday life at the turn of the century. Later it was labeled the century of atomic power by the physicists; of computers, by mathematicians; of synthetics, by chemists; of space flight, by the astronomers.

Yet for all their importance, great scientific discoveries have not given human society the direction of its development. The sciences themselves and their practical application depend conclusively upon the social system, upon those in control of a given society, those whose interests are being served by social development—upon the interests of the entire people, as under socialism, or of a few big private owners, as under capitalism.

The twentieth century's chief characteristic is profound social transformation, clearing the path to communism.

In our era, in fact, mankind is resolutely ending all forms of class and national oppression and rebuilding social relations on the basis of justice in a grim, difficult struggle against reaction, prejudice, and ignorance. It is firmly establishing on this earth the ideals of peace, labor, freedom, equality, brotherhood, and happiness for all peoples. Transition from capitalism to communism is our era's main content.

Our fatherland occupies a special place in this far-reaching historical process of social reconstruction: it has been the first to pave the way to communism for mankind. Reaching this goal depends to a considerable degree on today's students. You are taking over from your fathers and mothers, older brothers and sisters. You will be the organizers of the economy, creators of science and technology, literature and art, the managers of public affairs. Yours is not merely an enviable right to communism, but the duty to build it, a grave responsibility to history and future generations.

1

"Building" is an exceptionally good word for the social process taking place in our country. Building communism means erecting new plants, factories, and electric power stations; laying railroad lines, growing crops to supply an abundance of vitally needed industrial and agricultural products; it means inventing and placing in production complex mechanical and automatic devices that will make shorter work hours possible and bring joy and creativity into labor; it means erecting comfortable apartment houses, sanatoria, palaces of culture, stadiums to make long life, good health, and beauty in their daily surroundings possible for people; it means establishing new social relations among persons, raising and training the communist man to be a tireless creator, broadly educated and balanced in development, embodying spiritual richness, moral purity, and physical perfection.

Communist society thus comes into being as a result of millions working with purpose. "The building of communism," reads the *Theses of the Communist Party of the Soviet Union Central Committee*, issued on the centenary of Vladimir Il'ich Lenin's birth, "is all the people's cause. Upon their awareness, initiative, culture, and professional competence depends successful fulfillment of communism's economic program."

Communism is not an ordinary building project; it requires not merely working hands but warm hearts, not indifferent followers but enthusiasts, fully aware of what they are striving for and what they are building, with a scientific knowledge of society.

At present, several hundred scientific disciplines exist, each fascinating, one as important as another. Nowadays when production processes are based on scientific achievements, one cannot advance a single step without scientific knowledge,—without acquiring a profession, becoming a specialist. And this holds true not only for the person who has decided to be a scientist or teacher, engineer or physician, but also for those who will be working with machine tools, building new industrial plants and housing projects, producing abundant crops.

Even with the best intentions no one can master all the sciences; neither is it necessary. However, everyone must be familiar with social science.

First of all, and most important, one needs this knowledge to participate with awareness in building communism, to have a clear concept of what communism is and how to achieve it. It is also indispensable for proper understanding of the international situation and the Soviet state's foreign policy.

Knowing about society is also needed in daily activities. Irrespective of our place of work, we should not neglect to learn the principles underlying the organization of Soviet industry, how the Soviet state was established and is governed, what rights and duties the Soviet citizen has, and what the basic principles in human relations are.

Political literacy and ideological maturity and training are necessary in private life also, guarding one from mistakes, helping him to keep to the correct path.

In studying social science, at the very outset, it is important to realize that it does not consist in mechanical memorization of texts and learning formulas by rote. Marxism-Leninism is a creative science. It cannot be mastered by cramming. The goals in this case are to absorb completely the essence of the revolutionary theory, and to acquire the habit of thinking creatively and the ability to apply the knowledge thus gained in practical action. It is useless to remember that high-level labor productivity is needed for the victory of communism and at the same time shun work or do it in a slipshod manner. If, on the contrary, having once learned the principles of socialist management, one is concerned about progress in his plant or *kolkhoz* [collective farm], his study has not been in vain. The ability to combine theoretical knowledge with practical activity, that is what everyone should acquire from the course on social science.

In a famous speech at the Third Congress of the Young Communist League, V.I. Lenin defined youth's main task: study communism. Our youth is devotedly following Lenin's behest and learning communism, as it storms the heights of scientific knowledge and takes an active part in the entire people's creative work. Mastering the science of society is a required important stage in this learning process.

This textbook gives the minimum knowledge about society and its law of development indispensable to every young Soviet person for his better understanding of Communist Party policy and for his active, informed share in the struggle by all-the-people for communism. That is the reason for naming this course social science.

Examination of theory and practice in building socialism and communism is a principal part of the course. The text presents the teaching on the socialist revolution and the dictatorship of the proletariat, the controlling role of the Communist Party, a description of the economic and political system of the Soviet socialist society and of the main objectives and prospects of communist construction in the USSR. It also shows the triumph of Marxism-Leninism and the ideas of proletarian internationalism.

Part I: Principles of Marxism-Leninism

Introduction to Part I

Theoretical Basis of Communism

"A specter is haunting Europe—the specter of Communism," begins the famous "Manifesto of the Communist Party," in which K. Marx and F. Engels set forth the basic principles of the communist world outlook. Over one hundred years have since passed. Communism is no longer a specter; it is a mighty force reshaping the world and changing the face of our planet. Followers of Marxist-Leninist teaching increase in number annually; the whole of toiling humanity is rising under its battle flag.

Where does the strength of Marxism-Leninism come from? From the fact that its teaching faithfully reflects reality, that it equips us with knowledge of the laws governing the world's development and reveals to men the meaning of their lives, labor, and struggle. Marxist-Leninist teaching, indicator of the way to happiness and progress, constitutes *the theoretical foundation of communism.*

Result of the Great Quest

Marxism has been prepared by the entire history of mankind's long and arduous development. Under the burden of merciless exploitation the popular masses preserved a vision of a radiant future, expressing it in song and legend and, when angry, in uprisings and revolutions.

Mankind's best minds have striven to understand society's history, creating philosophical systems and economic theories and outlining schemes of an ideal social system that would reflect the popular faith in the triumph of justice. However, the backwardness of social relations and the scarcity of scientific knowledge gave these views a utopian character.

Circumstances favoring the emergence of the scientific communist world outlook matured only by the mid-nineteenth century. Capitalism's expansion graphically demonstrated the decisive influence of economics on society. Capitalism also produced the working class—the gravedigger of the exploiter system—whose appearance was signaled by revolutionary actions (the uprisings of weavers in Lyon and Silesia, the Chartist Movement). At the same time, growth in capitalist production promoted rapid development in the natural sciences, which had accumulated facts sufficient to create a scientific understanding of the world.

The ground for a new world outlook was prepared. Its urgency was confirmed by the evolution of philosophical and political theories. By that time progressive social thinkers, in expressing the needs of practical life, had already posed questions to which Marxist teaching was to provide the answer. German classical philosophy, English political economy, and French utopian socialism became the theoretical sources of Marxism.

G. Hegel and L. Feuerbach were prominent representatives of German classical philosophy. Hegel's contribution was elaboration of the theory of development. However, this teaching was limited by his assumption that it was not nature which was developing but a kind of absolute idea, which was the first principle and ultimate cause of the world. Feuerbach, by contrast, maintained that nature could be explained of itself, without resorting to mystical and antiscientific concepts of an absolute idea. He sharply criticized religion. But Feuerbach's views also had their limitations. He failed to grasp the significance of Hegel's theory of development and never applied it to nature and history. The views of Hegel and Feuerbach contained ideas that served as a point of departure for the formulation of Marxist philosophy.

In the field of political economy, the precursors of Marxism were the English economists, Smith and Ricardo. By demonstrating that labor constitutes the source of all wealth in society, they laid the groundwork for the creation of scientific political economy.

From your history courses you are familiar with the names of H. Saint-Simon, C. Fourier, and R. Owen—the great Utopian socialists of the nineteenth century. They criticized the capitalist system severely and worked out plans for an ideal society, one free from exploitation. Yet their teachings revealed no realistic method for achieving this goal. Utopian socialists naïvely believed that this ideal social system could be achieved by enlightening society and morally re-educating the exploiters. Nevertheless, their theories facilitated the creation of scientific socialism.

Marx and Engels did not merely develop the theories of their predecessors. They critically revised the ideological heritage of the past and created a fundamentally new doctrine reflecting the vital interests of that most progressive and revolutionary class, the proletariat.

The founders of Marxism caused a revolutionary upheaval in the thinking about society:

They created a solid scientific foundation for social theory, freed it of false ideas, fantastic notions, and utopian schemes. For the first time ideology, commonly understood as a system of social views, became a science concerned with studying objective laws of historical development.

They transformed a social theory into an ideology for a proletarian mass movement, bringing it out of the silence of the scholar's study, where it had been the domain of the "aristocracy of the spirit," to the wide arena of class battles for the toilers' interests.

They eliminated the metaphysical character of social thought, the separation of theory and practice, and they equipped the toilers with a powerful ideological weapon for transforming the world.

"Marx's teaching is all powerful, because it is true," said V.I. Lenin, defining the source of Marxism's unusual power and influence.

Components of Marxism

Transformation of the world according to Marxist principles requires scientific understanding. Therefore, one of Marxism's most significant components is *philosophy, the science concerned with the general laws of development in nature and society and the laws of cognition.*

Merely knowing these general laws, however, is not enough for understanding why one social system is replaced by another. The most important of all relations in society are economic production relations. Without mastering them it is impossible to answer the question of how the transition from capitalism to socialism and then to communism can be achieved.

That is why *political economy, the science of the development of production relations*, has become the second most important element of Marxism.

The theory of scientific communism is the third part of Marxism, one of greatest consequence. Based on Marxist philosophy and political economy, it discloses *the laws governing the origin and development of communist society.*

You have undoubtedly noticed that in discussing Marxism's components we have qualified them as "most significant," "most important," and "of greatest consequence." This is because Marxist thought has not confined itself to the development of philosophy and political economy and a doctrine about socialism. It has revolutionized all fields of knowledge about society: historical science, for example; ethics, aesthetics, the science of law, etc. To be precise, all these branches of knowledge, and many others, have acquired a genuinely scientific character only since furnishing themselves with Marxist methodology, i.e., the Marxist approach in the study of social phenomena.

Thus, *Marxism is a harmonious system of scientific views about the general developmental laws of nature and society, the victory of the socialist revolution, and the ways to build socialism and communism.*

It is important in studying Marxist philosophy or political economy and assimilating the theory of scientific communism to bear in mind that it is an indivisible system: all the components of Marxism are inseparably bound. Of the numerous writings of Marxism's founders, none may be called "purely" economic or "purely" philosophical. They used philosophy as a method for comprehensive analysis of social relations and subsequently made political conclusions on this basis. Profound study of economics and politics, in turn, provided them with a wealth of material for their philosophical generalizations.

A Creative and Developing Theory

Thinkers of the past sought to create conclusive theories, intending to provide the ultimate answer to all questions. But can any theory anticipate all of life's events? Hardly. Real life around us constantly develops, enriching human understanding without interruption. When a theory ceases to take notice of new facts and becomes a system of frozen dogma, it loses touch with life and is useless, even harmful, since it no longer offers a true image of reality. That is why theory must always be based on practice. Goethe was correct when he said: "Mere theory is dry, my friend. The tree of life is green and burgeoning."

All the attempts to create universal, definitive theories were doomed in advance to failure. Years passed and theories died with the eras that gave them birth; they became obsolete, along with the class whose interests they expressed. Only those ideas which most accurately reflected reality survived and are treasured in social thought, having been assimilated into new theories and tested by practical application.

Marxist teaching differs in character from preceding theories. "Marxism is not a dogma but a guide to action," V.I. Lenin was fond of saying. Marxist theoretical principles are being constantly enriched by social development in practice and by new scientific achievements. Marxism is a creative, developing teaching.

By the turn of the nineteenth century, history had entered upon a new era. The socialist revolution was approaching, its inevitability having been proven by Marxism's founders. The immediate task confronting the proletariat was the overthrow of capitalism by revolution. The international revolutionary movement had a valuable accumulation of experiences. Meanwhile, vigorous development in the natural sciences called for a general statement of new facts and discoveries by philosophy: the need for a creative development of Marxism became urgent. This great historic mission was fulfilled by V.I. Lenin.

In his conflict with the dogmatists who considered Marxism an ossified doctrine, V.I. Lenin gave an in-depth interpretation of the practical problems of the new historical era and of the philosophical meaning of the major discoveries in the natural sciences. He also enriched Marx's teachings with new ideas. He developed Marxist philosophy; investigated the laws governing imperialism, which is capitalism at its highest stage; worked out the theory of socialist revolution, the strategy and tactics of the international working-class movement, and Party teaching. By generalizing the first experience of socialist transformation, he created the theory of the method and means of building socialism and communism. V.I. Lenin developed all facets of Marxism, elevating it to a new level. That is why we speak of *Marxism-Leninism*.

Over forty years have passed since V.I. Lenin's death. During this time gigantic progress has been made in mankind's existence. The correlation of forces between socialism and capitalism has drastically changed. New conditions would have necessitated further development of Marxism-Leninism. The world's Marxist-Leninist parties collectively have been fulfilling this task. The Communist Party of the Soviet Union has made a major contribution to Marxist-Leninist teaching; its Program, the Twenty-third Congress resolutions, and other documents outline its plan to build communism in the USSR and the specific means of implementing this plan.

To understand the ways in which society develops in the direction towards communism, as set forth in the Party's documents, requires familiarity with the basic philosophical and economic ideas of Marxist-Leninist doctrine, if only in broad outline.

1

Philosophical Concepts About the World and Its Cognition

To one entering the world of scientific study, the word "philosophy" indicates something complex, difficult to understand but attractive in a persuasive way, promising to reveal the universe's innermost secrets. And, in fact, philosophy teaches one how to relate consciously and reflectively to reality. Not without reason, the word itself, "philosophy," translated from Greek, means "love of wisdom."

What is surrounding reality? What lies at the basis of all things and objects? What is the explanation of the definite order of all natural phenomena? What is man's place in the world? How does he come to know it? All these questions are the basis of a *world outlook*, i.e., *an integral system of views and concepts about the world.* Their answers come from philosophy, which generalizes the achievements of the natural and social sciences.

Matter and Motion

What is Matter?

As soon as we begin to ponder about the essential character of the surrounding world, the first philosophical question confronts us. Let us, in our imagination, glance at the objects and phenomena of nature. We shall see the minutest particles and gigantic stellar systems, the most simple monocellular organisms and highly organized living creatures. Objects differ in size, form, color, density, structural complexity, composition, and many other properties. Nature is extremely diversified; its wide variety of qualities is characteristic. In all this diversity, can anything unifying, anything common to all phenomena in the world, be found?

Since ancient times philosophers and natural scientists have striven to discover a principle fundamental to all of reality's objects and phenomena. Some saw it in water: everything originated from water and was reconverted to it, the ancient Greek philosopher Thales maintained. Others saw this principle in air, fire, or earth. Democritus, an important Greek philosopher, considered all substances to be composed of very minute, indivisible particles—atoms, "the primary building blocks" of the universe. Following their discovery of the atom (at the beginning of the twentieth century), scientists found it to have an extremely complicated structure. The electron, proton, neutron, positron, and a

13

number of other "elementary" particles were discovered next. It was soon learned that these particles were also complex, and no one of them could be considered the unique "construction material" of all objects. Nature's inexhaustible wealth cannot be reduced to simple "primary building blocks." However minute in size, each of the universe's known elements soon reveals complexity in its internal structure.

All natural objects and phenomena, whatever their complexity and properties, have independent existence or, to use a philosophical term, have *being*. To man they are *objects* of thought and action. They all share a common feature: they exist independently of what we think of them or whether we think of them at all. This is the characteristic uniting them into one general concept of *matter*, according to Marxist philosophy. Obviously, search for "pure" matter or matter "in general" would be futile. Matter exists in an infinite multitude of concrete objects and phenomena, each of which is part of a single material world.

But how do we determine whether this or that phenomenon exists independent of our consciousness, that its essence is material? In practice, first of all, we use our senses. A fearful person about to enter a dark room may feel uneasy, thinking a stranger is present. Upon switching on the light he realizes that his imagination has played a trick on him. Obviously, not everything can be seen or touched: a radio wave cannot be handled, ultrasonic vibration cannot be registered by the ear, the magnetic field cannot be detected by the sense organs. However, they are known by means of instruments; their existence is confirmed by scientific data. We perceive matter, in whatever form, ultimately through the senses.

In V.I. Lenin's definition, *matter is an objective reality that exists independent of consciousness and is imparted to man through his senses.*

Everyone knows from experience that there are no eternal objects and phenomena. Scientific data show that even celestial bodies billions and hundreds of billion years of age have a beginning and end, come into existence and perish. But *matter* as a whole is *infinite, timeless*. Objects do not disappear without trace when destroyed. Radioactive decay of an element's nucleus results in formation of other elements and free particles. Decomposition of one substance's molecules is the origin of another or several different substances. One generation of living organisms is succeeded by others, and even death does not cause an organism's composite atoms and molecules to disappear totally. With its discovery of the law of preservation, science confirms that matter, subject to truly fantastic transformation, never either disappears or ceases to exist. Similarly, mankind's experience of many centuries proves it is impossible for material objects to originate from nothing, meaning that matter has always existed and always will.

Not only is matter timeless, it is also *limitless in space*. Natural-science discoveries are constantly extending the spatial boundaries of the universe we know. Modern telescopes enable us to observe stars ten billion and more light-years away. To convert this distance into kilometers would require using a twenty-three digit number. And nowhere are there limits to the universe.

Every year scientific progress brings us deeper insights into the structure of matter. At the beginning of the last century only a single form of matter was known, a substance possessing an invariable mechanical mass. Then physicists discovered another form, the electromagnetic field. When at the turn of the century it was proven that the electron mass varies according to the velocity of its movement, there was confusion among the scientists who had related the concept of matter to invariability of mass. Availing themselves of this opportunity, certain bourgeois philosophers began talking about the "disappearance" of matter. V.I. Lenin denounced such unscientific views and pointed out that not matter but the limits of what we know about it had disappeared. Invariability of mass was found not to be common to all material objects, as previously thought. A new property was discovered, rapidly moving material particles. Thus, variability of mass depends on velocity of its motion. These or other forms of matter and its concrete properties must not be confused with matter itself.

As it penetrates the immense space of the universe and investigates the most complex intranuclear processes, science may yet disclose heretofore unknown forms of matter. However startlingly different their characteristics, these forms in fact exist as objective reality conveyed to us by our senses.

Motion—Mode of Matter's Existence

It is apparent, when we observe its multiple phenomena, that everything in nature is in motion and undergoes constant change. It may be categorically stated that any attempt to find a completely motionless object would fail. While it is true that certain bodies can exist in a state of rest, this state is always *relative.* Bodies are at rest only in relation to some system of coordinates conditionally assumed to be stationary. A stone on a road, for example, is motionless in relation to the earth. However, along with the earth, it rotates daily around the planet's axis and annually around the sun. The sun moves within the galaxy; the galaxy, in turn, follows a most complex trajectory among other stellar systems.

It can readily be seen that it is impossible to find an absolutely motionless object, even in the instance of the simplest mechanical form of motion. Physical and chemical changes occur constantly in all bodies: movement of atoms, molecules, elementary particles. Even more complicated movement takes place in animate nature and in society. Complex physiological processes are occurring in human and animal organisms. In animate nature some species are replaced by others. In mankind's history there is constant development and renewal of all aspects of social life. Not for a single day do men stop their perceptive activity.

With the development of social relations man changes also his views, ideas, moral character, and behavior.

The material world confronts us with a majestic scene of universal motion and change, where there is no place for what is rigid, invariable, and permanently fixed. As the ancient Greek philosopher Heraclitus said, everything in the world flows, everything changes.

The very fact of motion's universality suggests that matter and motion are indissolubly bound, are inseparable. In fact, contemporary science has established irrefutably that matter exists only in motion. If, suddenly, the impossible occurred and all processes were to stop for a time, this would be equivalent to complete disappearance of the world, of objective reality, of matter.

What is the nucleus of an atom, actually? You know that it is a complex system of elementary particles, nucleons, held together by nuclear energy generated in the process of their motion. Stopping this motion would result in the disintegration of the nucleus; the atom would cease to exist. Without motion the electromagnetic field is inconceivable, as is light, that stream of photon particles existing only in motion. Whatever material objects and phenomena we consider, we come to the same indisputable conclusion: to be, to exist, means to be in motion. *Motion, understood as change in general, an eternal process of renewal, is an integral, basic property of matter, a universal form (mode) of its existence.*

Arranging the basic forms of material motion which we know in increasing order of their complexity, we obtain the following sequence: mechanical (movement of material bodies or particles in space), physical (heat, electric, intra-atomic, and intranuclear motion), chemical (combination and separation of molecules), biological (life processes and development of organisms), and social (social life processes and society's development). A whole complex of various scientific disciplines is concerned with studying every form of matter's movement. As they discover processes of motion, change, and development in material objects, these sciences also gain insight into matter's inherent properties and structure.

There have been scientific attempts in the past, as there are now, to reduce higher forms of material movement to lower forms, for example, physical and chemical forms to mechanical displacement of atoms and molecules; and the social form to the biological (social Darwinism). This has been called "mechanism," which only misleads scientific thought, inasmuch as each higher form of movement of matter, while including the lower forms, possesses its own peculiar properties or features. These are the main characteristics by which a given form of movement of matter is understood.

Development and Universal Correlation of World Phenomena

Source of Motion

Observing motion in nature and society leads to the question: What is its source? It may occur to you that, simply, a push transmits motion from one object to another. It would seem that at first matter was inert and that some sort of supernatural power appeared and "gave it a push." The idea of a push as the universal source of motion inevitably leads to the religious myth of the "creation of the world."

External pushes do occur in nature, but they merely transmit motion from one body to another without ever being its original source. Consequently, the source of motion should be sought not external to, but within, material phenomena.

Let us recall the operational principles of a jet engine. Special substances, upon combustion, escape from the jet nozzle with enormous force, propelling the rocket in the opposite direction with equal force. Obviously, the presence of *opposing force* is indispensable for the rocket's take-off; their clash and counteraction provides the source of motion. And what is the situation in nature?

Apparently, all material objects contain opposites within them. If some objects seem to be absolutely homogeneous, it is only because their opposite aspects, elements, and tendencies are temporarily hidden from view. When these objects are examined in depth, opposite principles are immediately visible.

It is impossible to visualize even a simple mechanical motion not having opposites: action and counteraction, attraction and repulsion, centrifugal and centripetal forces. This is also true of more complicated physical forms of motion, where at every step we deal with the opposites of positive and negative electric charges, of electric and magnetic fields, and with opposites within objects as well as within fields. Any atom is composed of opposites; a positively charged nucleus and negatively charged electron shell. The atom's nucleus represents a unity of opposite particles; separating them requires great expenditure of energy. The main forms of chemical compounds, atomic and ionic, also have unity of opposites as their basis.

Similarly, in animate nature in every organism opposing processes of absorption and elimination of substances, of creation and destruction of living matter, of assimilation and dissimilation take place. Opposite forces also exist in society: progressive and revolutionary on the one hand, backward and conservative on the other.

The opposites are not isolated from each other. On the contrary, they occur within the same phenomena, function in unity, and cannot "exist" without each other. Separating opposites speculatively—assimilation from dissimilation, for example—results in the organism's extinction and, consequently, in the destruction of the very phenomenon under observation. Though joined and inseparable, opposites cannot at the same time remain "at peace" and "in agreement," exactly because they are opposites. Thus, there is constant conflict, struggle between opposite forces, a *contradiction* between them.

What is the role of contradictions in development? Take, for example, the interaction of heredity and variability in living organisms. All plants and animals have the ability to reproduce offspring similar to themselves and to transmit their own characteristics from one generation to another. However, life conditions of the descendants never exactly duplicate those of the parents. Variability, appearance in the descendants of certain properties not identical with the parental features, is the result of changing environmental conditions. As can be seen, heredity and variability are opposites, between which contradictions are continual. Variability is in conflict with heredity, destroys its conservatism, and stimulates new features into development. Heredity strengthens acquired useful qualities, transmitting them to subsequent generations. New species of animals and plants appear, and evolution takes place. Contradiction between heredity and variability thus is a source of animate nature's permanent evolution.

In social life contradiction between productive forces and production relations constitutes the basic source of development. In a society based on exploitation this contradiction is manifested in class contradictions and class struggle. This will be discussed in detail in subsequent chapters.

Because of intrinsic contradictions, material objects cannot be in a state of absolute rest. The struggle of opposites produces "unrest" in them, prevents them from congealing, and sets them in motion. It is precisely this struggle that constitutes the source of development of all objects and phenomena.

Transition from Quantity to Quality

Whatever the object under consideration, it is bound to possess a definite *quality* setting it apart from other objects and a definite *quantity* giving it characteristic size, volume, weight, etc.

Take an ordinary aluminum plate as an example. The specific weight of aluminum is 2.7; its atomic weight, 27; its nuclear charge, 13; its melting point, 659 degrees C. This is its quantitative description. At the same time, aluminum is a metal of silver-white color, maleable, a good conductor of electricity, trivalent in stable compounds, close to alkaline metals in activity, easily oxidized, etc. These are aluminum's qualitative features. Similarly, for any element, substance, or object, it is possible to give the quantitative description and establish the qualitative specifications.

Upon closer examination it is obvious that quantity and quality are interrelated. This is particularly striking in chemistry. Not without reason, F. Engels called chemistry the science of qualitative transformation of substances brought about by change in their quantitative composition. Oxygen and ozone, in fact, differ in chemical composition only quantitatively. Yet they are different substances, with different properties. Chemical compounds in the homologous methane series differ according to the number of their CH_2 groups. The extent to which their quality is thus affected can be judged by the fact that the series' first four compounds, from CH_4 through C_4H_{10}, are gases; the following eleven, liquids; and the rest, beginning with hydrocarbon, $C_{16}H_{34}$, are solids.

D.I. Mendeleyev's Periodic Table of Elements is based on the properties of chemical elements, their atomic weight, or more precisely, as contemporary science has shown, on the magnitude of the atom's nuclear charge. An increase of one unit in the charge—a quantitative change, in other words—causes transition to a new quality.

It may seem that in altering an object's quantitative property its quality is not materially affected. Thus, heating a solid by a few degrees does not change its aggregate state. But should its temperature be raised to the melting point, the solid will change into a liquid. Increasing the temperature to the boiling point will turn the liquid into gas. Quantitative variations lead to qualitative change.

This transition is readily seen in any substance in the process of radioactive decay. Release of a specific quantity of energy influences the state of the atomic nucleus, and the atoms of one substance change into atoms of another. Thus, decaying radium forms helium and rhodium. Absorption of energy by the atomic nuclei also eventually results in quantitative change.

Every chemical element has a number of isotopes of equal charge which have the same position in the periodic table but are quantitatively different according to atomic weight or, more precisely, according to the number of neutrons in the atomic nucleus. Adding one neutron to the nucleus of an isotope with the lowest atomic weight will cause a unit increase in weight but no profound qualitative alteration, and the basic properties of the given chemical element will be preserved. By continuing to add neutrons one at a time to the nucleus, the heaviest isotope is eventually obtained. What is the result of giving this isotope an additional neutron? A qualitative change takes place: One of the neutrons in the nucleus will change into a proton, emitting an electron simultaneously; the nuclear charge will receive a one unit increase; and there will be a transition to a new element occupying the next position in the periodic table. For example, when its nuclei are bombarded with neutrons, uranium isotope (Uranium 238) changes into neptunium, and the latter into plutonium.

In animate nature quantitative to qualitative change may be studied in the example of a butterfly's development, where several qualitative stages are clearly defined (caterpillar, chrysalis, and finally the actual butterfly). Transition from one stage to the next depends upon specific quantitative processes in the insect's organism. Here, too, quantitative changes prepare for qualitative.

Interrelation of quantitative and qualitative changes in society is discernible in the example of the system of cooperative production. Association of toilers into a single collective greatly exceeds in results the sum total of their strength and capability as individuals. An obvious example of transition to a new quality in social development is a social revolution, for which the preconditions gradually mature within society itself.

Quantitative changes, as is again apparent, bring about qualitative change, but only after certain limits are crossed. Formerly inconspicuous quantitative change then becomes qualitative; a leap occurs, i.e., there is transition from one quality to another. Knowing all this is helpful for understanding how matter develops in the course of universal motion and change, and how new phenomena appear.

If change from quantity to quality had never taken place, we may imagine what would have happened in animate nature. Academician V.L. Komarov has written:

If life on earth, once it had emerged, had increased only in quantity, the earth's surface would have been covered with a thick layer of jelly similar to that now produced by bacteria, amoebae, and other like organisms. But quantity has the property of changing into quality. In the process, the mass of substances which exists in various interrelationships (chemical, physical, etc.) with the environment acquires diverse qualities, undergoes differentiation. The homogeneous mass becomes heterogeneous.

Motion and change in matter are not merely quantitative exchanges of energy between various bodies, not merely simple growth. They are, rather, an eternal process of renewal of the material world, which passes from quantitative to qualitative changes. They are leaps, the destruction of the old and the emergence of the new.

From the Lower to the Higher,
from Simplicity to Complexity

Does the development of nature and society have direction? Or does it move in a circle, eternally retracing the same path covered previously many times, with no progress at all in this closed span?

Simple life experience, not to mention scientific data, lead us to conclude that there is progress, movement forward in the material world's development. A clear example of this is animate nature: by the very fact of its having emerged, nature has proven capable of passing from lower, inorganic forms to higher, more complex organic forms. It has traversed a lengthy route of progressive development from structureless living matter and primitive monocellular organisms to man. Each stage in this ascent has negated the preceding, as it were, and has been negated in its turn by the subsequent stage. A unique *negation of negation* has been taking place.

Negation in this context does not signify complete destruction of the entire contents of what existed before. First of all, simpler phenomena often continue to exist side by side with the new and more complex. Animate nature is an example: the most primitive animals exist together with the highly organized. Second, and more important, as the new emerges from the old in the very process of progressive development, it absorbs whatever was positive and valuable in the old.

In animate nature each new species assumes the useful properties accumulated by its predecessors in the evolutionary process.

In the history of society, each new social system emerges not in a vacuum but on the foundation of the assimilated material and spiritual wealth that preceding eras have created.

Upon the victory of the Great October Socialist Revolution there were those "ultrarevolutionaries" who proposed annihilating the old culture completely, because it had been a bourgeois culture, and creating a "proletarian culture," which would have nothing in common with the past. The most zealous even suggested that Pushkin be "thrown overboard." V.I. Lenin, severely critical of them, maintained that the proletariat was the custodian and worthy successor of the progressive, democratic traditions in the culture of the past. Since socialist culture cannot be created in a vacuum, to develop it and advance require enriching the memory by learning about all the treasures mankind has produced.

Thus, negation is not equivalent to the absence of *connection* or *continuity in development*. A phenomenon resulting from negation preserves everything that was of value in the preceding stage; at the same time something new and richer in content emerges. Due to this fact, development in nature, society, and cognition is not a marking-time process but a cause of progress and movement forward.

Certain developmental features in the chain of subsequent negations can be repeated, to the extent that the positive content of the lower levels of development is retained at the higher. An apparent return to the old on a higher level of progress occurs. For example, communal ownership of the means of production predominated under the conditions of primitive society. Its negation followed—private ownership and exploitation of man by man. With the victory of the socialist revolution, private ownership has been negated. Social ownership of the means of production has been established once again but on a basis unlike that of primitive society; on an incomparably higher basis.

Progressive development, then, as this example demonstrates, is not to be understood as a movement along a straight line but rather as a complex cyclic process, reminiscent of a spiral motion.

Development is a chain of negations, by which ascent is effected from the lower to the higher and from simple to complex.

Universal Correlation of Phenomena

From the study of the process of development it is evident that there is a definite interdependence between opposite sides of every object, between quantitative and qualitative change, and lower and higher developmental stages. Motion and development are impossible without *interaction* of opposite sides and phenomena, and *correlation* with environmental conditions.

Careful observation of reality as it develops reveals the close interconnection and mutual dependency of the most diverse objects and phenomena.

Look at a green leaf. It is really a full-fledged chemical plant, where carbon dioxide is transformed into oxygen with the aid of solar energy. Neither men nor animals could exist without it. K.A. Timiryazev rightly called plants the intermediary between heaven and earth and the true Prometheus, he who stole fire from heaven. What is the origin of the radiant energy that infuses life into all plants? It is the result of complex nuclear conversions occurring in the sun's depths. And this is not the whole story. Plants also need fertile soil, of which one part is developing organic nature and the other synthetic fertilizers produced by man in chemical plants. Moisture and proper climatic conditions are also needed for successful plant growth. Atmospheric phenomena are also included in the process of general interdependence. To present the connections of one plant with other objects in the world would require volumes, and the subject still would not be exhausted, since there is an infinite multitude of interconnections in nature.

However unique, however isolated they appear, these and other phenomena, as proven by the century-old experience of the human race and lengthy, tedious development of natural science and philosophy, all manifest that the world is one whole in its material nature.

Each object is connected with the rest of the world by thousands, millions, of ties, representing a totality that forms one single process of universal correlation and interaction of each entity with every other.

Interconnections between material world phenomena are extremely diversified.

If one were to undertake an indiscriminate study of all the interconnections between objects, he would be overwhelmed by the infinite variety of unique and accidental facts offering nothing or very little towards a grasp of the general situation. He must extract from the sum total of interconnections the general, most essential and necessary ties. In science they are called *lawlike, regular interconnections*.

Take for example the movement of small particles of black India ink in a drop of water (Brownian movement). At first it appears to be chaotic and disorderly. But, in fact, it is in strict conformity with a law discovered and formulated by molecular physics.

At the turn of the seventeenth century it seemed to many scientists that animate nature had no order. In the middle of the eighteenth century, however, C. Linnaeus, a Swedish physician and naturalist, established that a definite, systematic order was inherent in the multiformity of animate nature. Charles Darwin explained this order in the nineteenth century when he formulated his famous evolutionary theory of species. The multiplicity of chemical elements has rigid orderliness, as Mendeleyev's Periodic Table revealed. Objective order and consistency are also characteristic of the history of the human race, and their scientific expression has been found in Marxism-Leninism.

Inner objective relations exist in every area of reality, which permit understanding it as a single whole and which determine the nature and direction of its development. These inherent ties are reflected in developmental *laws*.

Many laws of nature discovered by science are well known: Newton's laws, Boyle-Mariotte's Law, the law of gravitation, laws of electricity, light reflection and refraction; Avogadro's Law, Mendeleyev's Periodic Table, and others. What does the notion of law convey?

Take the Archimedean principle. It expresses, first of all, a relationship, a connection between phenomena (between a solid body immersed in liquid and the liquid itself). Unquestionably, this relationship is *objective*: that means it must be accepted, whether we like it or not, and we do just that even when attaching a sinker to a fishing line. It is also clear that Archimedes' Law expresses not a specific connection between a particular solid body and a particular liquid but a *universally applicable* connection: immersing any body in any liquid produces the result corresponding to the law. This connection is *essential* and *indispensable*, disclosing, as it does, very important relations between solid bodies and liquids and its inevitability at each instance of their interaction. Finally, irrespective of the number of times this experiment is repeated, the principle is confirmed, meaning that it expresses a *permanent, recurrent* relation between phenomena.

Thus, to all understanding, the notion of law may be formulated as an *objective, universal, indispensable, and essential relationship between phenomena and objects, characterized by permanence and recurrence.*

Dialectics–Teaching About Development

Dialectics, the teaching about universal interrelation and development in the world, is concerned with studying the most general relationships inherent in all areas of reality and the most general features of development.

The word "dialectics" at first meant the art of debate, skill in revealing contradictions in an adversary's arguments. Even though the word is used in a much broader sense now, the study of contradictions within reality is the kernel, the essence of dialectics. This is quite understandable, since contradictions, after all, are the source, the internal motive force of all development.

V.I. Lenin described the basic tenets of dialectics:

It is development, an apparent repetition of previously traversed stages, but different and on a higher level ("negation of a negation")–development, so to speak, along a spiral and not along a straight line; a catastrophic, revolutionary development by leaps ("interruptions of graduality"); transformation of quantity into quality; internal developmental impulses generated by contradictions, by the clash of opposing forces and tendencies acting upon a given body, within a given phenomenon or within a given society; interdependence and the most intimate, inseparable connection of *all* aspects of each phenomenon (with history continuously discovering new aspects); a correlation producing the single, law-governed process of motion permeating the world. These are some of the features of dialectics conceived as . . . the teaching about development.

As the study of the universal interdependence and development of the world, dialectics functions as a scientific method of cognition. Having once satisfied ourselves that every phenomenon is related to others and in constant development, we must keep this fact in mind when studying any particular object. By committing us to study the world's interdependence and development, dialectics promotes in-depth investigation of reality.

Contemporary science reveals the relativity, mobility, and fluidity of limits in nature and in society. New discoveries often do not conform with customary concepts and schemes, calling for a new creative approach and elaboration of new "unusual" concepts and theories. The contemporary theory of elementary particles and the theory of relativity, for example: Could these new discoveries be understood if we were to limit ourselves to the laws of classical nineteenth-century mechanics?

Dialectics cautions against onesidedness, ossification of thinking, and dogmatism. It teaches not to give up helplessly in the face of contradictions but rather to explore their nature for new approaches, for fresh, deeper, and fuller explanations of correlations in nature and society.

Mastering the creative, dialectical way of thinking is indispensable, the more so as dialectics is inherent not only in the external world but in human consciousness and in the process of cognition of the world. Before examining this problem, it is imperative to understand the nature of consciousness, the correlation of the material with the spiritual.

Consciousness—A Property of Highly Organized Matter

Without Matter There Is No Consciousness

We know that the world is material. But what place have man's consciousness, thoughts, and feelings there? Could they not be considered a special form of matter?

To do so would be contradicting science. Material bodies have mechanical, physical, and chemical properties. Sensations and thoughts do not. They exist in the mind as spiritual images reflecting external objects and interconnections between them.

At the same time, our experience and scientific data testify to the fact that consciousness is impossible without matter. No one has ever experienced sensations and concepts that emanate under their own power, independently of matter. Consciousness exists only where there is a human brain, the organ of thought. Brain damage causes impairment of consciousness. Such chemical substances as aminazin or reserpine act upon the brain to suppress feelings of alarm, fear, uncertainty; other substances have the contrary effect, intensifying fear, even causing hallucinations. These facts confirm that consciousness is a property of highly organized matter, the human brain. What kind of property is it?

The very word "consciousness" suggests it is the means to acquire knowledge of the world, that one becomes conscious of what is happening. Thus, consciousness presupposes both the presence of a brain and the existence of material objects acting upon it.

Recall how the physiology of higher nervous activity explains the origin of sensations. Some external environmental factor (for example, a light ray reflected from an object) acts upon a sense organ (the eye). The energy from the outside excitant converted into a neural stimulation is transformed into a sensation. An image of the object arises in the consciousness.

Imagine for a moment a brain that does not receive signals from the outside world. However highly organized, it could not form a single sensation or thought. Of course no such brain exists. But there are instances of impairment of the brain's communication with the external world. There are disabled persons who are without sight and hearing and almost all cutaneous sensitivity. Most of the time their consciousness is inactive.

The brain may be compared, to a certain degree, to high-speed film on which pictures of reality are reflected. It is only necessary to cover the camera lens to shut the film off from the external world and leave it unexposed, without pictures. This analogy, of course, should not be taken literally. Objects are reflected on film according to physical and chemical laws. The reflection of reality in the human brain is a much more complex physiological and social process.

Thus, consciousness is not merely a property of the brain but rather of the brain's interaction with the material world. *Consciousness is the capacity of highly organized matter to reflect the external world in mental images*. Thanks to it, man cognizes the world around him and organizes his practical activity in a purposeful way.

How Man Cognizes the World

Cognition is not a simple act of a mirror reflecting the world in the human brain.

Let us consider how man cognizes the world. Familiarity with external objects begins from his first days of life. When an infant sees an electric bulb for the first time, the notion of it as a source of light is imprinted on his consciousness. As a schoolboy studying physics and gaining experience of the principles of electrical engineering, he comes to know the laws of electricity and the operational principles of electrical machinery. The range of his knowledge increases, and he has no difficulty in repairing a switch or installing a socket for a table lamp. With his schooling completed, the young man works in industry, studies electrical engineering, and becomes familiar with the latest advances in the field. Thus, his knowledge is being continuously expanded and strengthened.

The path taken by human society in cognizing the world resembles the individual in its development, to a certain degree.

In ancient times people knew nothing about the nature of electricity. A thunderstorm inspired terror and seemed to be the act of angry gods. Not by chance did Greek mythology depict Zeus as the Thunderer hurling lightning bolts at whoever dared oppose him. Gradually natural science accumulated facts about electrical phenomena. Study was made of the typical trait of certain bodies to become electrically charged when rubbed; laws of interaction between electrical charges were discovered. There were also mistakes in theory. For example, for some time attempts were made to explain electricity by motion of a weightless "electrical fluid." In the first half of the nineteenth century, science and experience had accumulated facts enough to make the discovery of electricity's fundamental laws. Man learned to convert energy from mechanical and thermal to electric, and back again. The first electric-power stations were built; the first electrical machinery was invented. Electricity, like steam, was put at man's service. The process of cognition did not stop here, however. In the second half of the century, J.C. Maxwell, an English physicist, developed the theory of the magnetic field, which integrated the heretofore separate areas of electricity, magnetism, and optics. And new horizons are just ahead: scientists are hypothesizing about unity of the electromagnetic, gravitational, and nuclear fields. Thus, one step at a time, scientific thinking penetrates phenomena ever more deeply.

As Lenin said, cognition is a complex thought process of advance from ignorance to knowledge, from incomplete, imprecise knowledge to what is fuller and more exact. Inasmuch as the world is infinite, cognition, knowing no limitations, is infinite, too.

Human cognition proceeds from observation, sensory perception—or as they say in philosophy, live reflection—to theoretical discovery of laws and their application in practice. This is the dialectical path of cognition of truth and objective reality.

We cognize the world primarily with the aid of the senses, the organs of sight, hearing, and touch. They represent channels, as it were, through which knowledge and information about the material world are conveyed to us.

But where is the assurance that the senses give reliable information? Is there no distortion in transmission, like in the child's game "out-of-order telephone"? Certainty of the reliability of our sensory images comes from having repeatedly verified them by experience in *practical activity*.

Imagine the chaos in life if people's sensations and perceptions did not correctly reflect the properties of external objects. It would simply be impossible to orient oneself in surrounding reality. There are instances, of course, when the senses do "deceive" us. A pencil half immersed in water appears to be broken. But this "deception" actually reflects the real properties of material phenomena, i.e., light rays are refracted in passing from a less dense to a more dense medium. The senses of healthy persons reflect objects in the external world correctly; they were developed during the evolution of animate nature as a means of orientation, as a means of better adaptation by the organism to its environment.

An object's reflection does not provide knowledge of its intrinsic developmental laws. Examining the crown of a tree, touching the branches, and listening to the leaves rustle do not bring an understanding of those profound interior processes occurring within the green leaf under the effect of solar rays. That these processes are invisible is not the point. We may penetrate the leaf's inner life with a microscope, but by limiting ourselves solely to observation we cannot understand it. What does "understand" mean? Discovering the laws, i.e., singling out from the total of complex interactions the essential connections (in this case, the laws of photosynthesis). The senses cannot perform this function. In sensory images, as we know, the essential aspects are fused, as it were, with the secondary.

To establish the laws of development of any phenomenon requires understanding and generalizing information received with the aid of the senses. And here we must have assistance from *abstract thinking or logical perception*, which, on the basis of sensory cognition, produces scientific abstractions, i.e., concepts expressing reality's essential relationships.

Physics operates with the concepts "velocity," "mass," "quantity of motion," "energy," etc., all of which are scientific abstractions. Velocity, energy, or mass in pure form are not found in nature, where material bodies move with different velocities and have varying effects on other bodies. Let us take the concept of valence in chemistry or heredity in biology. In actual reality it is possible to find atoms of various substances combining in fixed proportions and living organisms transmitting specific properties from one generation to another, but neither valence nor heredity will be seen in pure form. This is also true of the philosophical concepts of matter, motion, and law. As they elaborate scientific concepts or discover laws, scientists mentally single out intrinsic properties and relations, as though "abstracting" them from the actual material bodies. Hence the designation, *abstract thought*.

Scientific abstraction permits deeper understanding of reality. We disengage ourselves from many secondary aspects and properties of individual objects, but as a result we come to know their fundamental principle, their *essence*, and are able to orient ourselves in the mass of phenomena, discovering their basic and regular qualities.

In discussing Boyle-Mariotte's Law, for example, we must ignore the specific properties of one gas or another, the form of the vessel containing it, etc. In recompense we discover a very important correlation between gas pressure and volume, thus improving our understanding of the properties of gases in general.

Abstract thought is inextricably tied in with language. Usually, to express a thought we have recourse to words. Thinking is possible without pronouncing aloud, but it is still a process of clothing thoughts in words, as though one were talking to oneself. Why does this happen?

Abstract thinking arose in the process of people working together, and from the very beginning it has been a social product. There is a felt need among people at work to coordinate actions and exchange accumulated experience and knowledge. Arising from this need is articulate speech, language as means of communicating and safeguarding knowledge about surrounding reality that men have acquired in the course of their work.

Upon reading the word "fire" in a book or hearing it spoken by a radio announcer, even though there are neither flames, heat, nor crackle of beams burning around us in the room—nothing to arouse the image of fire in our consciousness—we clearly understand the reference. Why does a word acting on the hearing or sight produce a definite thought in the mind? The explanation is that in the course of centuries men have repeatedly encountered instances of fire in their practical activity and have isolated this phenomenon's general traits, have elaborated a concept of it, and connected it with the term "fire." In the very act of studying language we come into possession of the accumulated knowledge of many preceding generations. Each word, therefore, being more than mere sound, has specific meaning which one automatically grasps on hearing it.

Language is a priceless means of preserving, transmitting, and enlarging the treasury of human wisdom. Without it no one could read, study in school—or enrich his spiritual world with the treasures slowly accumulated by mankind. There would be no means available for people to ensure stability and continuity in the thinking process; their consciousness would hardly differ from the psyche of highly developed animals.

It may be readily understood how a person isolated from other human beings for one reason or another from childhood and incapable of speech could fail to develop the ability to think abstractly. An actual situation confirms this: In India a few years ago a girl was found who had been carried off shortly after birth by a shewolf. She had been living in a wolf pack for a number of years. She was, of course, unable to speak and lacked human thought entirely.

Abstract thinking is a powerful tool of cognition. The possibility for science to exist, to explain phenomena unintelligible to man and disclose the developmental laws of nature and society is thus given.

Truth and Its Criterion

The goal of man's cognition is to reach the *truth*, with the aid of which he may correctly orient himself in his environment, modifying it according to his needs.

What is truth? A philosopher never existed who did not ask this question.

The foremost thinkers of the past have devoted themselves to searching for and attaining truth.

In science we understand "truth," in its broadest application, to include any statement correctly reflecting reality, some characteristics of it, or a law governing it.

To ascertain whether a statement is in fact true is more complicated. In order to be certain of the truth of our knowledge, a *criterion* (an evaluating device) to confirm its accuracy is needed.

Frequently, in heated discussions each person is convinced that he is right and considers his opinion to be the truth. Who can judge? Where is the "litmus paper" that permits making an infallible distinction between true and false? When scientists or inventors are in disagreement, they turn for help to experimentation.

When a scientist asserts on the basis of theoretical investigation that an alloy of certain metals possesses particular properties, his conclusions can easily be verified by obtaining the alloy in question at the factory laboratory. If the alloy in fact does possess the properties the scientist claimed, then he was correct. If not, he was in error. The accuracy of D.I. Mendeleyev's Periodic Table was verified by practice when new elements were found whose existence and properties had been predicted on the basis of it. The practical success of artificial earth satellites and spaceships confirms the accuracy of theoretical calculations made by scientists and engineers engaged in space exploration.

The most reliable *criterion of truth is social practice*, i.e., the activity of persons transforming their environment, especially as producers.

Practice is the criterion of truth of not only natural but social-science theories. History has known many different social and political theories. They included a number of correct conclusions or conjectures, but on the whole they failed to withstand the test of practice. The Marxist-Leninist theory alone has been confirmed by the entire practice of social development, of the international revolutionary movement, and of the construction of socialism and communism.

Practice as Foundation of Cognition

Practice is not merely a criterion of truth. It is also the point of departure for cognition. "In the beginning there was a deed," wrote Goethe in *Faust*. Need for cognition of reality originated with man's practical needs. Since that time practice has set specific tasks for cognition. F. Engels said that the appearance of a technical need in society would advance science more than ten universities would. Human reasoning power is directed, first of all, to problems born of the demands of practical existence.

Even cognition itself is inconceivable without practice. Imagine restricting ourselves to simply observing the world around us, without intervening in its development in a practical way. We would then not be able to perceive material phenomena's developmental laws; it would be impossible to find out what is inside a nut without cracking its shell. Cognition of the internal laws that govern objects calls for turning them inside out, as it were, and looking at them from within. Clearly, this is possible only by means of practical action.

It is no accident that experimentation is a powerful means of scientific research of nature. Study of the atomic nucleus and its elementary particles or structure is inconceivable without an enormous amount of active experimentation. Powerful synchrophasotrons and other complex instruments used by scientists are the product of modern industrial experience.

The social sciences also develop on a practical basis. Marxism has formulated general conclusions based on the practical exercise of revolutionary struggle by the proletariat. Creative development of Marxist-Leninist theory in the program of the Communist Party of the Soviet Union and in the Party congress and plenum resolutions is the consequence of broad, practical understanding of building socialism and communism.

Thus, practical experience has a primary role in cognition, serving as its *basis*. Performance demonstrates man's capacity to know the world and discover the laws of its development. Matter is infinite and inexhaustible. Phenomena as yet unknown will therefore always exist, but none exist that are impossible of discovery. What was unknown yesterday we know quite well now, and those tasks over which scientific thought now struggles will be resolved tomorrow on the basis of new, practical achievements.

Practice is not something static in nature, immutable once and for all. Only a few years ago men could not cross the limits of the earth's atmosphere. Today earth satellites and spaceships cover cosmic space. Development of practice opens new vistas for ever broader knowledge of the world.

Practice definitely disproves relativism and dogmatism in the theory of knowledge.

Relativists maintain that all our knowledge of the world is relative, that nothing is stable and constant. What only yesterday seemed to be true today may appear false. Relativism contradicts practice. When science discovers the inner laws governing certain phenomena and those laws have been confirmed by practical experience, it means that they are correct and will remain so as long as the given phenomenon exists.

Dogmatists, on the contrary, assert that our knowledge is invariable. According to them, when certain laws are discovered, it is only necessary to confirm them and then apply them mechanically to reality, as though by rubber stamp, whatever the conditions. Dogmatism also contradicts practice by ignoring the fact that our knowledge can never exhaust the wealth of phenomena in the world. Together with the development of practical application, our knowledge, too, develops and broadens.

The laws of classical mechanics discovered by Newton are true. They have been repeatedly confirmed in a practical manner. However, in the twentieth century when speeds approximating the speed of light have become possible for mankind, it has been found that Newton's laws were only a specific case of more general laws discovered by A. Einstein. Obviously, the laws of classical mechanics did not subsequently become false. They continue correctly to reflect the mechanical interaction of bodies at comparatively low speeds. But now our knowledge has become broader, reflecting more general laws of interaction of bodies at all speeds, those close to the speed of light included.

This example illustrates the fact that in scientific knowledge there is always a stable kernel that remains true. But this nucleus is not invariable: in the process of development it becomes overgrown, so to speak, with new deductions and conclusions.

Unity of theory and practice is the key to understanding the active nature of human consciousness and its enormous transformative role. Consciousness is by no means a passive reflection of reality from somewhere, from outside. It penetrates the world and changes it by means of the practical activity of men.

As you look about, do you see many objects provided by nature alone, objects that are not products of creative activity inspired by man's consciousness? School desks, tables, physics instruments, the school building itself, industrial plants and factories, the most intricate machines—all have been created by people from raw materials and bear the imprint of fulfilled human needs. Even nature itself—forests, meadows, fields, the earth's atmosphere—is being transformed under the influence of practical action by society. The meaning and final cause of the emergence of consciousness are contained in the urge to transform reality according to man's needs. As Lenin observed, consciousness not only reflects the world, it also creates it. Man has never been satisfied with his surroundings; he has been changing objective reality. The active nature of consciousness becomes evident especially in the life of society. In our country Marxist-Leninist ideas as realized in the practical experience of communist construction are creating a new world, the world of communism.

Materialism and Idealism

We have learned, in a general way, about the Marxist philosophical theory concerning the world and how it is perceived. Let us now consider its position among other philosophical theories and its relationship to class struggle and to politics.

Two Trends in Philosophy

You may see from what has been said that as a philosophical theory Marxism's basic characteristic is explanation of the world within the framework of the world itself, without extraneous addition or invention. Nature and being[a] are taken as they are in reality. The teaching that considers the world to be one material whole, explaining everything in terms of matter, is called *materialism*. The Marxist philosophy is the highest form of materialism.

Materialism has a long history. It emerged as a philosophical theory in ancient times but was naïve in character, without basis in the exact sciences, since those sciences themselves were at an embryonic stage. The seventeenth and eighteenth centuries produced a new form of materialism which sought to unify all knowledge and equip science with a method for studying nature. At that time mechanics was the most highly developed of the sciences. This explains the *mechanical* nature of the materialism of those days, which reduced all laws of the universe, basically, to laws of mechanics. Backwardness in the sciences was the cause of another defect in seventeenth- and eighteenth-century materialism: it failed to carry to its logical conclusion the notion of the universe's development and interrelationship of all its phenomena, i.e., it was, as the philosophers say, *metaphysical*. Finally, this materialism was *reflective*, since it did not grasp the role of practical, revolutionary-transformative human activity.

The Marxist philosophical theory, as we have seen, maintains that the universe is in a condition of uninterrupted motion and development, with all phenomena connecting and interacting in the process. This means that in Marxism materialism is organically related to dialectics. Marxist philosphy as a whole, therefore, has been given the name *dialectical materialism*.

The interests that materialism serves may readily be understood. The materialist philosophy is intimately bound up with natural science and directed to the study of nature. It serves those social classes desiring scientific knowledge of the world for use in the interest of progress. Materialism, as a rule, is the philosophy of the advanced, progressive classes in society.

The most advanced and progressive class in modern society is the working class. It requires a clear scientific concept of the world for the purpose of its struggle with capitalism and construction of a communist society. This explains why dialectical materialism is the philosophical foundation of the working-class world-view.

Materialism is the leading, progressive trend in philosophy. But you have undoubtedly heard that in addition to materialism there is another trend in philosophy, *idealism*. Let us try to grasp its fundamental nature.

Idealists consider a spiritual principle, an idea, to be the fundamental principle of the universe. As opposed to the materialists, from the outset they reject any attempt to explain nature, matter, or being within the framework of these realities themselves.

For the idealists, consciousness, reason, god are the creators of nature and matter.

Idealism is divided into two basic trends: *subjective* and *objective*. Subjective

---

[a]Being, as has been mentioned, is a philosophical concept used to designate nature, matter, and the external world, as distinct from consciousness and thought.

idealists hold that all objects and phenomena in the external world are products of human consciousness. "The whole universe is the complex of my sensations" sums up the meaning of subjective idealism.

Objective idealists maintain that the material world is the product of some sort of universal mind existing somewhere outside human consciousness.

Idealism is disproved by the entire, massive data of natural science and by man's practical activity.

Modern natural science has proven that the earth, moon, and sun existed long before the emergence of man or any other being endowed with a psyche. Does not this argument confirm the external world's independence of human consciousness?

Concepts of a universal mind that "creates the world" are also in monstrous contradiction to natural science. Science has proven that consciousness is the product of highly organized matter, the brain. There can be no universal consciousness existing independent of highly organized matter. But even should its existence be agreed to, how could it create the world from nothing? Again, this contradicts all scientific laws. Man has begun to conquer outer space and penetrate the secrets of the microsmic world but nowhere encounters any trace whatever of activity of a universal mind. All phenomena are explained by natural causes.

In a conversation with Laplace, the famous astronomer, Napoleon asked why he made no mention of god in any of his works. "I had no need of that hypothesis," the scientist proudly answered. Since that era science has made many great discoveries and advances. Paraphrasing Laplace's words, we may say that mankind needs no fantastic tales about a world mind to explain the universe.

Why, then, does idealism endure, exerting an influence on many minds? As you know, it has its adherents even among scientists. Idealism, in fact, has roots both in human consciousness and social circumstances.

V.I. Lenin compared human cognition to a tree capable of producing sterile blossoms as well as fruit. Cognition, as has been stated, is a complex and contradictory process. Idealist theories, however, are based on a onesided approach to it.

Our sensations play an enormous role in cognition. But we must not forget that there are also abstract thought and practice. If its role is unduly expanded, there is risk of concluding that sensation is the only reality to be dealt with. This is precisely what the subjective idealists do when they say that sensations are "the elements" of the world. It would appear that sensations are not reflections of the properties of real objects but have an existence of their own, and people naïvely take them for objects of the external world. These are the roots of subjective idealism.

Everyone has seen and tasted apples, pears, oranges, and other fruit many times. But no one has ever seen and tasted "fruit" in general. The concept "fruit" is an abstraction, an imagined isolation of the common traits proper to apples, pears, and oranges. Abstractions are essential in the cognitive process; without them thought would be impossible. All sciences employ them. At no time should one forget, however, that these common traits, the content of abstraction, do not exist of themselves, distinct from individual objects. Otherwise one may easily imagine "fruit" in general as existing alongside apples, pears, and oranges, representing the essence of all real fruit as their basis. This is what the objective idealists do when they assert that a concept, an idea, has independent existence and engenders particular objects. This is the basis of objective idealism.

However, it is not simply a matter of the thought process being involved in a contradiction. Reasons for the persistence of idealism should be sought in social conditions also.

In contrast to materialism, idealism expresses, as a rule, the interests of the conservative classes who strive to preserve an obsolescent order, whereas cognition of the laws of the universe serves social progress. The departing classes, therefore, seize on idealism, which confuses the toilers, diverts them from finding solutions to actual needs and misleads them into a sphere of nebulous and lifeless abstractions. That the moribund classes cultivate and support idealist theories is the main reason idealism is preserved and there is an abundance of idealist theories in imperialist countries.

Idealism's antiscientific nature is strikingly clear in its kinship with religion.

Religion is a fantastic, distorted image of the world in man's consciousness, expressing his helplessness in the face of nature and his oppression by society. The religious concept of the world is directly opposed to the scientific; they are antipodes.

Science's struggle with religion runs through civilization's entire history. By its discoveries science undermines the foundations of church dogmas about the existence of god and his omnipotence. In explaining natural phenomena by natural causes, science leaves no room for god. The church persecuted scientists in the past, and not a few perished at the hands of churchmen. Now religion is being forced into retreat before the power of human reason. Members of the clergy usually do not deny that power as they once did, but now attempt to prove that god himself endowed man with ability to know the world.

From its first appearance down to our time, religion has played a reactionary role, and continues to do so. By seeking to instill into men the idea of life's fleeting nature and the pointlessness of struggling for happiness on this earth, it advocates passivity and indifference. It promises the faithful as recompense "the kingdom of heaven." Clearly, these ideas correspond perfectly with the interests of the exploiter classes, since they distract the toiling masses from the revolutionary struggle. The exploiter classes, therefore, have always supported religion and patronized the clergy. Religion has become the instrument of psychological enslavement of the masses. According to Marx's graphic phrase, religion is "the opium of the people."

The similarity between the basic tenets of idealism and religion is easily seen, of course. Idealism and the religious outlook are twins in their essence and social role; both resist science and materialism.

Thus, *materialism and idealism are two basic directions, two opposing trends, two irreconcilable camps in philosophy.*

Philosophy's Basic Question

The watershed between the two opposing camps, materialism and idealism, as can be seen, is their differing solution of the question of the *relationship of matter to consciousness*. Materialism's basic principle is recognition of matter's primacy and the secondary role of consciousness. Being determines consciousness, say the materialists, basing their argument on the entire practical experience of society and on natural science. The basic principle of idealism, by contrast, is recognition of the primacy of consciousness and the secondary role of matter or being.

In view of its exceptional significance in determining philosophical positions, the question of the relationship of matter and consciousness has been designated *philosophy's basic question*. All other problems of world outlook are resolved according to the answer to this question. In fact, if matter's primacy and independence from consciousness are accepted, then it is natural to consider motion, space, and time as objective forms of matter's existence. But if matter is considered secondary, as a derivative of consciousness, then motion, space, and time must be taken as forms of consciousness or spirit. Or consider the question of scientific laws. The materialist answer to philosophy's basic question directly leads to recognition of the objectivity of laws. The idealist answer compels one to consider laws either as the manifestation of universal reason or as the result of activity by man's consciousness. There is no philosophical problem which does not depend on solving the basic philosophical question.

Philosophy's basic question has another side: how our consciousness relates to the world. In other words, do we know the world? The contrast between materialism and idealism emerges in the answer to this question also. Materialists confidently reply: Yes, we do know the world. Among idealists there is no unanimity on this issue. The majority, including most contemporary bourgeois philosophers, deny the intelligibility of the world and advocate, basically, human reason's impotence. Certain idealists, while not denying the possibility of cognition, do not agree that cognition is matter's reflection in the thinking brain of man. Cognition in their view consists in reaching the world of pure ideas, in comprehending the activity of the absolute spirit; of god, in other words. Obviously, this interpretation of cognition does not try to investigate the objective laws in nature and society.

Certain philosophers, seeking to conceal the reactionary character of their views, assert that they belong to neither the materialists nor the idealists, that they have risen above the opposition level of the two main philosophical trends.

But, in your own judgment, how is it possible to avoid answering the question of the relation between being and consciousness? It is simply impossible. It is no accident that those philosophers who attempt to overcome the onesidedness of materialism and idealism are advocating, in fact, the purest idealism. At first they declare that the basic philosophical question, in their opinion, is meaningless and that philosophy's task is to analyze "sense data." Later it becomes evident that by "sense data" they mean sensations and perceptions. Sense data, i.e., sensations and perceptions, emerge as the only reality there is. Consequently, the basic question has been surreptitiously solved in favor of idealism: sensations and perceptions are regarded as primary in relation to material reality.

As has been stated, materialism and idealism are tied in with definite class interests. The former, based on science, expresses the interests of society's advanced, progressive classes; the latter is bound up with religion and defends conservative, reactionary class interest.

To assume that all idealists consciously and deliberately defend reactionary interests would, of course, be an oversimplification. There are those among them who adopt progressive attitudes on many sociopolitical questions; many idealist philosophers, for example, are waging an active struggle for peace. What is meant here is that the content of idealist teaching serves the interests of the reactionary classes, whether or not that is the intention of its authors.

An acute and irreconcilable struggle for the minds of men is raging between materialism and idealism. At first glance it may seem only very remotely connected to economic and political questions and to the class struggle seething within society. In fact the connection is not remote. Both basic trends are attempting to shape the person's world outlook, a definite thought pattern, on which his understanding of political goals depends. The contest between materialism and idealism, therefore, is in the final analysis bound up with class struggle.

It is evident then that the question of relationship between being and consciousness is basic not only because other philosophic questions depend on its answer. The solution of this basic question must reflect the *Party spirit* of philosophical theory and its connection with class struggle in society, with politics.

The Party spirit of dialectical materialism consists in the fact that it expresses the working-class interests. Bourgeois philosophers maintain that this Party spirit of dialectical materialism hampers objective cognition of the world. But this is not so. The working class is interested in scientific cognition of the world because it needs it for transforming the world. Class interest, therefore, in this instance does not interfere with scientific objective cognition but, on the contrary, promotes it. Bourgeois partisanship is another thing: it really does interfere with a scientific, objective approach to cognition of the world. The modern bourgeoisie is not interested in scientific cognition of the developmental laws of reality because these laws bring doom to capitalism. Since this is so, can any impartiality and objectivity be expected from bourgeois philosophers?

The Party spirit of Marxist philosophy, its relation with working-class interests and with politics is most clear in its teaching on the laws of social development.

Review Questions

1. What is matter? What forms of motion in matter do you know?
2. What is the philosophical meaning of the concept of motion?
3. How do motion and development occur in nature and society?
4. What is dialectics?
5. What is the role in cognition of live reflection, abstract thinking, practice?
6. What is the meaning of the Party spirit in philosophy?

Points to Consider and Discuss

1. You are taking part in a discussion during which two points of view about the role of philosophy are expressed. One side maintains that philosophy is quite superfluous, inasmuch as all knowledge of the world is supplied by exact sciences. The other side argues that philosophy is the science of all the sciences. It is your turn to take the floor.
2. You meet an adherent of subjective idealism. He maintains: "Men cannot say a thing about the existence of objects in the external world. As you know, we are only dealing with sensations and perceptions. I see a table, which means that I am experiencing visual sensations. Is there a real object behind them? We can approach a table and touch it. But this will be a tactile sensation, again. Man has no way to find out what is behind his sensations. Therefore, it is meaningless to talk about objects in the external world." What will be your objections to this reasoning?
3. You are visited by two friends who ask you to arbitrate an argument. One of them asserts that man knows the world with the aid of his senses, while the other maintains that this task is performed by reason, by abstract thinking. What will you tell these friends? What arguments will you put forward to clarify this problem to their satisfaction?

2

The Doctrine of Society's Development

Human history is complex and many-faceted. Revolutions, uprisings, coups d'état, bloody wars, and ideological struggle—a never-ending succession of historical facts. How are we to succeed in understanding this turbulent stream of events full of contrast and variety? Are they governed by any law? Or does the arbitrary game of chance cause them? These questions are answered by the Marxist teaching on society's development, *historical materialism*. It enables us to establish history's inner, objective logic and find our way in the complex network of social phenomena, selecting from among them what is most important and essential as a basis of understanding.

The Materialist Concept of History

Social Being and Social Consciousness

Society's history is essentially different from nature's development. In nature there are no conscious forces, and development occurs spontaneously. Not so in society, where human beings, with their endowments of consciousness and will, are the actors and set specific goals for themselves which they strive to reach. The illusion arises that consciousness, ideas, and goals determine the life of society.

This is not so, in fact. In order to exist man must satisfy his material needs for food, clothing, footwear, shelter, and so forth. These necessities force him to enter into definite relationships with nature and other men, whether he wishes to or not: he tills the fields, builds dwellings, sews clothing, makes production tools, and barters his labor's products. All this adds up to the material life of people, their social existence, with its own objective laws independent of whatever ideas and theories society has.

The main content of social existence is the labor of persons producing material goods. By his labor man is distinguished from the animal world. Animals do not produce material goods; they consume what they find ready in nature. But man's attitude toward nature is active; he transforms and creates the material goods he needs by his toil. Labor is the sole source of all the riches created by mankind in the course of its history. Not only man's brain but also his hand, to a certain extent, is the product of labor. The work of thousands of years has perfected it, making it a skillful organ capable of performing the most complex operations. Solely owing to labor, the human hand has attained such a high degree of perfection that it has been capable of bringing to life, in the words of F. Engels, Raphael's paintings, Thorvaldsen's sculpture, and Paganini's music.

Labor, the eternal and natural requirement of human life, has always constituted the main foundation of society's existence and development.

Men would never have been able to engage in science, politics, and art or create philosophical doctrines and political theories had they not satisfied their material needs with the help of production. Thus, man's social existence determines his consciousness.

What explains the fact that diverse social views and theories frequently exist in one society? Under capitalism, for example, there are bourgeois and socialist ideologies. The first defends the capitalist system, reflecting the position of the capitalist class and its interests within bourgeois society. The capitalists exploit the workers; absolute power is in their hands. They enjoy all the good things of life. Quite naturally, theories representing their interests declare capitalism to be the summit of justice and perfection.

Socialist ideology, by contrast, represents the proletariat's condition of oppression. Reflecting its class interests, it investigates the laws of capitalism's development, formulates the revolutionary tasks of the proletarian class struggle, and determines the ways and methods of overthrowing capitalism and completing the transition to socialism.

Thus, the content of social ideas is determined by the conditions of social existence of the classes whose interests they represent.

Whatever social theory we select, its roots always reach back to social existence, the material circumstances of society's life. Hence an important conclusion: the basis of social development must be sought not in men's consciousness but in their social being, in the development of the *production of material goods.*

Productive Forces and Production Relations

First of all, let us establish the constituent elements of production. Indispensable are raw materials, from which man's needs are produced: wood, coal, iron ore, any object upon which man actively works, an *object of labor.* Material goods cannot be produced with bare hands alone. Man performs even the simplest task with the help of a hammer, ax, or spade. Organizing modern production requires machine tools, machinery, and instruments. All these means by which men act upon an object of labor, using mechanical, physical, and chemical resources, are called *labor tools.* Emphasizing their importance in production, Marx called work tools production's bone-and-muscle system. Apart from work tools, necessities for production include plant buildings, depots, storehouses, railroads, power-transmission lines, irrigation canal systems, etc. Together with work tools they constitute the means of production, i.e., the total material conditions without which production is impossible.

Finally, production includes men's active labor. Without men machines are lifeless. They cannot produce material goods. The working people, the *producers of material goods*, are the most important factor in production.

The means of production created by society and by the persons with production experience and expertise constitute society's *productive forces*. Productive forces impart a definite character to material relations between society and nature. The level of development achieved by productive forces is an index of man's dominion over nature and his active impact upon it.

The development level of productive forces is judged, first and foremost, by production implements. They have a history of their own, from primitive man's simple wooden and stone work tools to modern complex machines which perform all the steps in production, leaving to men only the functions of control and adjustment. The more perfect the work tools, the greater the quantity of material goods that can be produced. Primitive man often needed the whole day to fell a tree with a stone ax, an operation that now can be performed in a few seconds with the help of an electric power saw. A heavy-duty excavator can move more ground in seven hours than a thousand men could equipped only with shovels.

The productive forces level is also measured by the power supply available for production. For many thousands of years muscle power of men and animals was practically the only source of energy. Now men get supplies of energy from mighty power stations, surpassing human muscle power many millions of times.

Men's production experience, their skill and expertise, is another indicator of the development level attained in productive forces. Modern productive forces differ from those of a hundred or a hundred and fifty years ago not only in the perfection of production tools but also in the workers' industrial training, higher level of education and qualifications. Contemporary production is simply inconceivable without science, which itself is becoming a direct productive force.

Production of material goods is impossible for the individual. Even if a recluse could be found who wished to withdraw from society and produce all his life needs personally, he would find it necessary to use production tools created and perfected by society and apply production experience and skill accumulated by many generations. Labor resources and production experience, as well as labor products, are the outcome of men working together, in the process of which by necessity they enter into *production relations*.

But what are production relations? In primitive society, as history shows, all members of the tribal commune had an identical part in social production: Together they secured the necessities of existence and gave mutual assistance; they consumed together whatever material goods were produced. Why was this so? Precisely because the means of production belonged to all of the society's members. Social relations in slaveholding, feudal, and capitalist societies are completely different. Groups of persons participate in social production in a variety of ways, some exploiting others. Also, the labor product is distributed unequally, with a handful of exploiters taking the lion's share of the material goods produced and the oppressed classes experiencing need and privation. What is the explanation? In the exploiter society production means belong to an insignificant minority, the exploiters. With the transition to socialism the picture of the relations among persons engaged in the production process again changes: relations among them are established on the basis of cooperative toil, and material goods are distributed according to the work performed. This is because under socialism the basic means of production belong to the whole of society.

To define production relations among persons requires, obviously, ascertaining the ownership of the means of production. First and foremost, production relations are *property relations.*

Men cannot survive without using the material goods they produce. Thus, they enter into property or ownership relations. Production is impossible without some form of ownership, the historic method of appropriating material goods. Bourgeois economists state that property is personal power over something. Actually, something becomes a property object only when persons engaged in the production process enter into social relations. Property may be compared to language. As the product of one individual person, language would be an absurdity, for there would be no one to talk to. Similarly, property does not exist independently of human social relations.

Private ownership of the production means begets relationships of exploitation. Public ownership establishes relationships of cooperative labor. The participation of various social groups in production and the distribution of the labor product are determined by the forms of ownership of the production means.

What is the interrelation and interaction of productive forces and production relations?

*Law of Correspondence Between Production
Relations and the Character of Productive
Forces*

From the time of human society's origin, material goods have been produced by men without interruption. Were it not so, society in a relatively short time would consume its total accumulated reserves and perish. As history shows, production improves by constant renewal, and change takes place in productive forces as well as in production relations.

In the early history of mankind the production level was very low. The club, stone ax, spear, and, later, the bow and arrow were the chief production tools.

Men could merely satisfy their minimal, indispensable needs with the greatest difficulty, and this only because they worked together. The production means and labor product under such conditions naturally did not belong to individual persons but to the collective. Social ownership was determined by the low development level of productive forces. Exploitation was also impossible, since a toiler could not produce more than necessary to support his life. Cooperative labor relations prevailed in the tribal community. Production relations corresponded to the level of development of productive forces.

The primitive communal system is sometimes called communist. But this was primitive communism, based on need and privation, not on abundance. This was the reason for its limitation and its inevitable collapse.

In the course of development, production tools gradually improved and metal tools appeared. Division of labor within society took place, with cattle-raising occurring side by side with agriculture and, later, handicrafts. Division of labor inevitably led to barter of products. The farmer and herdsman needed each other's product, and they were able to satisfy their reciprocal needs only through barter. Production relations of the primitive system, which encompassed only commune or tribe members, no longer corresponded to productive forces, being incompatible with division of labor and barter.

Progress in production made the failure of these relations inevitable. Use of improved work tools sharply increased the quantity of products, which could be turned out no longer only within the commune but also by the efforts of individual families. Simultaneously, ownership of the means of production also gradually passed to family units. Private property had its beginning, and with it economic inequality among men. Inequality also increased because the elders and leaders used their status for self-enrichment. With new means of production available, the toiler began to produce beyond his personal subsistence needs. There was exploitation of man by man. The rich enslaved the poor and prisoners of war were made slaves. The primitive communal system was replaced by the slaveholding system.

In slaveholding society the means of production are in the possession of the slaveowner, who owns the toiler (slave), a "talking work tool." Production relations in the early phase correspond to productive forces, of which the comparatively low level permits progress in material and intellectual culture only by the ruthless exploitation of vast slave masses. This creates the possibility for production to grow, the social division of labor to deepen, and culture to develop. Separation of intellectual from physical labor takes place. Liberated from physical toil, scholars, poets, sculptors, and philosophers have an opportunity to devote themselves to intellectual activity, and science and art flower.

However, like a tireless mole, history continues working imperceptibly. Productive forces are perfected: agricultural techniques advance, men make metals and metal tools with increasing success, the skills of craftsmen improve. Productive forces are increasingly hindred by slavery-based production relations.

The slave takes no interest in his work; under the lash of the slave driver he works inefficiently. The slaveholding type of production gradually becomes obsolete, to be replaced by feudal relations.

In feudal society the basic means of production are in the possession of the feudal landowners. The toilers (peasants) own only scant equipment for tillage and cattle-tending. By taking advantage of this circumstance, the landowner makes serfs of the peasants, compelling them to work for him. He grants them a plot of land and in exchange requires part of their crop (rent in crop shares or quit rent) and tillage of his property (rent in the form of unpaid labor or *corvée*).

At first new production relations correspond to the developmental level of productive forces, giving an opportunity for certain progress. The serf, after all, has some material interest in the results of his toil, since a portion of the crop remains his. He therefore works more carefully, using his tools with greater efficiency.

In time, however, new productive forces emerge within feudalism. Along with the development of towns comes handicraft production. Division of labor spreads, barter expands, and national markets gradually take shape. Commodity and money relations eat away the very core of the feudal system, and development goes on. Manufacturing begins and the master craftsman is forced out of existence. The first machines appear. Plants and factories mushroom.

The new technology creates the need for an industrial labor force that is free of the bonds of serfdom and comparatively well trained. Having become an obstacle to social progress, the feudal system gives way to the capitalist system.

The means of production under capitalism are concentrated in the hands of capitalists. The production worker, lacking them, is compelled to sell his labor power to the capitalist.

Capitalist production relations create wide opportunities for growth of productive forces. Technological progress has exceeded everything created in the course of man's preceding history. But by this vigorous development of productive forces, capitalism is preparing the material conditions of self-destruction. In the Procrustean bed of capitalist relations there is no room for these new productive forces. Capitalism is incapable of employing the rich potential of the new technology for mankind's good. It breeds sharp contradictions, furthermore, which are expressed in crises, unemployment, wars, and the destruction of productive forces. The time is ripe for the inevitable transition to socialism.

The history of productive forces and production relations proves that they have intrinsic unity: a given level in productive forces requires a definite type of production relations. Only by considering them in combination is it possible to demonstrate the manner and method used to produce material goods in any given historical period of society. Productive forces and production relations, in other words, taken together characterize the *mode of production* of material goods.

Productive forces represent, understandably, the most mobile and changeable feature of any production mode. As men create material goods, they constantly accumulate production experience, enabling them to improve existing industrial tools and invent new ones. Productive forces, therefore, are always in a state of flux. Production relations are a different matter: forms of property being comparatively stable, do not change from day to day. Social ownership of the means of production existed for hundreds of thousands of years under the primitive system; slaveholding ownership, for several thousand years; feudal, over a thousand years; and capitalist a few hundred years.

What happens as the result of this uneven development of the two aspects of the production mode? Production relations lag behind productive forces and a contradiction develops between them, becoming more serious as time passes, until it grows into a conflict. Production relations slow down the growth of productive forces. Conflict is resolved by replacing old production relations with new ones corresponding to the productive forces level. The new production relations create expanded opportunities for growth of productive forces, acting as stimulation for them, in the first phase. However, productive forces again outgrow production relations. Incompatibility reoccurs between the two aspects of the mode of production. History makes a new leap in development.

An important inner connection exists between the two aspects of the production mode, as can be seen. Production relations depend on productive forces and must be consistent with them: production development requires this. A lack of correspondence between them generates contradictions within the production mode, making a change of production relations inevitable and conformable to the new productive forces. This is the essence of the *law of correspondence between production relations and the character of productive forces*, the mainspring of historical progress.

History is an enactment of the passions and emotions of political leaders, monarchs, diplomats, and military men clashing and seething in a storm of events. To the inexperienced observer they create history according to their whims. He does not even suspect the existence of profound historical processes, the effect of the developmental laws of the production mode and the result of the interaction of productive forces with production relations. In fact, these processes are the real foundation of human history.

Socioeconomic Formation

The Economic System and Society's Spiritual Life

Having learned the laws governing the development of production, let us consider the question of how social being, the material life of society, determines social consciousness, the spiritual life.

Let us reflect on how productive forces and production relations influence the development of social consciousness, beginning with productive forces. Perfecting the means of production and accumulating production experience facilitate man's growth in scientific knowledge of nature. It would be absurd, however, to try to deduce social ideas and theories directly from the development of productive forces. In fact, machine tools used in production in the Soviet Union and in many capitalist countries are identical, while our political system, ideology, and moral principles are radically opposed to those of the capitalist countries. Consequently, the basis of social theories, of political systems, and of moral relations should not be sought directly in productive forces.

What is the role of production relations, for example, in capitalist society? Production relations are capitalistic since they are based on private ownership and bourgeois exploitation of the workers. The political system fully corresponds to these production relations, with the state power belonging to the bourgeoisie, who occupies the dominant position in the economy. Bourgeois ethics is permeated with the huckster, the business spirit, reflecting production relations motivated chiefly by desire for gain, pursuit of profits. Bourgeois philosophical and political theories and views are, in the final analysis, subordinate to the interest of capital. It may be objected that progressive theories and views representing the interests of the working class and other progressive forces exist under capitalism also. True. But they do not develop in a vacuum. They reflect the contradictions in the capitalist system.

When comparing capitalist with socialist society, it is seen that a new type of production relations is established among men, built on social ownership. How does this affect spiritual and political life, ideological attitudes and social consciousness? In conformity with the new production relations, they have changed, too. Our country has a socialist state. Communist moral principles are being manifested in personal relations. Marxism-Leninism, our society's ideology, reflects the people's interest.

It may be correctly concluded that the system of production relations forming a society's economic structure is the foundation of its ideological life. The economic system is the *basis*, of a sort, upon which rises the *superstructure* of various social ideas and theories, different ideological relations, and political, juridical, and cultural institutions and organizations.

Role of the Ideological Superstructure

Social life is full of variety. It may not be reduced to economics; it is, rather, a complex interrelationship of economic, political, moral, legal, and other human factors. Without doubt, social ideas, theories, and attitudes have an important part in history. In reflecting the economic system, they give direction to human activity, thereby influencing society's development, including its economics.

Karl Marx said that ideas become a material force when they take hold of the masses. How powerful a force the ideas of Marxism-Leninism have become in our own time is well known.

There are, of course, all sorts of ideas. If progressive ideas accelerate social development, reactionary ideas hamper it.

Guided by specific ideas, men enter ideological relations, forming different kinds of social institutions and organizations. Ideological relations and institutions also have an influence on economics.

Thus, the ideological superstructure is not a passive reflection of the economic system, registering automatically whatever change occurs within it. It has an active influence in return and is an organic part of the social development process. Any attempt to reduce historical events to economics alone would inevitably substitute a sterile scheme for the riches and many colorful facets of social life, simplifying and vulgarizing Marxism.

For example, why did Russian realistic art flower during the nineteenth century? To explain it satisfactorily by the economic system alone is impossible without distorting the facts. With the backward system of feudal serfdom existing in our country at that time, how were superior works of literature, painting, and music created on such a basis? The unusual soaring of artistic thought is understandable if, along with economics, we take into consideration other aspects of life. The ideological content of Russian realistic art was determined, first of all, by the acute political struggle against serfdom that was growing in intensity in the country. Populist traditions, progressive ideological currents from the West, and a great many other factors affected it. But what of the decisive role of economics? It must not be forgotten that the political struggle in Russia, the populist traditions, and progressive currents in social thought in other countries all depended on and were rooted in the economic system. Thus, the economic system had a determining role in this case, too, but only as the ultimate factor, affecting art through politics, ethics, philosophy, etc.

The Great October Socialist Revolution is an outstanding event in mankind's history. Can this revolution be considered, however, to have occurred solely as the result of developments in economics or productive forces? Could the revolution have been successful if the working class in Russia had not accumulated great political experience, had not been through the stern schooling of 1905, and had not forged a lasting political alliance with the peasantry? Assuredly not. The success of the revolution is impossible to imagine without the Bolshevik party, which as battle headquarters for the revolution directed the struggle of the working class. In the final analysis, of course, the October Revolution was an expression of economic necessity visible not only in the political class struggle but also in the Party's activity and in the ideological struggle led by V.I. Lenin against the bourgeois ideology and opportunism of the right and the "left."

Society's development, as you can see, is the interaction of economics with politics, ideology, and all other aspects of social life. It would be absurd to deny their role. In this interaction, however, one must not lose sight of the economic basis running through it like a red thread and making it possible to understand the development of society in conformity with social laws.

What Is a Socioeconomic Formation?

When we try to create a mental picture of social life in its entirety, it ceases to be a chaotic mass of facts and events or a disordered tangle of human actions. In the system of production relations we discovered what one may call society's skeleton, which gives it unity and integrity. Men's ideological attitudes, spiritual activity and views, political interests, and moral ideas clothe the skeleton with flesh and blood, combining with it to make up a living and developing social organism. Thus, at every stage of its historical development, a society, taken as a sum total of all its elements, together with its proper economic system and ideological and political superstructure, constitutes an integral *socioeconomic formation.*

The history of society is one of development and sequence of socioeconomic formations. The process takes place according to objective laws independent of, and in fact the cause of, men's consciousness and will. There are five formations in all as is well known: the primitive-communal, the slaveholding, the feudal, the capitalist, and the communist. Replacement of the production mode means transformation of society's economic structure. Thereupon a relatively speedy upheaval occurs in the entire ideological superstructure. One socioeconomic formation gives way to another. And each subsequent formation indicates a new stage in mankind's history.

Bourgeois sociology offers theories of the historical cycle, according to which history is a series of consecutive cycles, each supposedly repeating its predecessor, with no forward movement on the whole. But this is not so.

Comparison of the developmental level in the productive forces of various formations convinces one that with the transition from one formation to another the developmental level constantly rises. Without question, progress is observable in the development of spiritual culture also.

In certain historical periods there is stagnation and even regression in the development of culture. In Europe, for example, during the transition from slaveholding to feudal society a decline in artistic development was to be seen at first. This is another illustration of the fact that social consciousness does not depend mechanically on the economic system. However, taking culture as a whole, not individual areas, and comparing complete socioeconomic formations, not individual historical periods, it is clear that each formation represents a step forward in relation to its predecessor in the area of cultural development.

Social development is not circular but ascendant, from the lower to the higher. This is the path of *social progress.*

Classes and Class Struggle

What Are Classes?

Every society, with the exception of the primitive-communal society, is composed of large groups of persons that differ in many essential characteristics. Slaves and slaveholders, feudal lords and peasants, capitalists and workers—all belong to social groups called *classes*. What are the basic characteristics of a class?

Let us take bourgeois society and analyze the differences between workers and capitalists. They differ in their life circumstances, political views, and moral make-up, and sometimes even in their language, dress, and manners. All these characteristics are significant but still do not reveal basic class distinctions that clarify the difference between worker and capitalist views and way of life. If we say this is so because the capitalist has a larger income, we arrive at deeper class distinctions, those of economics: the worker and capitalist differ in how they obtain their incomes and in size of income. But a new question arises: Why does the capitalist receive more social wealth than the worker? Only because the means of production are in his hands. As a result, the capitalist occupies the dominant position in the economy and is able to exploit the workers by appropriating the fruits of their labor.

Relationship to the means of production is the chief sign of class distinction. Other signs derive from it: the place of a class in the system of social production and its role in the social organization of labor; and the manner in which the class obtains the share of social wealth at its disposal and the size of that share. Also, political, moral, psychological, and ideological characteristics and features of the class derive from it.

Classes exist, as can be easily seen, only where various groups of persons differ in their relationship to the means of production. Classes do not last forever. In the primitive-communal society where property did not exist, there could be no classes. They emerged with the appearance of private property and will gradually disappear following its abolition.

Instrument of Class Domination

Since they possess the means of production, the exploiting classes wield great economic power, which they use to impose their will on society. Private ownership of the means of production, a system that enables the majority to exploit the minority, is declared to represent society's unshakable foundation. Any action directed against the interests of the exploiters is held illegal and is prosecuted by law. Social relations in a class society are regulated by laws and juridical norms expressing the will of the ruling class. The sum total of these laws and norms is called *the law*.

But why are all obliged to submit to the will of the ruling class and to abide by its laws? The reason is that the ruling class has the organs of power in its hands, such as the police, the army, the courts, prisons. All these organs constitute the state, i.e., the political apparatus which is the machinery for restraining the oppressed classes. In all socioeconomic formations based on private property and exploitation, *the state is the instrument of class domination by the exploiters of the exploited.*

The state originated with society's division into classes. Previously, social affairs were administered by all of the people together, and administrative authority was not removed from the people. The authority of elders and tribal chiefs rested on their personal qualities, their great experience, wisdom, courage, and so forth. With the appearance of private property, the propertied class seized political control of society. From this moment on political power was separated from the people and transformed into state power belonging to the exploiters, whose main function became the suppression of the resistance of the oppressed masses.

Replacement of the socioeconomic formation naturally causes change in the class character of the state. Accordingly, there are three distinct basic types of exploiting states: the slaveholding, the feudal, and the bourgeois.

Let us compare several bourgeois states. In England there is a constitutional monarchy; in the United States, a presidential government; in Spain, a Francoist dictatorship. All are of the same type, and still they differ. How? In form. A state's form depends, first of all, on *the form of government*, and, second, on *the political regime.* There are two basic forms of government: monarchy and republic.

Monarchy is rule by a single person (king, czar, emperor) with hereditary succession. A monarch relies on the ruling class and carries out its will. If his actions or intentions begin to diverge from the interests of the ruling class, the latter finds ways to replace one monarch by another more obliging. When the Russian emperor Paul I attempted to conclude an alliance with Napoleon, he was murdered by the nobles: an alliance with bourgeois France contradicted the interests of the landowning aristocracy. Referring to this event, a historian has remarked that Russia was an "autocracy limited by regicide."

A *republic* (from Latin, "common cause") is power implemented by elective organs. Understandably, in an exploiter society a republic, also, expresses the interests of the ruling class.

The political regime is reflected by the methods of rule. The ruling exploiter class may resort to openly terroristic methods of suppressing the oppressed classes, or it may govern by democratic methods, but in most instances it uses the "policy of the stick and carrot."

Let us now examine a very important concept, *democracy.* It is a state system that secures participation of the popular masses in the government and personal freedom, i.e., the possibility for citizens to enjoy political rights (equality of all before the law, freedom of speech, of the press, and of assembly; inviolability of the home, etc.).

In exploiter societies democracy is limited. In the slaveholding democratic republics of Athens and in early Rome, as you know quite well, a large segment of the population—the slaves—were completely deprived of all rights. In the medieval city republics, Venice and Florence in Italy and Novgorod in Russia, the wealthy merchants or craft—guild masters held the reins of power. In contemporary bourgeois democracies, despite the right of universal suffrage, power is held by the wealthy bourgeoisie, which uses its total economic might to control all branches of the state apparatus and means of propaganda. It is not reluctant to resort to bribery, fraud, and falsification in order to prevent the toiling masses from governing the state. Thus, the existence of democratic institutions does not change the class character of the state.

In the exploiter society the state, because of its very composition, is always a control instrument of the exploiters, and democracy is merely one of the forms of that control.

At the same time, under the conditions of an exploiter society, even this limited and formal democracy represents the most acceptable state form for the toilers. Democratic institutions are the conquests of the masses, which for a millenium have struggled for their rights and wrestled concessions from the ruling classes.

Despite its class limitations, bourgeois democracy offers possibilities for the struggle to improve the condition of the working class. By using political liberties proclaimed by a constitution, the working class can better organize itself for the revolutionary struggle to overthrow the capitalist system. Understandably, therefore, the monopolist bourgeoisie in fear of the growing revolutionary movement strives to get rid of democracy and establish its own overt dictatorship. This is why one of the most important tasks of the working class is the struggle to preserve and broaden democracy.

Genuine democracy is only possible under the conditions created by socialism, where the main democratic principles—the people's rule and personal freedom—find solid basis in economic relations.

Motive Force of History

From your studies you have become convinced that history is full of class struggle. The slaveholding states of the East, Greece, and Rome often shuddered under the blows of rebelling slaves. During the epoch of feudalism there were mass peasant uprisings: Wat Tyler's Rebellion in England, the Jacquerie revolt in France, the Peasants' War in Germany, the uprisings of Bolotnikov, Razin, and Pugachev in Russia, the peasant wars in China. From the beginning of the nineteenth century right up to our day, class battles by the proletariat have been raging in capitalist countries.

What are the causes of class struggle and what is its role in society's history?

Class struggle inevitably grows out of the social antagonism[a] that exists between the exploiters and the exploited. The very position of the oppressed classes in society, persecuted as they are by their oppressors, forces them into revolutionary struggle.

Bourgeois ideologists assert that the interests of the opposed classes can be reconciled. Judge for yourselves: How can the oppressor and the oppressed be reconciled? To achieve this the exploiters would have to give up their ownership of the means of production voluntarily. But the crux of the matter is that they have never done so, and they never will. Only by class struggle can the means of production be wrested from them and exploitation eliminated.

Replacement of a socioeconomic formation, as has been noted, takes place as a result of solving the conflict between productive forces and obsolete production relations. What is the attitude of the different classes toward this conflict? Clearly, the exploiter classes do not want elimination of obsolete production relations. They cling to them with all their might in order to protect their wealth and power. Remember how furiously the landowning aristocrats fought to preserve their privileges, how stubbornly they opposed bourgeois revolutions? And what of the contemporary imperialists? Is it possible to expect that they will voluntarily abandon the capitalist system? All their actions show that they will defend its existence to the last.

This means that the replacement of a social system by one more progressive cannot occur spontaneously, even if production relations have become an obstacle to social progress. It requires crushing the resistance of the reactionary classes who defend the old production relations. This is the historical meaning of the revolutionary struggle of the oppressed classes, who sweep from the path of social progress obstacles and obstructions raised by the reactionary classes. *Class struggle is the motive force of history in all exploiter formations.* In an antagonistic society social progress is impossible without it.

Class struggle reaches the highest level of acuteness in periods of social revolutions.

Social Revolution

In society's history periods of gradual development differ sharply from those of sudden breakup of an entire social system.

After the fall of the Roman Empire in Europe the years of the dark Middle Ages tediously dragged on. One royal dynasty succeeded another; there were wars and palace revolts; feudal possessions were repeatedly cut up, but all these events did not change the nature of the feudal system. And though from time to

[a]By *antagonism* is meant contradictions between classes whose interests are opposed and irreconcilable.

time the conflagrations of peasant revolts enveloped entire countries, threatening to engulf the landowning feudal lords and monarchs, the aristocrats, taking advantage of the backwardness and ignorance of the peasantry, split their ranks and drowned their uprisings in blood.

But the epoch of great social convulsions followed. In the sixteenth century, the Low Countries; in the seventeenth, England; in the eighteenth, France. The social structure of the leading European powers suffered radical change in only three centuries. Within a comparatively short period of time feudalism was replaced by capitalism.

Radical breakup of social order which brings about the transition from one socioeconomic formation to another is called social revolution. Its economic basis is conflict between productive forces and production relations. Progressive forces try to solve this conflict by abolishing old production relations. Reactionary classes oppose the resolution of this conflict. The ruling class uses the state's entire power in the struggle against the revolutionary movement. *Therefore the main problem of every revolution is that of power.* Once it has conquered the power of the state, the revolutionary class uses it to demolish the old system completely and establish a new order.

Historical experience shows that a revolution is not made to order. Its indispensable prerequisite is the *revolutionary situation*, i.e., a condition of society in which the ruling classes can no longer rule by old methods and in which the oppressed classes refuse to continue living according to the old ways. By no means does every revolutionary situation develop into a revolution. Mass political forces are needed to translate it into reality.

They develop from among those classes interested in liquidating the existing order and capable of bringing the revolution to a victorious conclusion. These classes represent the *motive forces of the revolution.* In order to rally political forces for revolution, the revolutionary classes must acquire certain experience in class struggle, form political parties and organizations, produce revolutionary commanders and leaders, and be ready for selfless actions.

Revolutions differ in character according to the tasks to be accomplished. If a revolution establishes bourgeois relations, then it is a bourgeois revolution; if, however, it leads to establishment of the socialist system, its character is socialist.

The vast role of the oppressed and exploited classes is revealed with unusual force in social revolutions. By heroic struggle these classes tear down the foundations of the old society. It is precisely these classes which produce the shock battalions of the revolution, storming the bastions of the state power of the reactionary classes and with selfless determination defending revolutionary conquests from the encroachments of counterrevolution.

The oppressed classes are the principal motive of all great revolutions. Revolutions, V.I. Lenin said, are holidays for the oppressed and the exploited. As a result of the active participation of the popular masses in political life, events are now moving with inconceivable speed. Social revolution may be compared to a purifying thunderstorm after which one can breathe freely. Revolutions sweep obstacles from the path of social progress. Not in vain did K. Marx call them locomotives of history.

Historical Forms of Human Communities

Clan and Tribe

From time immemorial, historical forms of communal living have existed alongside class and social differences separating people into distinct social groups.

The primary forms of communities—clan and tribe—originated in the blood relationship. The Russian term for clan (*rod*) indicates the common origin of its members. In the early stages of human history people were united and thought of themselves as being united, first of all, by ties of blood, by origin from a common ancestor. (Kinship was by either patrilineal or matrilineal descent.) Such groups lived together in communes. This did not result from either caprice or an especially strong clan feeling; it was necessary because of collective housekeeping, accumulated work habits, and the upbringing of the young.

As time went by, the clan grew larger and other communities branched off. Kinship and economic connections were preserved, and broader unions of clans—tribes—appeared. A tribe would number hundreds and even thousands of persons. In order to live and hunt, the tribe occupied a definite territory. Its members had language, religious beliefs, customs, and ceremonies in common. Clan and tribe life was built on spontaneously democratic principles. Leadership of the clan commune was entrusted to the elders elected by all its adult members. The tribe was governed by a council elected by the tribal meeting.

In subsequent stages of development, unions began forming among the tribes, dictated by both economic and military requirements. As before, however, kinship by blood remained the principal uniting link. Substitution of kinship by the territorial connection, which happened with economic development, led to formation of nationalities and, later, nations.

Nationality and Nation

A union of tribes was too broad an organization to last for a long time, since its basis was blood relationship. With developing economic relations, territorial proximity became more important, even when it linked persons not otherwise related. Common territory, language, and customs determined the identical historical fate of large groups of people and produced a single psychological character type and culture. Thus, *nationality* originated.

Nationality emerged during the slaveholding and feudal epochs. During the slaveholding era, for example, the nationalities of ancient Egypt and Greece were formed. During the feudal period Western European nationalities appeared. In the ninth century Eastern Slavic tribes established the Old Russian nationality.

Nationality was a comparatively unstable form of community. Many ancient nationalities disintegrated, others subsequently gave birth to various nations. Thus, the Old Russian nationality was the origin of Russians, Ukrainians, and Belorussians. The comparative precariousness of ties uniting one nationality can be explained by the absence of a single economy. Also, nationality has rather strong local differences within its common culture, and its language is divided into a number of dialects.

Consolidation of nationalities into nations takes place during the development of capitalist relations. Capitalism breaks down local barriers, creates a common national market, binds one or several nationalities by the common interest of its economic life. As a result, territorial unity is supplemented by economic unity, and on this foundation a common national culture comes into being and national awareness and patriotic sentiments develop. *A nation is a stable community of people united by economic, territorial, linguistic, and cultural-psychological ties.*

National relations play a great role in the social development. They are apparent in economics, politics, and culture.

Two Tendencies in the Development of Nations

National relations are characterized by two contradictory tendencies: awakening of national life, striving for national self-reliance and independence; and broadening of international relations, breaking down of national barriers and internationalization of the social life.

Essentially, these tendencies are both progressive. Flowering of nations and their close friendship equally foster the enrichment of humanity's common civilization. However, under capitalism these tendencies encounter strong resistance, and they succeed only by means of acute international conflict. The striving for national independence is opposed by the ruling classes of the oppressor nations and can only be achieved by stubborn struggle. Under the conditions of capitalism international relations take the form of antagonism: enslavement of certain nations and nationalities by others.

Clearly, therefore, the questions of national liberation and development are inseparable from social progress. The struggle of oppressed nations for their national independence and rebirth is closely interwoven with the revolutionary movement of the international working class for mankind's social liberation from the yoke of capital. Only in this way are all nations able to attain genuine national equality and full development of all their capacities and talents. Conditions will thus be created for friendship and the gradual drawing together of nations. Ultimately, once communist society has been developed and victorious over the entire planet, the result will be elimination of national distinctions and formation of a higher international community, a single human race.

Bourgeois Nationalism and Proletarian Internationalism

As has been stated, nations were born at the time that capitalism originated. Naturally, the bourgeoisie, in pursuit of its own class interests, from the very first has tried to take advantage of the rise of national consciousness and sentiments. The nation is proclaimed to be a higher form of community, and theories are advanced about the superiority of one nation or another over all the rest. The bourgeoisie attempts to stupefy the masses with nationalism in order to hinder the growing class consciousness of the proletariat and introduce international discord into the toilers' ranks.

Of course, in evaluating nationalism's historical role, a realistic approach is needed. The nationalism of an oppressed nation struggling against colonialism has an all-democratic, progressive content. In this case nationalist ideas and feelings come to the fore as expressions of protest against imperialism. Even under these circumstances, however, nationalism has inherent negative characteristics along with the positive. Its progressive content may continue to develop only when based on an increasingly consistent defense of the interests of the toiling classes and strata of the population—the majority of the nation—so as to counterbalance the interests of the reactionaries, who do not hesitate to betray the cause of national liberation in order to preserve their class privileges.

To nationalism the working class opposes *proletarian internationalism*, i.e., the class solidarity of the toilers of all nations and races in the struggle against the rule of capital and for liberation from all forms of social and national oppression. The famous slogan "Proletarians of the world, unite!" has become the battle cry of the international brotherhood of toilers.

Proletarian internationalism is deeply rooted in the actual conditions of the working class in capitalist society. Capital is an international force and exploits the workers irrespective of their nationality or skin color. Profits flowing into the safes of billionaires are created by the labor of workers of many different countries. International union of the working class—of all the toilers—is needed to tear down the power of the world's capital. The principle of proletarian internationalism has been consciously made the foundation of the activities of the revolutionary vanguard of the working class, i.e., the Marxist-Leninist parties.

Proletarian internationalism has nothing in common with national nihilism, which does not take account of the real existence of nations, their characteristic life style, culture, and feelings of national pride. The problem is not to deny the existence of national interests but to combine them correctly with the international class interest of the toilers.

While paying lip service to the nation, bourgeois nationalism, in fact, damages its vital interests. Under the banner of nationalism and chauvinism imperialist wars were unleashed, leading to the greatest national calamities. In the name of nationalism and racism German fascism plunged humanity into the Second World War, which became a national tragedy for the German people. By separating and setting nations against each other, nationalism sows hatred and enmity among peoples.

Proletarian internationalism links the fate of nations with the social emancipation of toilers. It awakens vital forces in each nation, opens to each of them perspectives of prosperity in the international union of equal peoples. While it champions the common interests of the international working class—the leading force of history—proletarian internationalism embodies the genuine interests of all nations.

Historical Necessity and Human Activity

Men Alone Create History

With the understanding that society, like nature, develops according to objective laws, it is legitimate to ask: What is the role of men in the historical process? Isn't man really just a blind tool of historical necessity?

Ancient mythology has tales about an implacable fate wielding power over men and gods. Man is incapable of changing what has been ordained for him by the goddesses of fate, the Moerae. Is it possible that historical necessity is similar to fate? And if that is true, would it not be better to withdraw from social affairs and passively wait for the inevitable outcome of events?

In their attempts to discredit it, bourgeois ideologists assert that Marxism-Leninism supposedly leads to *fatalism*, i.e., a world outlook according to which historical events are predetermined. Why struggle for socialism and communism, they reason, if all laws of history inevitably lead to communism? No one would struggle for the coming of spring or summer.

The laws of history differ from those of nature precisely in that they assert themselves necessarily by means of human actions. Historical necessity is reflected not in fatal processes distinct from men's actions but in the fact that with the development of production in society new material needs become urgent, forcing persons to act in large groups in a definite direction.

When feudal relationships turned into fetters of productive forces, there was a material need to destroy them. This need found its expression in the revolutionary actions of the bourgeoisie and peasantry, both of which had suffered the oppression of feudal relationships, and their revolutionary struggle swept away the feudal system. The soldiers of the revolution stormed the Bastille boldly and courageously, and they defended the new order from feudal counterrevolution. If it were not for their revolutionary struggle, the feudal system would not have collapsed by itself. This is a clear example that the laws of history do not operate automatically. Men create their history themselves, not arbitrarily but under the influence of environmental circumstances, among which economic necessity is paramount. It comes to the fore through the actions of individuals who are to some degree aware of the current requirements of social development.

Society as a whole does not struggle for the realization of progressive change. The forces of reaction oppose historical necessity since it threatens their prosperity and power. The activity of the reactionaries obstructs social progress but cannot stop it. For example, imperialists' attempts to preserve colonialism by all available means delayed the emancipation of the colonial peoples but could not extinguish the fire of the movement for national liberation and stave off the collapse of the colonial system.

V.I. Lenin strongly opposed the opportunists who underestimated the importance of active revolutionary struggle for socialism and the role of socialist consciousness, of a revolutionary theory, and of the Party in this struggle. Obviously, the more aware the revolutionary forces are of the necessity of victory for the new order, the more actively they struggle for it, and the more quickly social progress is brought about.

Historical Necessity and Freedom

Bourgeois ideologists usually presume that historical necessity deprives people of their freedom. From their point of view freedom is incompatible with necessity.

Let us seek to understand this matter by relying on our own experience. Suppose that two people should lose their way in a dense forest. One ignores the necessary connections existing in nature and, considering himself free, proceeds in the first possible direction. He may console himself that any time he is "free" to change direction and go the other way. And only after wandering around aimlessly for hours and failing to find the correct way, does he understand that his "freedom" has deluded him. Actually he is not free; he finds himself completely dependent on the environmental conditions, which fill him with fear and despair. The second person who was lost acts differently. He knows that in nature there are necessary connections between the four cardinal points and the positions of celestial bodies. Recollecting all he learned about these connections from his studies and his own experience, he chooses the path that soon will lead him home. Understanding necessity and acting accordingly help this man to orient himself in his surroundings. In reality he will be free in relation to necessity.

Knowledge of objective necessity gives men their freedom of historical action. The best example is the activities of our nation under the leadership of the Communist party. The Party is equipped with the knowledge of the laws of social development; it organizes the activities of our people in accordance with the historical necessity that leads to communism. The results are well known; socialism has been built in our country, we feel secure as to our future, and we are moving forward on the straight road that has been mapped out in the Program of the Communist Party of the Soviet Union and in the decisions of Party congresses in accordance with the laws of history. We are selecting the direction in which to move as freely and accurately as the man in the countryside who finds his orientation.

Of course, the socialist system of itself does not guarantee absence of errors in the field of economics, politics, culture, and ideology. That is why Marxism-Leninism requires serious consideration and careful study of objective laws, as well as decisions and actions strictly conforming to the needs of the development of society.

Thus, necessity by no means excludes freedom and, conversely, freedom does not exclude necessity. *Freedom consists in understanding necessity and in its practical use.*

The Popular Masses and Personality

In our history textbook we find several hundred names of persons who have left an unusually deep imprint on the life of society, great scientists, military commanders, persons active in public life, artists and thinkers of genius, and leaders of the revolutionary movements. Who does not know the names of Alexander the Great, Julius Caesar, Spartacus, Peter the First, Napoleon? It may seem that they are the only makers of history.

Beyond question, outstanding personalities play a great role in history. Is it possible for example, to deny the influence of Robespierre in the history of France? But where did his strength lie? Study of his actions, speeches, and decrees shows that he represented the interests of the mass movement of the French people against feudalism. That was the reason the masses elected him their leader and assured him of their support. On the other hand, what was Robespierre's weakness that led him to the same guillotine on which he had executed the enemies of the revolution? During the last stage of his activities he lost the support of the masses. The historical actions of great men, clearly, are supported by movements of the popular masses caused by profound needs of a society or nation in development.

There were many brave and able men among the Russian *narodniki* [populists] of the eighteen-seventies. But they were individualistic heroes, far from the people. Therefore their activities failed to bring the desired results. Even though outstanding for its individual qualities, a personality unavoidably suffers defeat if, removed from the masses, it does not reflect the urgent developmental needs of society.

One may ask: How would history have evolved if one or another of the great men had failed to appear in its arena? Is it possible that the bourgeois revolution in England would not have taken place if Cromwell had died in childhood? Of course it would have happened. As you know, history has been shaped by basic objective laws of development of socioeconomic formations. The seventeenth-century bourgeois revolution in England was a historical necessity. Had Cromwell not existed, other men would have taken his place. Many an historic event probably would then have developed in a different way and at a different time, but the fundamental direction of historical development would have remained the same.

The role of a great personality consists in having a clear awareness of, and giving precise expression to, the needs of society; he organizes the progressive forces and leads their struggle for the fulfillment of these needs.

In comparing distinguished leaders of various periods, it is easily established that the historical significance of their actions was determined by the scope of the social movement whose objectives they represented. The revolutionary movement of the proletariat, whose part in human history cannot be compared to that of any other social movement, makes exceedingly high demands of its commanders and leaders.

The workers' movement has brought forward the great creators of communist ideology and leaders of the toilers of the entire world: K. Marx, F. Engels, and V.I. Lenin. The founders of Marxism-Leninism had outstanding qualities: the gift of great scientific foresight, the ability to generalize the revolutionary movement experience creatively, the facility to combine theory and practice, organizational talent, the unswerving will for victory, and personal courage and charm. Mankind pays them the tribute of deep respect for the tremendous contribution they have made to the cause of the struggle for the toilers' liberation.

As great as the role of prominent leaders has been, there is nothing supernatural in it. Bourgeois ideologists, while denying the part the masses have played in history, attempt to shroud the actions of great men in mystical secrecy, ascribing to them an ability to mold history at will and glorifying them with blind worship. The cult of personality is totally alien to the materialist conception of history, which teaches one to look for the foundation of history in material production, in *the activity of the popular masses.*

K. Marx, F. Engels, and V.I. Lenin always condemned exaggerated glorification and eulogizing of individual leaders. They were implacable enemies of the cult of personality, and they explained the tremendous damage it could inflict upon the revolutionary movement.

The historical framework of any great man's activities is circumscribed by the social needs of a given epoch. Even in the fields of science, art, and culture, where personal ability has special meaning, the cultural process is determined in the final analysis by society's needs. Great scientists make discoveries that have been anticipated by the practical needs of society; great artists give expression in their works to the social views of their epoch.

Beyond a doubt, Darwin's theory of evolution was prepared by the progress of agricultural practice. Ideas voiced by Darwin's predecessors reveal that the need for formulating this theory had matured. Darwin's genius completed their work by generalizing the experience of the development of biological science.

In the field of classical art it is hardly possible to find a work that would not somehow present society's interests. And it is not by chance that the periods of sharp turns in history produced great works of art. The Renaissance brought a whole galaxy of great poets and painters.

But what is the origin of the social needs that produce great men? These needs emerge, first and foremost, as a result of the development of production. This being the case, we must conclude that the decisive role in history belongs to the persons occupied in production of material goods. This signal historical task has always been performed by the toilers.

Let us now turn to political matters. It may be said with certainty that in history no critical period can be found in which the masses did not take the decisive part. The people have always had the last word in revolutions and in wars of liberation. But even in peacetime the people exercised their influence on politics despite the effort by the ruling classes to prevent their participation. Kings, presidents, and ministers defending the interest of the exploiters have been compelled to take into consideration the people's demands. By their struggle the toiling masses limited the appetites of the ruling classes, often forcing them to make concessions.

At first glance, the spiritual sphere is the exclusive domain of prominent individuals. Scientists, writers, poets, painters, musicians form an unbroken chain of great men. But what is the source of ideas and inspiration for those great intellects? It is well known that science develops on the basis of practice and success in production. The sources of scientific ideas thus are hidden in the tremendous production experience gradually being accumulated by the direct producers of material goods—the popular masses.

As for classical art, we know from the history of literature that it has a profoundly popular character. Who is there among us who is not enraptured by folksongs, *bylinas* [Russian epic poems], and legends? The people is the great poet, artist, and musician. Genuine artistic masters draw their ideas, content, and artistic images from the people's life and creativity. "Zeus was created by the people," said M. Gorky. "Phidias incarnated him in marble."

As can readily be seen, there is no area of social life in which the decisive role does not belong to the people. And its role is growing throughout the historical development process. It is especially great during the present epoch, when mankind is accomplishing its transition to communism. The great historical task of constructing a communist society could not be achieved if the broadest masses of the toilers were not to join in this effort.

Intellectual Instrument of the Proletariat

Having learned the fundamental tenets of Marxist philosophy—dialectical and historical materialism—let us now consider its social significance.

Philosophy has existed for many centuries. Until the time of the appearance of dialectical and historical materialism it was remote from the masses and the revolutionary struggle.

According to a legend, the ancient philosopher Diogenes spent his entire life in a barrel. He had but one concern, that people not disturb him with worldly cares and obstruct his thoughts. Of course, not all philosophers of the past were like Diogenes. Many actively participated in the political and social life of their times. However, even the most progressive philosophical teachings were not consistently scientific. In their views about society, the philosophers of the past took the position of idealism. Their philosophical systems could not show the masses the way out of their poverty, the path of liberation from exploitation.

Marxist philosophy emerged as the expression of the interests of the proletariat, the class whose historical mission consists in liquidating the exploiter system and constructing communism. How is this to be accomplished? That is the question philosophy needed to answer. "Philosophers *were* merely *explaining* the world in many different ways," wrote K. Marx, "but the problem is to *change* it."

Marxist philosophy has become the intellectual instrument of the proletariat because it has provided scientific understanding of the world and revealed the laws of social development. It has become the brain of the liberation movement, whose heart is the working class. As the philosophy of the popular masses, Marxism has acquired the active character lacking in the philosophic systems of the past. Dialectical and historical materialism has become the ideological foundation of the class struggle of the proletariat, the theoretical basis for building communism. The communist and workers' parties rely on it in formulating their policies under the complex conditions of the contemporary epoch.

Applying the dialectical-materialist philosophy as a tool of scientific research, the founders of Marxism subjected the economic system of capitalism to thorough analysis, uncovered the causes and mechanism of capitalist exploitation, and substantiated the inevitability of the downfall of the last antagonistic socioeconomic formation, capitalism.

Review Questions

1. What do we understand by social being and social consciousness?
2. What is the interaction of productive forces and production relations?
3. Why is the class struggle within an antagonistic society the motive force of history?
4. How does replacement of socioeconomic formations occur?
5. Whom do we call great historical personalities? How is their activity connected with the activities of the popular masses?
6. What does Marxist-Leninist philosophy offer the working class and the toiling masses?

Points to Consider and Discuss

1. Bourgeois sociologists maintain that the main motive force of history is consciousness. "As you know, the actions of men are always premeditated," they say. "Even while taking part in the production process, men act consciously. When a man changes production tools, he has in mind a previously planned goal; he is aware of why he needs them." What will be your objections to this reasoning?
2. Imagine that you are having a talk with a person who says that the Marxist understanding of history seems to him to be onesided, inasmuch as it ascribes to economy the determining role in the life of society. What is your reply?
3. You happen to participate in a discussion about the nature of genius. Some participants maintain that a genius is gifted with exceptional natural talents. Others contend that the genius is the product of his epoch. Still others say that a genius is the product of labor. What are your thoughts on this topic?
4. Certain reactionary ideologists assert that revolution is a social illness of a kind, that it causes great damage to society, inasmuch as it distracts people from their day-to-day pursuits, makes victims, and disturbs the operations of governing bodies. Using historical facts, try to refute this slander of the revolution.

3 Capitalism and Its Decline

In his work of genius, *Capital*, K. Marx wrote: "In this work the topic of my study is the capitalist mode of production and corresponding production and exchange relations." Having brought to light the laws governing the production and distribution of material goods, Marx showed that the causes of the unavoidable downfall of capitalism and the victory of socialism are rooted in the economic conditions of social life.

Capitalist Commodity Production

The unlimited sway of *commodity production* is characteristic of capitalism. Commodity—or rather, the exchange of one commodity for another—causes all the contradictions in bourgeois society.

Even though the exchange of commodities existed long before capitalism, the economy of precapitalist formations was basically a natural one. Every feudal household existed in isolation, seldom resorting to exchange with the outside world, since serf labor and manor artisans produced almost all the needs of the landlord and his servants. Peasants had a natural economy. They not only cultivated crops and raised cattle but also wove cloth, made footwear and household tools. Of course, even natural economy called for exchange of some labor products (salt, iron, spices, objects of luxury) as market commodities, but this exchange played a secondary role, since only an insignificant number of products were earmarked for sale.

Let us recall the description of the country estates of Russian landowners by N.V. Gogol in *Dead Souls*. Neither Manilov, Sobakevich, Korobochka, Plyushkin and Nozdrev, nor their serfs, had any practical need for market products. If Nozdrev had a passion for trade, this was a gentleman's whim, not an economic necessity.

Under capitalism, however, factories, plants, and farms, as a rule, produce their goods for sale. All aspects of life in a capitalist society are permeated with the commodity-money relationship. Commodity exchange is the most widespread and commonplace relationship, and it is encountered billions of times in a bourgeois society. Everything becomes the object of buying and selling: "homes, land, honors, rank, countries, kingdoms, desires, pleasures, conscience, honor, wives, husbands, children, masters, servants, life, blood, bodies, and souls," wrote the English writer John Bunyon about bourgeois society.

Commodity Production

What is commodity production? Commodity production is a type of economic organization of society in which goods are produced not for personal consumption but for sale.

How are labor products converted into commodities?

Two social conditions must exist. First, there must be social division of labor, under which every person ceases to produce all his needs and is engaged in one kind of production only. Secondly, the means of production must become the property of individual persons or groups. Under these two conditions sale and purchase of goods become an economic necessity.

There are three forms of commodity production: *direct commodity production*, under which goods are made by independent small producers, artisans, or peasants; *capitalist commodity production*, managed by capitalists exploiting the labor of hired workers; and *socialist commodity production*, as it exists in a socialist society (described in Chapter 4).

Direct commodity production is not connected with any specific socio-economic formation. It has existed and continues to exist within various production modes. It appeared during the disintegration of the primitive communal system, existed under the conditions of slaveholding society and feudalism, and continues under capitalism and even in the present period of transition to socialism.

Intensification of the social division of labor between artisanship and agriculture and between city and village led to increased dependence of the feudal economy upon market relations and to its control by money. Development of commodity relations was thus preparing the ground for feudalism's disintegration. Long before the walls of feudal castles were being pierced by cannon balls of the new artillery, Engels wrote, their foundations had been undermined by money. Capitalist commodity production thus emerged from direct commodity production during the period of feudalism's decay.

Let us compare the basic characteristics of direct commodity production and capitalist commodity production.

Direct commodity production, as well as its capitalist counterpart, is based on social division of labor and private ownership of the means of production and of the labor product. This is their point of similarity. However, direct commodity production of craftsmen and peasants differs from capitalist production in that the labor of craftsmen and peasants are their property. Under capitalism the products of labor are the private property of those who did not produce them or spend a single minute of labor time in their production but happen to be the owners of the means of production. This is the basic difference between capitalist and direct commodity production.

A commodity is a labor product made for exchange. Clearly, it must satisfy some human need; otherwise there would be no purchaser. An object's ability to satisfy one or another of people's needs is called *consumer value*.

The consumer value of bread, sugar, butter, milk, meat, or sausage lies in the fact that they satisfy people's food requirements. The consumer value of boots, slippers, and shoes exists in the fact that they satisfy people's need for footwear. Labor products directly satisfying people's personal needs are not the only ones with consumer value. This value also applies to the means of production of material goods.

The use of commodities may be obtained by purchasing them. For the same amount of money, for example, one may purchase a refrigerator, four men's suits, or three sewing machines. In other words, one refrigerator costs as much as four suits of clothing. What does that signify? Completely different commodities possess something in common that permits comparing them in a definite ratio. This common element is not the physical, chemical, or any other natural property of things. Commodities possess only one common property: *they are all products of human labor*. This makes them commensurable. In comparing commodities people in fact compare the labor expended on them. The labor embodied in it constitutes the *value* of a commodity. However, labor itself is not value but only creates it under the condition of commodity exchange production.

It is not easy to understand what constitutes value, since, according to Marx's saying in his *Capital*, it does not include even a grain of matter. Nevertheless, let us make a gradual approach to clarifying the notion of value.

If value constitutes labor embodied in a commodity, then its magnitude depends upon the amount of labor spent on the commodity's production. The labor amount is measured by its duration or the working time. Consequently, working time is the measure of both labor and value. The working time itself is measured by hours, days, and so on.

The more labor expended in producing an item, the higher its value. A simple example proves this. A miner mines iron ore worth $10. From this ore a metal worker smelts pig iron which costs $30. Steel costing $90 is made from the pig iron. Pins costing $300, blades for pocketknives at $900, or watch springs for $3,000 can be made out of this steel. The same amount of steel was used for each of these commodities. Why then would the blades be more expensive than the pins, and the watch springs more expensive than the blades? Because a different quantity of labor was required to produce each of them.

Producers of commodities work under unequal conditions, using different production tools and varying skills; hence they spend different amounts of time to produce identical items. However, on the market identical commodities have the same value. Consequently, the magnitude of commodity value does not depend upon specific characteristics of the production process and the producer but is determined by the prevailing labor conditions, i.e., *the socially indispensable work time*.

Let us assume that there are three groups of producers of footwear. The first makes a pair of boots in seven hours, the second in ten, and the third in fourteen. The first and third production groups are small and supply the market with insignificant quantities of footwear, while the second group produces the bulk of the output.

Whose work time should be considered socially indispensable? That of the second group, that is, ten hours. Because socially indispensable time approaches or is identical with the work time of those enterprises (whether better or inferior) which produce the bulk of the commodities of a given production branch.

Now we are able to define the concept of value. *Value is the socially indispensable labor expended to produce commodities.*

Value is a historical phenomenon inherent only in commodity production. Under the conditions of a natural economy, value did not exist, and it will disappear in the higher phase of communist society, since commodity production will then wither away. Therefore, since it is not a quality of the objects themselves, value only expresses social relations among men producing commodities.

Socially indispensable time spent to produce a commodity unit does not remain invariable. It is reduced as production forces, technology, and science develop.

Thus, in England in 1784, the price of yarn exceeded 130 pence per pound but dropped to almost 11 pence in 1823. Following the invention and wide use of the spinning machine, the bulk of the yarn was produced in factories, its value being fixed by machine production. Hand weavers working independently with spinning wheels spent much more work time to produce yarn than the factories, and the value of their production dropped to the level of the factory-made yarn. Unable to meet the competition, the weavers were ruined.

As can be seen, the value of a commodity unit depends upon *labor productivity*. The higher the labor productivity, the less time spent in production and, as a result, the lower the commodity value.

Labor productivity is measured by the amount of production per time unit (hour or day). It depends primarily upon work tools and their level of technical perfection: the more perfect the machines, the more successful the labor of the workers. Labor productivity is affected by the workers' technical qualifications and ability to use equipment. The level of scientific development is also of great importance: the faster the latest scientific advances are incorporated into production processes, the higher labor productivity becomes in society. Finally, labor productivity depends upon natural conditions: in agriculture, upon soil fertility and favorable climate; in the mining industry, upon mineral wealth and oil wells.

The growth rate of labor productivity is not equal in all enterprises; as a rule, it increases first in individual capitalist enterprises with progressive technology, whose owners thus increase their profits.

Let us assume that in the overwhelming majority of enterprises of any one production branch a worker produces eight commodity units per eight-hour day. In one work hour he produces one new unit valued at $2; in an entire day, eight units valued at $16.

Should production improvement be introduced in one of the enterprises—a new tool or work method—its use will double labor productivity. As a result, a worker in that enterprise will produce not eight but sixteen commodity units during an eight-hour work day. The individual value of one commodity unit will then drop from $2 to $1.

However, the social value of this commodity is not changed by the increase in labor productivity in one outstanding enterprise. As before, it equals $2 per unit. The capitalist who applies the new production method continues to sell his commodity on the basis of its social value, thus gaining $1 on each commodity unit compared to other capitalists. This figure represents the difference between the social value of the commodity and its individual value.

Other capitalists also strive after larger profits; they attempt to reach the level of the technically advanced enterprise and find means to improve their production methods and increase labor productivity. However, the general rise of labor productivity results in lowering the commodity value.

If the majority of enterprises of a given production branch improves labor productivity to the extent that the normal, typical social production rate per worker is no longer eight but sixteen commodity units per day, then the socially indispensable time for production of one unit will decrease from one hour to a half hour, and its social value will decrease by one half.

As a result, all the capitalists will find themselves in an identical situation. In order to increase their gains over other capitalists, the big capitalists will again attempt to increase labor productivity in their enterprises, and the entire process will repeat itself, but now on a higher level of development of productive forces.

Growth in labor productivity is an economic necessity for all formations, since it represents the basic prerequisite for society's economic and cultural development. It expresses the new developmental level of productive forces, as well as the character of production relations, i.e., production mode, features, movement, and development.

Every production mode, compared with its predecessor, creates higher labor productivity, assures a larger supply of products, and increases society's wealth. Superiority of the new social system over the old is apparent in the increase of labor productivity.

V.I. Lenin pointed out that "in the final analysis, labor productivity is the most important—the central—factor in the victory of the new social order. Capitalism created labor productivity unheard of under serfdom. Capitalism can and will eventually be defeated by creation of the new, much higher labor productivity by socialism."

Money

The existence of money is inevitable in a society that has commodity exchange. Money is a commodity spontaneously singled out from among other commodities as the generally accepted equivalent of the value that all the others have. With the emergence of money came a new economic force whose possession brought wealth and power. "The ultimate commodity was invented," said Engels, "which in hidden form contains all the other commodities, a magic means which can at will change into any tempting, desirable object. Whoever possessed it controlled the world of production." With the development of the commodity-money relationship, money's power in society has grown. In bourgeois society, with its highly developed commodity production, money rules over men and enslaves them. "In this world," Balzac wrote, "the holy, noble, reverend, eternally youthful, all-powerful five-franc coin stands above the Constitution."

Money only makes sense as an expression of social and production relations. When Robinson Crusoe, the hero of Daniel Defoe's novel, found himself in the loneliness of an uninhabited island, he made good use of everything he salvaged from the wrecked ship, except the money. There was no one with whom Robinson could enter into an exchange relationship, and money, the most important valuable in a bourgeois society, lost its power and became a quite ordinary—actually, useless—object. "Useless trash," said Robinson, "what do I need it for now? It is not worth even my bending down to pick it up from the floor."

Gold is a universally recognized monetary commodity. Its natural properties make it the most convenient means to fulfill money's social functions. It can be easily divided into small quantities and massed together again without losing value; it can be stored quite safely, as it does not oxidize, and it has small volume and weight in relation to its value. A fixed amount by weight is used as a monetary unit in some countries, e.g., one dollar equals 0.888671 grams of gold.

Money performs many functions. First of all, it serves as *the measure of value*, i.e., it measures the value of all other commodities.

Every commodity is sold for a definite sum of money, which expresses the commodity value. Commodity value expressed in money is called *price*. Commodity prices—monetary expression of value—if demand equals supply, depend upon two quantities: the value of the commodities themselves and the value of gold. The lower the commodity value, the lower its price; the higher its value, the higher the price. And, conversely, the lower the price of gold, the higher the commodity price. Thus, commodity price changes in direct proportion to the commodity value and is inversely proportionate to the value of gold.

Price changes of precious metals have played a significant role in the history of prices, especially the price revolution following the discovery of America. Rich deposits discovered there led to a decreased gold price, thus causing a rise in commodity prices.

Money ideally fulfills the function of measuring values. Thus, one does not actually have to have money in cash to measure a commodity value. As a result of frequently repeated purchases and sales—i.e., exchange of commodities for money—both sellers and buyers mentally compare commodities to definite amounts of money (gold) corresponding to their value.

When it is used in commodity exchange, money serves as a *circulation medium*. To fulfill this function money must not be abstract but must be real. In the circulation process money changes hands without interruption. Today a commodity producer receives it for the sale of his merchandise, tomorrow he spends it to buy someone else's product. In its role of circulation medium, money functions as a temporary intermediary in commodity exchange. Therefore, it may be substituted by symbols or tokens of value, that is, by paper money. The only significant factor is the seller's certainty that the paper money he receives will also be accepted by others when he passes it on in exchange for commodities. That is why acceptance of paper money is mandatory on the territory of a given state.

The quantity of money needed for circulation is determined by the sum total of commodity prices divided by circulation frequency of the monetary unit. For example, if in a country the sum total of all commodity prices realizable in a year's time amounts to one hundred billion monetary units, and each monetary unit performs an average of five exchanges in the course of that year, then the quantity of money needed for circulation equals twenty billions. If, again, each monetary unit is expected to change hands ten times, only ten billions would be needed. Thus, the faster money circulates, the fewer the units required for circulation.

Newspapers frequently contain special terms for disorders in money circulation in the capitalist world. It is therefore advisable to become familiar, if only in general outline, with the most characteristic phenomena in this field.

If paper money is issued in proportion to the quantity of gold necessary for circulation, its purchasing power will equal that of gold coins. However, ignoring commodity exchange requirements, bourgeois states usually issue superfluous quantities of paper money in order to cover expenses for war, crises, and other shocks. This oversupply of paper money causes its depreciation, or *inflation*.

Inflation puts a heavy burden on the toiling masses, especially workers and employees, inasmuch as their wages and salaries rise more slowly than the prices of the necessities of life. Inflation also harms small commodity producers, farmers, and peasants. The bourgeoisie is only slightly touched by it, while big capitalists even come out winners.

When inflation begins to threaten the capitalist economy, the bourgeois state takes measures to strengthen its monetary system. With this aim in view various monetary reforms are introduced; *devaluation*, first of all, that is, the lowering of the gold content in a currency unit.

Money also functions as a *means of accumulation*, that is, as a means of creating *wealth*. This function follows from the fact that any desired object may be purchased with money; it therefore becomes a general embodiment of society's wealth, a means of its accumulation. Thus, a portion is withdrawn from circulation and becomes immobilized as treasure, which can only consist of money fully backed by gold and objects made of gold, silver, and precious stones.

Money does not always exist as cash. The sale-purchase of goods frequently takes place on terms of credit. This is caused by the unequal production time of various commodities, the seasonal character of their production and sale. For example, a capitalist industrialist makes a tractor in the spring and puts it on the market. A farmer needs it, but he will have money enough only in the fall after harvesting his crops. He buys the tractor on credit, by deferred payment. In this case money functions as the means of payment. It has a similar function in other transactions unconnected with commodity exchange, payment of taxes, for example.

In economic relations between states money becomes *world currency*. In this capacity it loses its national character and returns to its original form of gold bars. When economic accounts between states are settled, gold is accepted by weight.

National currency may also be used as world currency, if upon request by any state this currency is exchanged without difficulty for gold at the determined rate, in other words, if it is freely convertible. Until World War I the British pound sterling functioned as the foremost world currency. This role later passed to the American dollar. Following World War II the dollar was considered to be as good as gold, but actually it was above gold because it controlled the value of the metal. The fixed gold price of 1934 has been maintained at the same stable level of $35 per troy ounce (31.1 grams) of gold. However, prices of world trade commodities in dollars have increased during the last thirty-plus years on the average of 2.5 to 3 times. As a result, gold has been artificially underpriced.

At present the problem of supplying a sufficient amount of gold and convertible currency for international exchange has become extremely acute. This has resulted in a currency-financial crisis that has shaken the capitalist world. In 1967 the exchange value of the pound sterling was decreased by 14.3 percent. The French franc followed, with the lowering of its exchange value by 12.5 percent. In 1969 several other countries followed France by devaluating their currencies at the same rate. The currency-financial situation of many capitalist countries, particularly that of the United States, remains quite tense despite feverish measures to arrest further development of the currency crisis.

The Law of Value

Capitalists most frequently organize their production independent of one another, on their own responsibility and at their own risk. Therefore, no one knows in advance how many enterprises will engage in producing the same type of commodity, what volume of goods will be produced within a year or two, what quantity of goods will be thrown on the market, and how much the population will be able to buy. This causes spontaneous development and *production anarchy*, or lack of organization and planning throughout the capitalist economy. Though the sole owner of his enterprise, the capitalist remains the slave of the market, ruled by spontaneously operating economic laws.

Competition, the desperate struggle among capitalists for more advantageous conditions of production and sale, as well as for higher profits, is closely associated with production anarchy.

How can production of this kind exist and develop?

The law automatically regulating capitalist production is the *law of value*.

Under the law of value exchange of commodities corresponds to the amount of socially indispensable labor expended on their production. The price paid for the commodity ought to be related to its value. However, market prices are shaped spontaneously by the interaction of supply and demand. If more commodities are offered than are in demand, the price falls below the value, and vice versa. When supply and demand coincide, price and value coincide. Influenced by the fluctuation of prices, capitalists transfer their capital from branches in which commodity prices are below value to those where they are higher.

Let us assume that the value of an automobile is $4,000 but that there is no corresponding demand on the market: the capitalist, not knowing how many automobiles customers would need, produced more than necessary. The market responds immediately by a spontaneous fluctuation of prices. As a result of competition, automobile prices drop below value and are no longer $4,000; they are only $3,000. The price slump below value forces the owners of automobile enterprises to curtail production, and many capitalists who cannot meet the competition are compelled to transfer their capital into other production branches where prices are above value. Whereas in the past they produced 250,000 cars, now they will turn out, let us say, 170,000. It appears, however, that this time, too, the capitalists' guess was wrong: the demand was for 200,000 cars. Again the price increases over the value, reaching $4,500. Then there is an expansion in production and influx of capital and manpower from other branches. The prices fluctuate again, falling below value. Production is once again curtailed, prices rise above value, and so on.

Spontaneous fluctuation of prices in relation to value is the only possible mechanism to regulate capitalist commodity production. Price fluctuation, making production in one or another branch relatively profitable, determines expansion or curtailment of production volume. This is the essence of the *law of value which under capitalism regulates exchange of commodities and distribution of the means of production and labor among the various production branches*.

Market fluctuation of prices, of supply and demand, leads to inequality among producers, ruins some and enriches the others, unavoidable results of the operation of the law of value. The capitalist who does not want to be pushed out of the arena of capitalist competition, does not want to be ruined, must lower the price of his goods, increase labor productivity in his enterprise, and improve the technological level of production.

Let us assume that a commodity is sold according to its value for $2 per unit. The demand for the item equals the supply, because only under this condition does price equal value. When labor productivity doubles in an outstanding enterprise and output consequently doubles, the supply of the commodity will then exceed the demand, and its price will inevitably drop below its value, to $1.50 per item, for instance.

The owner of the outstanding enterprise is not afraid of the price slump, since even under these circumstances he will sell his product at a price higher than the cost to him. However, this price slump is fraught with grave danger for owners of medium-size enterprises. The income they receive is sharply curtailed, making them noncompetitive and possibly leading to their ruin. Therefore, if they want to remain capitalists, they are compelled to introduce new production methods and install new equipment.

To a certain extent competitive struggle stimulates introduction of new technology and production modernization. At the same time, competition and production anarchy cause destruction of productive forces, bringing incalculable misery to the toilers. We will understand how this happens when we learn about the mechanism of capital's exploitation of labor.

Exploitation of Labor by Capital

Surplus Value

Capitalist production is subordinated to a single aim: enrichment of the capitalists. How is this achieved, and at whose expense?

Before goods can be sold on the market and earnings realized, the goods must be produced; but labor and only labor can create their value. The capitalist is not a slaveholder or a feudal lord; he does not have slaves and serfs to whom he can give orders as if they were his property. He does however own the means of production, and in society there also exists a class of proletarians deprived of these means. The worker is free of personal dependence upon the capitalist, but in order to survive he must hire himself out to the capitalist and sell him his *manpower*. By purchasing it the capitalist acquires the only commodity capable of creating value.

Manpower is sold as a commodity for a definte price. A person is fit to work only if his vital needs are satisfied. The worker consumes a certain amount of bread, meat, butter, sugar every day; he wears out a certain amount of clothing and footwear; he uses a certain amount of wood or coal to heat his apartment; he must support his family, where a new live "commodity" is growing for the capitalist. Hence manpower's value equals the value of the necessities of life required to support the worker and his family.

Manpower value varies in different countries at different times, depending upon natural conditions and upon the toilers' living standard as historically developed. It is also influenced by economic causes: the development level of production, technical progress, etc. On the one hand, increase of labor productivity lowers the worker's cost of living and, consequently, the value of manpower. On the other hand, transportation expenses increase with expansion of city areas. Expenses for new services, telephone and gas for example, grow. New cultural needs appear. The contemporary worker in advanced capitalist countries cannot do without newspapers, motion-picture theaters, radio, television, etc. With the growing needs of workers and their families the value of manpower increases.

But the main influence on manpower value is the class struggle of the proletariat against the bourgeoisie for improved living conditions.

Once he has purchased manpower, the capitalist combines it with his means of production. With factory buildings erected and raw materials supplied, the worker takes his place at the machine and production begins.

The role of manpower differs from that of the means of production. Manpower creates new values, while means of production cannot. The value of the means of production is preserved by the workers' effort and transferred to the newly made commodities according to the rate of wear of the production tools. If a machine operates for ten years, then annually it loses one tenth of its value, which is transferred to the value of the newly created commodity. Raw material—cotton, for example—in its processed form is completely transferred into the new product, cotton fabric, and its value is also transferred into the fabric's value.

If the value of cloth needed for a topcoat together with lining, buttons, etc. equals $50 and the tailor charges $30 for his work, the value of the finished coat will amount to $80. The former value of $50 has been preserved and transferred to the topcoat by means of the tailor's labor. The additional value created by the tailor in his labor process equals $30.

The new value created by the worker in the capitalist production process exceeds his manpower value.

Let us assume that in an hour's labor the worker produces a new value equivalent to $2, while the daily cost of manpower is $6. In this case the worker should labor for three hours in compensation. However, the worker has sold not a definite amount of labor but his manpower, and its purchaser disposes of it as he pleases. Therefore, the proletarian must labor the whole work day. If an average work day is eight hours, then the worker creates new value amounting to

$16 during that space of time. Thus, in the production process the worker by his toil creates a value greater than that of his manpower.

The difference between these two values is gratuitously appropriated by the capitalist and represents the source of his enrichment. It is the *surplus value*.

Thus, the *essence of capitalist exploitation is production of surplus value and its appropriation by the capitalists*. The system of hired labor is a system of hired slavery.

We can readily see that the work day may be divided into two parts. During the first part (the indispensable work time) the worker produces the value equal to his manpower value; during the second (surplus work time) he creates surplus value for the capitalist. Therefore, the more time he works for himself, the less he labors for the capitalist, and vice versa. Understandably, the capitalist always strives to increase the surplus time as much as he can, expand exploitation of the workers, and extract higher profits from their labor as a result.

Acquiring surplus value is the main stimulus of activity for the capitalist. In most cases he is quite indifferent to what he produces: commodities useful for people like clothing, footwear, meat, bread, and sugar, or guns that bring death and destruction. He must produce usable values, since this is the indispensable condition for producing surplus value. Steel production, as Marx wrote, is only a pretext for production of surplus value.

Production of surplus value through exploitation of hired workers is the *basic economic law of capitalism*. Clearly, this law reveals both the aim of capitalist production and the means of achieving it.

Surplus value is created only in the area of material production, and at first glance it may appear that it is entirely appropriated by the capitalist industrialist.

In fact, distribution of surplus value takes place among the various groups of capitalists by way of constant struggle and desperate competition. At first, the surplus value is entirely at the disposal of the industrialists, from whom the merchants and bankers obtain their share. But commodities must be sold as well as produced. The industrialist, as a rule, sells his products wholesale to the trading capitalist, who channels them to the consumer. If the industrialist were to take care of marketing his commodities himself, he would have to invest additional funds in commercial buildings, hire sales personnel, etc. So the industrialists let the trade capitalist do the marketing of commodities, and in compensation for this they must cede him a portion of the surplus value.

Consequently, all kinds of indirect income in capitalist society—trade profits, loan interest, bank profits—are forms of surplus value, while the sole source of all indirect income is the surplus labor of workers engaged in the production of material goods. Thus, not only the capitalists for whom they work but the capitalist class as a whole exploits the workers.

Capital

In capitalist society the means of production are sold and bought for money; they are commodities with their own value. The production process begins with purchase of the means of production and manpower by the capitalist. The result of combining them is commodity production. The capitalist then sells the products of his enterprise for an amount higher than that spent on their production. *The value that brings surplus value by exploiting hired labor is capital.*

Bourgeois ideologists claim that capital first appeared as a result of industriousness and other virtues of its owners: the thrifty became capitalists, while the idlers and squanderers became hired hands. Marx unmasked this fabrication aimed at simpletons. Capital appeared as a result of plunder, coercion, expropriation of land from the peasants, and pillage of colonies. But even should we agree that the first capital did originate in labor, that does not change its present nature, since after several years all capital, whatever its origin, was replaced by surplus value, the result of exploitation. Capitalists must cover their expenditures from the surplus value. If it were not for exploitation of hired workers who create surplus value, the capitalists would have soon exhausted their original capital and be left with nothing.

Let us assume that all funds invested in a capitalist enterprise, the entire capital, equals $100,000 and that the hired workers annually produce surplus value amounting to $20,000. Let us further assume that the capitalist spends the entire surplus value. In this case, the surplus value funds spent in the course of five years would equal the original capital figure. Consequently, without exploitation of hired workers nothing would have been left of the capitalist's funds over the five-year period: the owner retains his capital with the help of the surplus value squeezed from his workers.

In practice, the owners do not throw all their surplus value to the winds. Thirst for profits induces them to expand production, and they spend a portion of their profits for that purpose. Production expansion and increase in the number of exploited workers lead to growth of surplus value accruing to the capitalist. Such bliss would hardly be found even in a fairy tale: the owner lives in greater and greater luxury, with his wealth constantly growing.

This leads to two conclusions: first, all capital is the result of exploitation; second, no given sum of money, no matter how large, constitutes capital of itself, nor does the sum total of the means of production—factories, plants, raw materials, fuel and machines. They may become capital only under definite conditions: when there exists both a class of private owners of the means of production and a class of hired workers who sell their manpower as a commodity. Therefore, *capital represents the social relationship between the capitalist and the worker, and its essence is exploitation of labor.*

When the capitalist system is liquidated, the means of production become social property. Manpower ceases to be a commodity and capital as an historic category ceases to exist.

Capital Accumulation and the Proletariat's Deteriorating Situation

Surplus value is the source of capital accumulation, of which capitalists spend a certain part for their personal needs and the remaining part for expansion of production. This second part is converted into capital, through capitalization. This process is called *capital accumulation*.

Surplus value acquired by the capitalist grows with the expansion of production. He is given the opportunity to expand production, exploit more workers, and appropriate an ever-growing amount of surplus value. While tremendous wealth is concentrated at one pole of society, and the luxury and parasitism of the exploiter classes are increasing, at the other pole exploitation of the proletariat increases. The gap between those who by their labor create all the wealth and those who appropriate this wealth is widening. This is the *law of capital accumulation*.

At the dawn of capitalism the new entrepreneur not only extorted all he could from the proletariat, he frequently economized on trifles in order to multiply his capital. In literature, hardly by chance, spendthrift aristocrats who squander tremendous fortunes are contrasted with prudent and thrifty industrialists, bankers, and moneylenders like Dombey, and Nusingen, and Gobseck. The capitalist of this period frequently spent days and nights at his factory. He knew his workers by name, attended to his own bookkeeping.

As capital accumulated, the most successful businessmen amassed gigantic fortunes and no longer burdened themselves with hard work. The heirs of Dombey, Nusingen, and Gobseck, who possess billions of francs, dollars, and pounds sterling, do not need to economize. They "go mad from over-abundance," literally: build palaces with swimming pools covered with gold plated tiles, buy castles in England and ship them to America, give parties for their pet dogs, and even leave them inheritances.

Capitalism not only assures a small group of parasites the means of living in luxury at the expense of exploited labor, it also condemns a part of the proletarians to unemployment and poverty, depriving them of the means of livelihood.

Unemployment is the inevitable companion of the capitalist system. It appeared in the early stages of capitalist development. Technical progress and the use of more productive machines led to curtailed demand for manpower. And if, at first, unemployment was temporary and disappeared relatively quickly, later it became permanent. A whole army of people deprived of work has appeared in society, the so-called reserve army of labor. In the United States, for example, in recent years the number of unemployed has ranged from three to ive million persons. What are the reasons for unemployment? Is it due to new equipment that a certain number of working people have been deprived of their daily bread? As we know from history, that was exactly what the Luddites thought when they turned their wrath against the machines. But obviously machines have nothing to do with it. The most convincing proof of this is the fact that in the socialist countries where new machines are introduced into the production process on a mass scale, there is no unemployment, and cannot be.

The reason for unemployment is hidden in the capitalist economic system. Technical progress, affording an opportunity to increase production with less expenditure of labor, makes possible the reduced work day and wage increases. The capitalist, however, modernizes his equipment not for the workers' sake, but in order to enlarge his own profits. Therefore, he does just the opposite: dismisses some workers and thus forces the others to work even more intensively. How does he succeed in doing that? Because the larger the number of unemployed, the more the employed group clings to its jobs. Fear of losing a livelihood is stronger than any stick. Thus unemployment is used as a means of pressure over the employed segment of the working class.

The newspaper of the magnates of American capital, the *Wall Street Journal*, wrote openly on this subject: "A bricklayer who sees at the gate two unemployed eager to take his place will lay more brick without requesting any additional wages or bonuses."

And, to realize what the loss of work means in the United States, one should read a letter written by a certain David Hume to an American newspaper:

I am an engineer by profession. For six years I worked in a metallurgical plant near Philadelphia. On November 30, last year, I was given notice of dismissal as of December 30. I begged to stay on, considering my poor health and the fact that my wife was expecting a baby. The company coldly rejected my request. My wife and I were shaken by the misfortune that had befallen us. I went to a hospital, but after a week I had to leave, since my wife had fallen ill from worry. The child was born prematurely and died twelve hours later. I was again hospitalized. And all of this must be paid for. Payment must go to the attending physician, for the hospital bed, for the bed in the maternity ward, and the baby's funeral. Soon we will lose our home and all our possessions. We have nowhere to go. We do not want to live.

Contemporary technology is a miraculous invention of the human mind, capable of facilitating labor and providing people with a more prosperous life. However, its capitalist use leads to the deterioration of the proletariat's situation. And the unemployed are by no means the only ones to suffer. For increased intensity of work means nothing else but the premature exhaustion of manpower. Many proletarians subjected to the so-called assembly-line labor used in the capitalist production system turn into invalids at forty or forty-five.

The deteriorating situation of the proletariat is not a direct and uninterrupted process. It may intensify or diminish according to specific conditions and characteristics of different countries. Capitalism's offensive against the vital rights of the toilers meets firm resistance from the working class. By drastic measures (strikes, etc.) the proletariat succeeds in obtaining partial concessions, such as wage increases or a reduced work day. All this, however, does not compensate for the fact that the exploitation of the proletariat is on the increase, as a whole, in the capitalist world.

Economic crises, those catastrophic drops in production, bring the toilers particularly severe hardship. At all times the capitalists attempt to increase output, induced not only by their desire for profits but by the competitive struggle as well. But the income of the general public is increasing very slowly, if at all. In other words, the public demand and ability to pay for commodities lag further and further behind their production. Periodically the lag reaches a point at which tremendous stockpiles of goods accumulate, medium-sized farmers and capitalists are ruined, thousands of enterprises are closed down, unemployment rises sharply, and wages drop.

At first glance it would seem that overproduction is the reason for crisis. Actually, the goods find no buyers not because they are not needed but because there is no way to pay for them. Consumer capacity is not determined by an empty stomach but by the contents of the purse. The result is so unnatural a phenomenon as hunger in the midst of plenty. Stores and warehouses are loaded with produce and commodities, but capitalists find it more to their advantage to let the goods rot than to sell them at a fraction of their price. They take pains to stop the price drop by any means, so as to be compensated later for their losses.

In 1934 a total of 2,400,000 people starved to death in capitalist countries. But in the United States more than 1,000,000 carloads of grain (enough to feed 100 million people for a year), 267,000 carloads of coffee, 258,000 tons of sugar, 26,000 tons of rice, 25,000 tons of meat, and a large quantity of various other products were destroyed.

Crises clearly show the predatory nature of capitalism. They give proof that capitalism slows down the development of productive forces and in many ways undoes mankind's progress. Now that capitalism is going through the last stage of its existence, this has become particularly clear.

Imperialism

Capitalism's Final Stage

At the end of the nineteenth century the attention of the entire world was riveted on Central America and South Africa, where the Spanish-American and the Anglo-Boer wars were raging. They were the bloody turning points marking capitalism's entry into the higher and final stage of its development—*imperialism*.

The concept of imperialism should not be linked only with conquest by force of other countries. Capitalism's development led to serious changes in the economic and political structure of bourgeois society. Therefore, we speak of capitalism as entering the last stage of development.

At the same time imperialism does not represent a separate social system different from the capitalist system. As heretofore, the economic basis of bourgeois society in the epoch of imperialism is the capitalist ownership of the means of production, irrespective of specific forms (individual, corporate, or state-capitalist ownership). Production of surplus value and exploitation of the class of hired workers by the capitalist class remain the cornerstones of the economy.

The same capitalist laws of economy continue to operate under imperialism: the law of surplus value, the general law of capital accumulation, laws of competition, and others.

V.I. Lenin gave a comprehensive definition of imperialism. He showed that imperialism is first of all, a monopoly capitalism; second, a parasitic or decaying capitalism; third, a dying capitalism. The briefest possible definition of imperialism he said, is *monopoly capitalism*.

What are monopolies and what is the difference between monopoly and premonopoly capitalism? Monopolies are gigantic capitalist associations which have exclusive control over one or even several branches of the economy. They emerged as the natural result of concentration of production and of capital.

Free competition in the era of industrial capitalism leads to the exclusion and replacement of smaller enterprises by large ones. There is concentration of production in increasingly larger enterprises. There is also concentration of capital, which grows as part of the surplus value is added to it. Simultaneously with concentration of capital, its centralization takes place. It is either a voluntary or a coercive amalgamation: voluntary when new share- or stock-holding companies are formed, coercive when smaller companies are absorbed by larger ones in the course of competitive struggle.

Competition is particularly acute and destructive between big capitalists, with each trying to capture the market and wipe out his competitors. When this proves impossible, the capitalists attempt to reach agreement on the volume of production output, prices, and so forth. A few dozen gigantic enterprises can more easily reach agreement than hundreds and thousands of smaller ones. Thus, concentration and centralization of capital and production lead to the rise of monopolies.

As early as the beginning of the twentieth century, gigantic, empirelike monopolistic corporations of coal, oil, and steel were formed in the advanced capitalist countries. In the metallurgy industry in the United States five monopolies predominate, the largest of which are United States Steel and

Bethlehem Steel Corporation. They produce more than four-fifths of the steel output of the country. One of the largest trusts in the world, Standard Oil, dominates the oil industry. The chemical industry is controlled by the Du Pont de Nemours concern; the electric industry by General Electric Co.; the automotive industry is dominated by three monopolies: General Motors, Ford, and Chrysler.

In West Germany the chemical industry is dominated by the successors of the I.G. Farben Industrie; the machine-building industry by Mannesmann and Lenkner; the steel production is controlled by the Flick, Thyssen companies and others.

In England, hegemony in the various branches of industry is held by the Vickers military-metallurgical concern, the Imperial Chemical Industries trust, and the Royal Dutch Shell Oil monopoly. In France, 80 percent of the steel output is concentrated in the hands of four monopolistic groups. The Eugene Pechiney trust completely controls the entire production of aluminum; the Boussac textile company, 70 percent of cotton fabric production.

Big monopolies also dominate the financial system and trade. For example, in the United States a few powerful financial groups rule the country's whole economy and determine its policies. These include the Morgans, Rockefellers, du Ponts, Mellons, and others. International monopolies are also formed, economic associations uniting capitalists of different countries, which divide the consumer markets and raw material sources among themselves.

The fact that under imperialism free competition is replaced by the monopolies does not mean that all competition is abolished. Many medium-sized and small enterprises and masses of small commodity producers—peasants and artisans—still preserve their existence in the capitalist countries. Obviously, they are incapable of fighting the conglomerations and must pay a kind of tribute to the monopolies. Thus, in the United States most farmers sell their produce wholesale to big commercial companies, which then resell it to the retailers. The farmer is helpless when confronted by the monopolies: he must accept the price they fix. Taking advantage of this, the monopolists lower the wholesale prices and increase the retail prices. This price differential (the so-called "scissors") brings them fabulous profits. Meanwhile, every year thousands of farmers are ruined.

This example helps us to understand the mechanism of monopolistic pricing. In the era of imperialism the bulk of commodities is not sold at prices freely established in the market: the monopolists are able to impose higher prices, permitting them to earn excessive profits by robbing the workers and the other toiling strata of the population.

Having accumulated tremendous excess capital, the monopolists try to put it into circulation. However, it becomes increasingly difficult to find a profitable use for it in economically advanced capitalist countries. The monopolists then search feverishly for new fields of activity; they *export capital* in ever-growing amounts and invest it in industrial and trade enterprises abroad.

Prior to World War II capital was exported mostly to the colonies and underdeveloped and economically backward countries, where its use brought particularly high returns, since wages were much lower than in Europe or the United States.

The monopolists invested their capital in colonial countries, receiving in return an endless stream of African gold and diamonds, oil from the Near and Middle East, natural rubber from Malaya, coffee and fruit from South American countries. It is quite understandable that the monopolies of those countries with colonial possessions were in the most advantageous position. As Lenin said, those who were late getting seated at the imperialist dining table demanded their "share" in the plunder of the colonies with increasing insistence. This was the reason for imperialist wars waged for the reapportionment of the world.

The situation has been aggravated by the fact that the capitalist countries have developed quite unevenly, reminding one of a long-distance race in which the runners' positions are constantly changing. The countries that only yesterday were economically and militarily the strongest today must stand aside and let their competitors move ahead. And tomorrow the correlation of forces among imperialist powers again will change. Each one in its forward push tries to use its advantages (if only temporary) for redistribution of markets, spheres of influences, and territories. The strongest among them even make claims to world domination. The *law of the uneven development of capitalism during the epoch of imperialism*, discovered by V.I. Lenin, forms hostile groups of imperialist states rent by acute contradictions.

Changes in the economy of capitalism cause changes in its policies.

V.I. Lenin more than once noted that "a turn from democracy to reaction" is characteristic of imperialism. In its intensification of the exploitation of toilers, the monopolistic bourgeoisie repeatedly resorts to terroristic administrative methods to suppress the resistance of the popular masses. Fascism is the most overt form of the terroristic regimes. The working class, all the progressive forces of society capable of preventing the victory of reaction, are resisting the monopolies.

State-Monopoly Capitalism

As early as the first decades of the twentieth century, symptoms of fusion of capitalist monopolies with the bourgeois state appeared. On this basis V.I. Lenin made a conclusion about the gradual transformation of monopoly capitalism into state-monopoly capitalism.

What is its nature? In answer one should trace the changes that occurrred in the relations, first of all, between the monopolies and the bourgeois state; and second, in the role of the state in imperialist countries.

From its very inception the bourgeois state has been the tool of class domination by the capitalists, expressing the will and the interests of this class as a whole. Naturally, the big bourgeoisie exercised the greatest influence on state affairs and the course of internal and external policies. However, during the period of free competition, there was struggle between the different strata of the ruling class for predominance in the exercise of power. This struggle ceased only during those periods when the exploiters united their forces to suppress the revolutionary actions of the toilers. The situation changed with capitalism's entry into its imperialist stage. Concentration of production and centralization of capital have given the monopolistic ruling clique such economic might that other strata of the bourgeoisie cannot compete with it in the struggle for power.

The more the economic domination by the monopolies was strengthened, the more open was their striving for undivided power, for complete submission of the government apparatus. And if during the early stages the magnates of capital acted mostly through their agents (financing members of parliaments and cabinet ministers, bribing leaders of political parties), as time went on they became less and less inhibited. They left the backstage and began personally to assume the highest government posts. In recent years this process has been in full swing.

President Eisenhower's administration was known in the United States as the cabinet of seventeen millionaires. In the administrations that followed big capitalists also held important posts. Of course, this does not mean that monopolies have renounced their former methods; they continue to use them. Thus, the overwhelming majority in the United States Congress consists of bourgeois lawyers who are in the service of, or are getting bribes from, big corporations. Both principal political parties of the country, the Republican and Democratic parties, defend the interests of monopoly capital; and many billionaires, so as not to miscalculate, simultaneously make large financial contributions to the treasuries of both political parties.

In our times large associations of monopolies are not stingy and spend dollars, pounds sterling, marks, and francs in order to get influential and comfortable government jobs for themselves or their trusted friends. But of course it is not just a matter of their personal participation in the government. Of incomparably greater significance is the fact that the associations that unite the biggest monopolists exercise decisive influence on the policies of the bourgeois governments. The Chamber of Commerce and the National Association of Manufacturers, representing the interests of "big business," are in fact determining the political course of the United States. An identical situation exists in Great Britain, West Germany, and other capitalist countries.

Having the government machinery at their disposal, the monopolies succeeded in making it a perfect servant of their goals inside the country and in the international arena. The fundamental change of the role of the bourgeois state takes place under the influence of monopolies, to a considerable extent. Why do we say "to a considerable extent"? Because this process is influenced by other factors also. The working class, all the toiling strata of society, are resolutely fighting domination by the monopolies, and in a number of areas they are achieving essential successes. But changes in the actions of the bourgeois state are mainly caused by the specific interests of the monopolies.

These changes find their expression first and foremost in increasing intervention by the bourgeois state in economic matters. It is well to recall how this matter looked in the past. In the period of free competition the state interfered with the economy only slightly, leaving unlimited freedom to private entrepreneurs, the capitalists. The bourgeois theoreticians of that time called the state a "night watchman," thus stressing the fact that the state was there to protect the existing order, exclusively. The contemporary imperialist state actively intrudes into the sphere of relations between labor and capital, makes attempts at programing economic development on nationwide scale, undertakes the financing of scientific research, redistributes a portion of the national income, and owns a production sector that is sometimes quite substantial.

At first glance all this apparently corresponds to the pressing needs of social development. After all, the social character of modern production urgently requires introduction of planning into the economy, and this cannot be achieved without increasing the state's regulatory role. From this point of view the processes taking place in contemporary capitalist society represent preparation of the material prerequisites for the transition to socialism. But this is only one side of the problem. On the other side, state intervention in economic life under the conditions of subordination of the government apparatus to the monopolies serves the interests of the monopolies, first of all.

By intervening in the relations between labor and capital, the contemporary bourgeois state allegedly acts as an unbiased arbiter, a judge before whom the interests of both parties are equal. Actually, the state power and authority are fully on the side of the capitalists. Thus, the Taft-Hartley Act and other antilabor bills in the United States were passed to allow the government to bar strikes on the basis of their "endangering the state security," and to "freeze" workers' wages regardless of rising prices.

State agencies in many capitalist countries now work on economic development programs. Their purpose is to stabilize capitalist production, cut unemployment, and at least partially overcome the destructive influence of economic anarchy and competition. This kind of programing brings definite results, but it is implemented so as not to infringe upon the monopolists' interests. Moreover, the monopolists use it as a camouflage device. They continue to enrich themselves while they formally take part in carrying out certain state recommendations, allegedly serving in this way the general national interests.

Bourgeois programing must not be equated with socialist economic planning. Plans devised by bourgeois states are not binding on privately owned capitalist companies; they are mostly in the nature of recommendations, prognoses. Private enterprises and large associations of monopolies do not receive specific production assignments from the state, and since they are engaged in competitive struggle, they are not in a position to coordinate their activities in a planned way so as to ensure balanced economic development.

Redistribution of the national income by the device of the state budget plays a major role in the enrichment of the monopolies. While the bourgeois state collects gigantic amounts of money through taxation imposed on the toilers, it spends only an insignificant part of these funds on education, public health, and other public services. The United States now allocates eighty billion dollars a year for military expenditures. Thus, the toilers bear the whole burden of militarism, while sums of money spent by the government for military production are channeled into the safes of large industrial corporations specializing in arms manufacture. Contemporary bourgeois states also spend considerable sums to finance scientific research.

Increase of state-owned property is bound up with state-monopoly capitalism. By its class nature, this property is state-monopoly property, inasmuch as the bourgeois states themselves act merely as "executive committees" of the monopoly bourgeoisie. This property is amassed in three different ways: by construction of new enterprises (mostly military) financed by the state budget, by government purchase of shares in capitalist corporations, or bourgeois nationalization of individual enterprises or of entire branches of industry. This expansion of state-monopoly property frequently is caused by the tendency to take over production branches requiring large capital investments (for example, the atomic industry) or those not profitable enough (coal mining and the power industry).

In England the coal-mining industry, gas plants and electric power generation are concentrated in the hands of the state. More than 20 percent of workers and employees are on the payroll of government-owned enterprises. In France the state sector supplies nearly 15 percent of the country's entire industrial output. Nearly 80 percent of the aircraft industry, almost the entire coal-mining industry and electric-power generation, are concentrated in the hands of the state. In Italy over 20 percent of the total labor force works in government-owned enterprises.

As they unmask the capitalist nature of state-monopoly property, the working-class and communist parties are struggling for removal of the most important production branches from the control of private capital at the same time. After World War II this struggle was of great importance in nationalizing various production branches in England and France, as well as in nationalizing the electric-power industry in Italy in 1962. At present most of the programs of communist and workers' parties contain demands for nationalization. Nevertheless, communists struggle not merely for nationalization but also for genuine democratic control over state enterprises.

State-monopoly capitalism is also characterized by the creation of interstate monopoly associations, such as the European Economic Community (Common Market), the European Free Trade Association, and others.

To sum up, as we can see, state-monopoly capitalism represents the joint forces of the monopolies with those of the state in order to consolidate the position of the monopoly bourgeoisie and to increase the life of the capitalist system. Transformation of monopoly capitalism into state-monopoly capitalism does not mean transition to a new stage different from imperialism. It is still the same capitalism, now in its imperialist stage of development.

The concept of "state-monopoly capitalism" should not be identified with the broader concept of "state capitalism." State-monopoly capitalism exists only in advanced capitalist countries, while state capitalism has a specific structure and may exist in economically underdeveloped countries. Moreover, state capitalism was one of the temporary structures in the economy of the Soviet Union and certain other socialist countries during their transition period from capitalism to socialism.

Capitalism's General Crisis

Intensification of Capitalist Contradictions

The conflict between productive forces and production relations constitutes the inner spring of the historical process, the economic foundation of social revolutions, resulting in transition from one production mode to another. An example of this conflict, which is becoming increasingly acute before our very eyes, is the *contradiction between the social character of production and the private capitalist form of appropriation*—the basic contradiction of capitalism.

As capitalism develops, the degree of labor socialization constantly increases, and economic ties and interdependence are strengthened among individual enterprises, among entire production branches, and within the whole economy.

For a modern factory to produce a pair of shoes requires raising cattle and processing the leather at a tannery and coloring it with chemical dyes. Other factories must produce fabric and thread; machinery plants must supply equipment and machines for the shoe factories. These plants, in turn, require ore and steel. At the same time all these enterprises need fuel, electric power, lubricants, etc.

By large-scale pooling of labor, capitalism imparts a social character to production. Despite production's social character, however, the form of appropriation continues to remain private: since the means of production belong to the capitalists, the labor product becomes their property. Private ownership impedes production growth; development of productive forces is slowed down.

Thus, despite the high level and great possibilities of the economy in advanced capitalist countries, their production grows slowly, and during some years not at all. Chronic failure to use production capacities fully is a usual phenomenon of contemporary capitalism, the ugly character of which is particularly evident in the militarization of the economy. It is caused not only by the imperialists' aggressive designs but also by their insatiable thirst for profits. It is their fault that highly developed productive forces that could ensure a happy life for hundreds of millions within a short time are being used to a considerable degree against the interests of humanity for production of the means of extermination and destruction. This happens because these productive forces are at the disposal of the exploiting minority—the bourgeoisie—instead of the toilers, instead of society as a whole.

Capitalist production relations have long since ceased to correspond to the character of the productive forces and are in conflict with them. Antagonistic, irreconcilable contradiction between the social character of production and the private form of appropriation has now reached an extremely acute stage. State-monopoly capitalism has prepared all the *material prerequisites for the transition to socialism*. Large-scale, machine-equipped industry and an exceptionally high degree of socialized production have created conditions for ending economic anarchy and crises and for assuring planned development of productive forces in the interest of society as a whole. Private ownership of the means of production, the capitalist system, must be abolished.

Characterizing imperialism as moribund capitalism does not, of course, mean that it will automatically die without a decisive struggle by the popular masses under the leadership of the working class. Having defined imperialism as moribund capitalism, V.I. Lenin also called it the *eve of the socialist revolution*. To be sure, the monopoly bourgeoisie does not surrender without a fight. It makes every effort to save the capitalist system. However, it is powerless to ward off the inevitable: capitalist contradictions, coming to a head, lead to downfall.

As it intensifies exploitation of the toilers, the monopoly bourgeoisie meets growing resistance from them. *The revolutionary movement of the proletariat* for liberation from capitalist oppression and for the socialist transformation of society is spreading and becoming more and more powerful.

In enslaving the peoples of colonial and dependent countries, the monopoly bourgeoisie condemns millions to slow extinction and leaves them no choice but to win their independence or perish. Hence the swelling wave of the *national liberation movement* against imperialist servitude.

In raising the fascists to power and unleashing wars, the monopoly bourgeoisie sacrifices millions of human lives out of greed and destroys the wealth created by peoples' labor over long years. Hence the intensification of the *peoples' struggle for democracy and peace*.

In one mighty stream these powerful forces unite to destroy imperialism. The inevitable decline of the capitalist system, the epoch of transition from capitalism to socialism, is setting in.

Inasmuch as the development of capitalism is uneven, society's transition to socialism cannot occur everywhere at the same time. The downfall of capitalism and the victory of socialism is a slow process taking in a whole era, the era of the *general crisis of capitalism*.

Stages in Capitalism's General Crisis

During the general crisis of capitalism intensification of internal contradictions in the capitalist system reaches a level at which this system is powerless to maintain control over individual countries, which one by one break away and enter upon the socialist path. On the other hand, the very emergence, growth, and consolidation of the socialist system hastens the decay of imperialism.

The first stage in capitalism's general crisis began as a result of World War I and the victory of the October Socialist Revolution. The October Revolution had a tremendous influence on the workers' and national-liberation movements, and it gave a powerful thrust to the whole development of society. After October 1917, it may be said the locomotive of history moved onto the main track and sped full steam ahead toward communism.

World War II led to intensification and deepening of capitalism's general crisis; the breakaway of a number of countries in Europe and Asia from the capitalist system inaugurated the *second stage* of this crisis. Socialism spread beyond one country's borders and was transformed into a world system. At the same time national-liberation revolutions led to the creation of independent countries replacing former colonies and semicolonies.

The *third stage* began in the second half of the fifties. It is unique in that it did not begin with a world war. Until this time capitalism had enough strength in time of peace to effectively stifle the socialist movement of the toilers and the national-liberation movement of enslaved peoples. Only when weakened by strife among themselves or busy with world wars were the imperialists left powerless to prevent the great victories of the liberation movements.

Now they are unable to do that even in peacetime, as vividly demonstrated by the dissolution of the colonial system. It is particularly worth noting that the heroic people of small Cuba, next door to the largest imperialist power, not only won its independence but also embarked on the road to socialism.

The general crisis should not be confused with periodic economic crises. It is called *general* precisely because it affects not only the economy but also the politics and ideology of capitalist society. In the political sphere the monopoly bourgeoisie is forced more frequently than ever to resort to the use of bayonets to preserve its rule. The bourgeoisie is hopelessly losing the struggle for the minds of men because it has flouted the ideals by which in the past it managed to influence the masses.

Without Ideals

For many decades bourgeois ideologists boasted about the existence of freedom of thought in their countries.[a] In imperialist countries at present there are

---
[a]Mark Twain, the great American writer, wrote on this subject with bitterness: "In our country there are three things beyond dispute: freedom of speech, freedom of thought, and prudence which keeps us from using them."

numerous campaigns organized against Marxism-Leninism. Why is this so? Because the imperialists are mortally afraid of our revolutionary teaching, because they lack ideas which they could oppose to the noble ideas of Marxism-Leninism.

When the bourgeoisie reached for power, it won over the masses by the slogans of liberty, equality, and fraternity, which still appear in bourgeois constitutions. But the toilers by now know their value. Liberty for the capitalists means exploiting the workers; liberty for reactionaries is committing political murders; liberty for newspaper magnates is fanning war hysteria. And "liberty" for the workers is to bend their spines; "liberty" for communists means sitting behind bars; "liberty" for peace fighters means being clubbed by police truncheons.

The slogan of equality sounds no less shameful in the mouths of the bourgeois ideologists. Can we speak of equality between lords and slaves, between the well fed and the hungry? Billionaire Mellon manages to spend a million dollars for one ball. Wealthy psychopathic women, "mad from over-abundance," keep servants to care for their Pomeranians and poodles. Meanwhile many thousands of persons in the poorly developed countries suffer from want and hunger.

The last shred of conscience must be discarded by the person who wishes to preach brotherhood in the world of imperialism, in the United States, where Negroes are being lynched, where bombing peaceful Vietnamese towns and villages and exterminating women and children is found possible.

In our time the bourgeoisie has completely abandoned, has stamped upon, the ideals once inscribed on its banners. Ever broader masses of people now are becoming convinced that genuine liberty, equality, and fraternity can be secured only by the socialist, communist system. The more active the struggle of the working class and peoples against the total control of the monopolies, the more frequently do imperialist governments resort to measures of social demogoguery, agreeing to partial concessions in order to preserve and strengthen the foundations of the capitalist system. Repressive measures, directed first and foremost against communists, are not being neglected, either. The rights of communist parties and their members are restricted in a number of countries; their activity is proscribed.

Anticommunism represents one of the most obvious signs of the intensifying crisis of bourgeois ideology.

It also finds expression in the decline of culture. The bookstore shelves, theater stages, motion-picture and television screens are flooded by low-grade works glorifying cruelty and violence, praising depravity, appealing to the lowest instincts. In painting, senseless piling up of lines and spots claimed as opening up the secrets of human psychology is a fashionable trend. In music, a wild cacophony of sounds replaces melody and harmony. In sculpture appear constructions monstrous in their absurdity, producing repulsive impressions.

In speaking of the decadence of bourgeois culture, it would be unfair not to admit that there are many honest artists in capitalist countries who sincerely strive to support the victory of justice and goodness. But the fact is that their creative work cannot be wholly related to bourgeois culture: the logic of life leads honest artists to unmask the vices of the capitalist system and search for the way out of the blind alley into which dying capitalism is dragging its peoples. It is only natural that the most prominent cultural leaders have come to recognize the greatness of communist ideas. Among them are Romain Rolland, Theodore Dreiser, Thomas Mann and Heinrich Mann, Joliot-Curie, Paul Langevin, Bernard Shaw, Pablo Neruda, Nicolas Guillén, and many others. Is it not significant that the greatest French painter, Pablo Picasso, is a member of the Communist party? The progressive intelligentsia breaks with capitalism and devotes its efforts to the struggle for the victory of communism.

Obviously, in talking about the spiritual poverty of imperialism, it would be mistaken to underestimate its efforts in the ideological struggle. The monopoly bourgeoisie and its state have at their disposal a gigantic propaganda machine and powerful means of communication, which all are serving their aims, striving by all possible means to slander socialism, on the one hand, and, on the other, to present contemporary capitalism as a "paradise" for the toiler, as the world of "freedom" and prosperity.

Imperialist propaganda is especially active in advertising the high standard of living in the United States, England, and a few other economically advanced capitalist countries, boasting that qualified workers there are able to own private automobiles or standard small family homes.

As a rule, this is made possible by means of credit. A person who receives an expensive item for his use pays for it over a number of years. It would seem that credit sales as such are convenient and advantageous to the consumer. However, the capitalists resort to giving credit not because of eagerness to assist the population. They are forced to do it by the narrow market and lack of demand for goods. Credit is not accessible to all and is accompanied by harsh conditions: if a man acquires an item and then loses his job and is unable to pay consecutive installments, he forfeits his property right.

Those toilers who receive comparatively high wages do live under material conditions that are not bad. However, one cannot judge the whole by its part, if the whole is not homogeneous. In capitalist countries millions of unemployed or partially employed exist side by side with those who work. There are qualified workers, farmhands, and laborers who can barely make both ends meet. Side by side with whites, there are millions of toilers in the United States—Negroes, Mexicans, Puerto Ricans—who receive wages many times lower for identical work. American authorities willingly show foreign tourists comfortable small homes inhabited by the workers of Ford automobile plants, but they prefer to keep these tourists out of Harlem, the Negro slum of New York City, where people live in horrible misery and where, according to an American journalist, "rats are feeding on people."

Finally, just as one cannot judge about the situation of all toilers from the condition of part of the working class, so one cannot judge about the standard of living in the capitalist world as a whole from the standard of living of the population in one capitalist country (or even in one group of such countries). "Next door" to the United States lies the South American continent, whose toiling population lives in poverty. In the long-suffering countries of Asia and Africa, plundered by imperialism, the average per-capita income is scores of times lower than in the United States and Western European countries.

Zealous bourgeois propaganda will never be able to hide the innate defects of capitalism, which is and will remain the system of exploitation of man by man and of oppression of nation by nation, a system of social inequality.

History has passed the verdict of Guilty on capitalism. It is doomed, because the objective laws of society's development have put the revolutionary transition to socialism on the agenda of our century.

From Capitalism to Socialism

Historic Mission of the Working Class

Having discovered the economic laws that govern the development of capitalism, the founders of Marxism proved that the system itself is raising its own gravedigger, the proletariat.

Why is it specifically the proletariat which is leading the fight against capitalism? Because its working and living conditions make the proletariat the most advanced, the most revolutionary class of bourgeois society.

The workers have to deal with machines requiring certain definite skills and a broad outlook. Of course, the capitalists would prefer that the workers not think at all, that they work like living robots only capable of performing labor operations. They must give the worker a minimum knowledge, however, lest he be unable to operate machinery. And the more complex a person's work, the higher his degree of consciousness, the higher his aspiration to understand facts of life and grasp the causes of his disastrous condition, and fight for his own liberation.

The proletariat is not only the *most conscious* of the toiling classes but also the *best organized*. All workers toil in plants and factories in which the very labor process depends upon their common effort. Day in and day out each person becomes accustomed to working shoulder to shoulder with his comrades and considers himself a minute part of that great army of toilers subject, like himself, to forced labor. By taking part in strikes, the proletarians learn by experience that unity and ability to undertake organized actions are powerful weapons in the struggle against the class enemy.

Consciousness and organization make the proletariat the *most revolutionary class*. The fact that under capitalism the proletariat has nothing that it fears to lose also contributes to this. The other toiling class, the peasantry, has also been subjected to cruel exploitation. However, since the peasant owns his plot of land, there is conflict in his consciousness between the attitude of a toiler and that of a small proprietor: the first attracts him to socialism; the second pulls him back toward capitalism. The proletarians possess nothing but manpower. As Marx said, they have nothing to lose but their chains, and they have the whole world to gain.

Note that Marx did not say "country" but, precisely, "the whole world." The point here is that the proletarians of all countries have one common goal, and in order to attain it they must unite their forces not merely in one country but all over the world. Therefore, the inspiring phrase from the "Manifesto of the Communist Party"—*"Proletarians of all countries unite"*—which is the motto of our Communist party, too, is the most important slogan of the communist movement.

The Socialist Revolution

In fulfillment of its historic mission, the proletariat becomes the main motive force and leader of the *socialist revolution*, this most far-reaching social revolution, whose task consists in liquidating private ownership of the means of production and exploitation of man by man. In achieving the socialist revolution, the proletariat liberates not only itself but all toilers and society as a whole. Since the basic interests of all toilers coincide with those of the proletarians, it is only natural that the broad popular masses and, primarily, the toiling peasantry take part in the socialist revolution. Lenin said that the revolutionary union of workers and peasants is the guarantee of victory over capitalism. The socialist revolution is not a plot or an elitist coup d'état carried out by a group of "activist" revolutionaries, but a movement and a struggle of millions headed by the working class, which is lead by the Marxist-Leninist party.

The following question may arise: What are the tasks of the proletariat in the countries where the remnants of feudalism still exist—private ownership of large landed estates, division of society into strata, absence of universal suffrage and other democratic rights and freedoms? The dogmatists, to whom the Russian Mensheviks belonged, claimed that the struggle against feudalism was the business of the bourgeoisie: let the bourgeoisie carry out the bourgeois revolution, establish capitalist relations, and then will come the turn of the proletariat to overthrow capitalism. In opposition to this sterile scheme V.I. Lenin brought forward the idea of proletarian hegemony in a bourgeois-democratic revolution. In the epoch of imperialism, the bourgeoisie is incapable of carrying on a consistent struggle against feudalism. It fears the proletariat more than fire, and consequently it tries to stop the bourgeois-democratic revolution at the halfway point and make a compromise with the feudal lords, concluding an alliance with them against the people. Only the proletariat allied with the peasantry is capable of bringing a bourgeois-democratic revolution to a successful conclusion. And after achieving full control over the revolution, the proletariat naturally will not limit itself to democratic solutions. It will lead the toilers onward until all exploitation is abolished. The bourgeois-democratic revolution will turn into a socialist revolution.

We have already said that the main problem of every revolution is power. The working class has to take power into its own hands in order to complete all the far-reaching tasks facing it. How this is to be accomplished depends upon the specific historical conditions of the country where the revolution is taking place. If, in their struggle against the mass revolutionary movement, the exploiter classes resort to open violence, using the entire might of the repressive military-bureaucratic apparatus for this purpose, then the working class is compelled to seize power by armed revolt.

However, the exploiter classes cannot always resort to violence. When the working class has obvious power superiority and the exploiter classes are not capable of or decide against using armed violence, the transition of power may be peaceful. To be sure, both peaceful and nonpeaceful ways require the revolutionary struggle of the people under the leadership of the working class, in other words, establishment of the *dictatorship of the proletariat*.

Dictatorship of the Proletariat

The premise that the transition from capitalism to socialism requires the control of society by the proletarian state is the main idea in all of Marxist-Leninist teaching about the socialist revolution. In fact, let us imagine for a moment that after having achieved power and decreed that the means of production were henceforth social property, the working class would "retire." What would happen then? The very next day the bourgeoisie would again return to power, and everything would continue as before.

No. Transition from capitalism to socialism will never be accomplished by decree. Behind the decrees must stand the organized power of the popular masses, which can put them into effect and actually fulfill the tasks of the revolution. Social property and the interests of the toiling people must be protected from the exploiter classes, who will desperately oppose the revolution, utilizing every means at their disposal, often including armed struggle.

And this is by no means the whole story. After the means of production become social property, there are new problems: the economy must be organized on a scientific basis, rapid growth of productive forces must be ensured, the toilers must be mobilized to take up many other measures connected with building socialism. All this is impossible without the proletarian state.

There is nothing strange in the fact that the bourgeoisie and its hangers-on from the labor movement have singled out the dictatorship of the proletariat as the chief target for their attacks on Marxism. By their hypocritical condemnation of violence, they count on disarming the working class. When the Paris Commune existed, it dealt quite mildly with the enemies of the revolution. And the very same bourgeois whom the Commune had spared exterminated the best sons of the French proletariat with the help of Prussian interventionists. All the while, the bourgeois press around the world called the Communards oppressors and murderers.

The entire history of capitalism is one of constant violence and unheard-of cruelty toward the toilers and peoples of colonies and dependent countries. It is hardly necessary to state that the brief violence of the proletarian revolution, whose purpose, in the final analysis, is elimination of all violence, cannot be compared with capitalist violence. The socialist revolution resolutely liberates society from the tormenting evils of capitalism like a surgeon who, by a bold operation, cures a patient from a protracted and serious ailment.

Vengeance on exploiters for their criminal acts against the toilers is not the most important aim in this operation. The proletariat gives the former owners every opportunity to work and earn a livelihood on equal terms with other members of society. But if they engage in counterrevolutionary activities, encroaching upon the people's conquests, they are suppressed. In this consists the higher justice and humane character of the dictatorship of the proletariat, which protects the interests of the popular masses from a small group of parasites.

While it is *dictatorship in relation to the exploiters*, proletarian power is *democracy for the toilers*.

It cannot be otherwise. The proletariat and other toiling classes and strata of the population share common interests. In carrying out its leadership of society through control of the state, the working class does not claim any privileges for itself; on the contrary, it is always in the front line of the most difficult sectors of socialist construction; it inspires the masses by its example, it imbues them with its revolutionary enthusiasm.

How should the proletariat organize its dictatorship so as to accomplish the tasks history has assigned to it? Would it not be possible to use the ready-made machinery of the bourgeois state by simply turning it in the opposite direction? Let the bureaucrats who have a practised hand in administrative matters go on doing their paperwork (though now only according to the new instructions issued by the proletarian regime). Let the judges try cases and pass sentences (now only on the basis of revolutionary laws). Let the generals command their troops (now on orders from the proletarian headquarters). Let the prison guards keep prisoners behind bars (but only those who encroach upon the revolution, and criminals).

This decision would mean that the state machinery would be idiing, with its employees sabotaging and frustrating the will of the proletarian government. The generals would begin organizing conspiracies against the revolution; judges would distort revolutionary laws. The whole mechanism of the bourgeois state is constructed to oppress the working people, and government jobs are only held by representatives of the exploiter classes or by employees who in the majority are devoted to the old order.

Consequently, the proletariat is faced with the task of *crushing the bourgeois state machine and creating a new socialist state*. Historically, it is a state of a higher type, whose forms of organization and activities are subordinated to the interests of the toilers and to the construction of a communist society.

In order to attack the capitalist regime successfully, the proletariat must be armed with a deep understanding of its own immediate needs and final objectives, an understanding provided by the theory of scientific communism. Lacking this, the workers' movement would work in darkness, groping "by touch" for the correct path. Who could then combine the workers' movement and the science of communism, explain to the toilers the causes of their disastrous situation, and show them the way to escape? Not one or even several persons, no matter how brilliant and courageous, could ever successfully solve this task. It only could have been solved by the *Party, the leading detachment, vanguard, of the working class, which unites the most conscious revolutionaries, those who are the most steadfast and devoted to the cause of communism*.

The role of the Party is not limited to spreading the tenets of the Marxist-Leninist science. Regardless of how conscious the fighters or builders may be, regardless of how well they understand what they must fight for and build, the success of their activities will depend conclusively upon whether they have knowledgable and experienced leadership, capable of organizing the struggle and the building, capable of foreseeing the obstacles that may appear and mobilizing the people to overcome them. The Communist party is that courageous commander of the army of fighters for the revolution, that wise engineer of the building of communist society.

Necessity of a Transition Period

The victory of the October Revolution presented the Russian proletariat and its Communist party with a multitude of complex problems. Ultimately, they amounted to the question of where to begin. The very statement of the question indicates the basic difference between the socialist revolution and all the preceding types. The bourgeois revolution triumphed after the foundations of capitalism had already been established in society; its task was to remove the obstacles of feudalism from the path of capitalist production relations and ensure their unhindered development. The socialist revolution does not find any parts of the new structure ready made: socialist relations cannot develop under capitalism as capitalist relations did under feudalism. Relying on the appropriate material prerequisites (chiefly, the social character of production), it must create socialist economic forms and secure the establishment and development of socialist relations.

Because of these great creative objectives of the socialist revolution, there was need for a *transition period* from capitalism to socialism, a period of breaking down the old, capitalist relations and consolidating the new, socialist relations. In answer to the question of where to begin, it was necessary to formulate the basic aims of the transition period and find the most effective means for their realization. In other words, the real-life situation called for a scientifically based plan for establishing socialism. This plan, as worked out by V.I. Lenin, was adopted by the Party as the foundation of all its activities. Industrialization of the country, collectivization of agriculture, cultural revolution—these were the three general tasks for the transition period, the three fundamental ideas of the Leninist plan of building socialism.

V.I. Lenin considered industrialization the only way of re-equipping all branches of the economy with modern technology, achieving rapid growth in labor productivity, and raising the living standard. Only industrialization could transform miserable and weak Russia into a powerful and flourishing socialist state, ensure prosperity for the working people, and create an economic foundation without which the transition from the lower to the higher stage of communism is impossible.

This idea was clearly expressed in V.I. Lenin's famous formula: *"Communism is the Soviet power plus electrification of the whole country."* This idea reveals, first of all, the political side of communism: the Soviet power is the form of political organization that allows the broad popular masses to control all public affairs by themselves. This awakens their creative energies and provides opportunities to carry out the most far-reaching plans for transforming nature in the working man's interest. Secondly, it shows the economic aspects of communism: electrification of the entire country and gigantic development of productive forces will lead to the creation of communist economy, ensure abundance of material goods, and permit the noble principles of communist social relations to be put into practice. The GOELRO plan [State Commission for the Electrification of Russia] set up under V.I. Lenin's leadership foresaw not only construction of a network of electric-power stations but complex and coordinated development of all branches of industry. The GOELRO plan was, in fact, a plan for industrialization and became the foundation for the first of several five-year plans for development of the USSR economy.

The creation of heavy industry facilitated the solution of another highly complex problem of the transition period, the *reorganization of the individual, isolated, small peasant holdings into the large-scale, socially owned, socialist farm economy.*

The essence of Lenin's cooperative plan is that the Soviet state create a powerful socialist industry capable of reorganizing agricultural production, of supplying it with modern equipment. Gradually, the peasant will acquire collectivist habits with the help of the simplest cooperative forms, i.e., combining manpower and resources. Once persuaded by practical experience of the advantages of collective labor based on the use of tractors, combines, and other mechanical farm machinery, the peasants will voluntarily unite into *kolkhozes* and abandon private farming.

Finally, building socialism requires bringing about a *cultural revolution*, without which it is impossible to make life for the toilers materially prosperous or spiritually rich. A cultural revolution together with industrialization of the country and collectivization of agriculture lays the foundation itself upon which socialism will grow.

The essence of cultural revolution consists in broadly disseminating culture (making all the treasures of science and art accessible to the large popular masses) and developing it *in depth* (promoting our science, technology, and art to the front ranks and assuring that they mature).

But first illiteracy and ignorance had to be eradicated. Three-fourths of the population of prerevolutionary Russia was illiterate, and four-fifths of the youth of both sexes. One magazine estimated that at the rate of development of education in Russia at that time no less than one hundred and twenty-five years would be needed to achieve universal elementary education, and no less than four thousand six hundred years to teach the peoples of Central Asia how to read and write.

This was why the campaign against illiteracy and for an organized public education was so critical a problem.

The Soviet government considered it one of the most important tasks to win over to its side the specialists in science and technology who had been trained in capitalist Russia. They had to be persuaded, made to realize the greatness of the people's cause.

"Tell the intelligentsia," said V.I. Lenin to Maxim Gorky, "to come join us. According to you they sincerely serve the interests of justice. What's the matter then? Welcome to our side: it is we who have undertaken the colossal job of putting the people on their feet and telling the world the whole truth about life. It is we who are showing peoples the direction to a human life, the path away from slavery, poverty, and humiliation."

It was necessary to train hundreds of thousands of young specialists, and to achieve this goal required broad development of higher and secondary specialized education.

Our Party went ahead to solve the problems of socialist construction, unafraid of innovations and the far-reaching dimensions of the problems it encountered, unafraid of difficulties and temporary setbacks. The Leninist plan for building the new society has also been widely and irrefutably confirmed by the rich experience of other socialist countries.

To sum up, we can now clearly see the ways of the transition from capitalism to socialism as Marxism-Leninism has scientifically formulated them.

To put an end to social inequality, poverty, and the calamities afflicting the popular masses, the means of production owned by private persons must first of all be transferred to social ownership by the whole society. This can be accomplished only by the revolution of the oppressed and destitute classes under the leadership of the proletariat and the Communist party. Revolution cannot succeed without the dictatorship of the proletariat and without scrapping the bourgeois state machinery and creating the new socialist state.

All known revolutions in the past led to the replacement of one form of exploitation by another. *The socialist revolution puts an end forever to the oppression of man by man, opens to society wide vistas to a radiant future.* In this lies its historic meaning, its unfading greatness.

In our own time these truths have long ago passed from the realm of theory into practice. Under the leadership of the working class and its communist vanguard, the toilers of our country have transformed, according to socialist principles, the economic base, social relations, political superstructure, and ideology of our society. They have built socialism. The same tasks are now being carried out in a number of other countries where the socialist revolution has been victorious. Their collective experience constitutes the living embodiment of Marxist-Leninist teaching.

In the second part of this textbook you will study the economic and sociopolitical system of Soviet socialist society. You will learn about the tasks of communist construction, toward the realization of which the Soviet people are now working.

Review Questions

1. How does the law of value control capitalist production?
2. What is the essence of capitalist exploitation?
3. Why is imperialism a dying capitalism? Demonstrate by means of contemporary facts.
4. What are the basic characteristics of state-monopoly capitalism?
5. What is the historic mission of the working class?
6. What are the tasks of the socialist revolution?
7. Why is the dictatorship of the proletariat indispensable?

Points to Consider and Discuss

1. Exchange views on the following question: What has been preserved and what changed in the economic structure of capitalism since its entry into the stage of imperialism?

2. Thanks to a stubborn struggle for its rights and to the influence of the example of socialist countries, the working class of advanced capitalist countries has recently achieved some improvement of its material condition. Does that mean that it is now less exploited?
3. Helped by your knowledge of history, try to answer the question as to how the socialist revolution differs from all previous revolutions.
4. The reformists maintain that the transition to a new system may be accomplished without revolution, by way of capitalism's "gradual transformation" into socialism. Prove that these views are false.

Part II: Socialism and Communism

4 Economic System of Socialism

In accordance with Lenin's teaching, the essence of socialism is in the transfer of the means of production to ownership by the people, in the replacement of the capitalist economic system by planned production in the interest of all members of society. Socialism presupposes a labor system with capitalists excluded, with the strictest control by the state and social organizations over the amount of labor and consumption.

Ownership

Economic Basis of Socialism

In our country the means of production belong to society. This determines the character of production relations, of the economic structure of socialism. We have neither a class deprived of the means of production nor one of private owners. Regarding ownership of the means of production, no one occupies a privileged position or, on the contrary, a disadvantageous position in comparison with another. As a result, transformation of the means of production into capital, and manpower into commodity, has vanished. *Social ownership excludes the exploitation of man by man.*

Where there is no exploitation, no possibility to appropriate the fruits of labor by others for oneself, the only source of livelihood is personal labor. Social ownership prevents parasitism and loafing. It promotes the same obligation of work for all, based on the principle: "He who does not work does not eat."

Inasmuch as the fruits of labor are at the disposal of society and then distributed among the people, the amount of compensation for work depends entirely upon the level of social wealth: the richer the society, the better its members live. They are all interested in the development of socialist production, and a common economic interest unites people, bringing them closer together. Production relations of socialism are relations of comradeship and mutual aid between toilers who are free of exploitation.

The development of socialist economy is determined by the single will of the entire society, the owner of the means of production, and not by uncoordinated and contradictory activities of individual groups or persons. Social ownership precludes production anarchy, crises, and unemployment; it offers the opportunity (and creates the necessity) for a purposeful system of production

103

planning. In other words, dominance of social ownership means that blind, spontaneous laws of capitalism have ceased to regulate production and the *economic laws of socialism* have become operative.

These are the most important characteristics of the economic system of socialism, and they are determined by social ownership.

Ownership, as you already know, is a social relationship that reflects the conditions of production, distribution, and consumption of material wealth. In daily life property relations are expressed as the *right of ownership*, an order secured by law, where individual persons or groups of persons, or the state, own, use, and dispose of property. The most important characteristic of the right of ownership is possession of property. An owner may transfer to other persons or organizations the right to use and, to a certain extent, manage his property without relinquishing his ownership. He loses all ownership rights only if he abandons possession (by sale or gift of his property).

Social ownership in our country is expressed above all in the fact that the overwhelming mass of the means of production and other material goods are in the possession of the socialist state. By mandate of the people and in its name, the state enjoys all property rights, including the right to dispose of property (for example, the sale of machinery and other commodities to foreign states).

All Soviet citizens make direct use of state property: the toilers in the course of their work use machines and machine tools; the scientists use the equipment of institutes and laboratories; you students use school buildings, tools in shops, and instruments in laboratories.

But the people as a whole do not manage state property. It is administered by state agencies and enterprises that are part of the large, overall governmental state structure.

The directors of enterprises and institutions are entrusted by the state with powers entitling them to manage material goods, while the collectives are given the right to check on the actions of the directors.

The power and right to manage state property is granted not on a personal basis to Comrade Ivanov, Petrov, or Semenov, but to the director, other managerial personnel—the collective. For this reason we are fully justified in saying that the collective is the proprietor of its enterprise or institution.

The production collective manages the property entrusted to it only within limits established by the state. Thus, for example, the "Regulations Concerning The Socialist State Production Enterprise" stipulate that the enterprise may sell surplus production equipment only in case a higher state organ responsible for redistribution of such surplus production equipment relinquishes its prerogative.

The state may allow citizens use of property that belongs to the entire society through its organizations (plants, institutes, schools—all these, after all, are state organizations) and directly, as well. Thus, housing in cities and in workers' settlements belonging to the state are given to the Soviet people for their use. In all cases, however, the state remains the owner and overall manager of the property.

Why in this instance do we speak of "state" and not "social" property? Because part of the means of production and other material goods (including right of ownership) belongs not to the entire people but to work associations of peasants, the *kolkhozes*.

Two Forms of Socialist Ownership

State and *kolkhoz* ownership are essentially of the same type. In socialist society they are therefore known as two different forms of social property. They preclude the existence of parasitic classes and exploitation of man by man; they are the basis of the production relations dominant under socialism.

Inasmuch as industry plays a decisive role in the economy of modern society, the socioeconomic nature of cooperative ownership depends entirely upon who is the owner of industrial enterprises, banks, transportation facilities, and other basic means of production. There are many cooperatives in capitalist countries now. However, under the conditions of private ownership, they are not, and never could be, socialist enterprises, even though they may ease the situation of toilers, farmers, and artisans. Frequently, such cooperatives become bankrupt, unable to meet competition from big capitalists and landowners. Or they may fall apart because certain members, once they become rich, take control of the whole cooperative enterprise.

Under the dominance of social ownership of the means of production, when power belongs to the toilers, cooperative ownership not only excludes ruin, exploitation of labor, etc., but even becomes a pillar of the new social relations. Its nature is entirely socialist.

The main distinguishing feature of the two forms of socialist ownership is the degree of socialization of the means of production. State ownership socializes the means of production on a countrywide scale, making them the property of the entire people. *Kolkhoz* ownership socializes the means of production within the limits of a single agricultural enterprise, making them the property of a group of persons.

State (all-people's) property	*Cooperative-kolkhoz (group) property*
Land, mineral resources, water, forests, industrial enterprises and their production, large agricultural enterprises organized by the state [*sovkhozes*] and their produce, maintenance and repair stations, banks, transportation facilities, means of communication, communal service and cultural establishments (hospitals, polyclinics, rest homes, schools, institutes, sports stadiums, etc.), basic housing in cities and industrial centers.	Community enterprises of *kolkhozes* and cooperatives with their livestock (cattle, poultry), equipment, and production tools (tractors, combines, etc.), production and community buildings. (The land used by *kolkhozes* has been granted to them in perpetuity, free of charge.)

It is quite understandable that state ownership plays the leading role in the system of socialist ownership. And not only because it embraces all the basic means of production. State ownership also affords the opportunity to organize the development of the economy according to a single plan. It encourages individuals to be guided by the interest of the entire people and trains them to think in terms of the state as a whole.

This does not at all mean that persons who are toiling on *kolkhoz* property are in an inferior position. As part of the entire people they are co-owners of state property. Moreover, the *kolkhoz* form of ownership fully corresponds to the present level of development of productive forces in the rural areas; it creates all the conditions for further increase of production.

The differences between state enterprises and *kolkhozes* are related to the two forms of socialist ownership.

The employees of state enterprises earn wages paid only in cash.

Kolkhoz toilers are paid both in cash and in kind, proportionate to their contribution to the community enterprise and according to the collective's income. Additional source of income for *kolkhoz* members is their work in their subsidiary household economy.

A guaranteed wage for the labor of *kolkhoz* members was recently introduced by a decision of the Party and the government, bringing compensation of labor in agriculture closer to wages being paid in industry.

The financial resources from which *kolkhoz* peasants are paid are known as the *consumption fund*. The remainder of *kolkhoz* income goes into the *unshared fund*. It consists of the basic means of production, that is, agricultural machinery, motors, equipment, *kolkhoz* electric-power stations, transportation facilities, buildings and installations for production and cultural use, livestock (draft and productive), materials and cash earmarked for expansion of *kolkhoz* production. This fund is indivisible, since it cannot be used as a consumption fund to be distributed on the basis of workdays among *kolkhoz* members. Also, it is not subject to distribution as payment to *kolkhoz* members in case they leave the *kolkhoz*.

The unshared funds have been accumulated by the labor of *kolkhoz* members with the help of the entire Soviet people. Thirty years ago *kolkhoz* property consisted of the socialized means of production owned by peasant farms: horses, plows, wooden plows, harrows, and other implements. Current unshared *kolkhoz* funds are mostly tractors, combines, trucks, and other machinery.

Unshared funds are increased from the income deductions made each current year and from direct expenditure of labor by the *kolkhoz* members in creating the means of production and in building cultural facilities. Thus, in 1958 unshared funds amounted to 24.2 billion rubles, and in 1969 nearly 53 billion.

The two types of socialist enterprises differ fundamentally in form of management.

The director of an in industrial enterprise is appointed by and responsible to

Unshared Funds

Basic production funds: buildings (structures for production purposes), tractors, combines and other machinery, motors, electric-power stations, draft and breed cattle, means of transportation, irrigation installations, production and farm equipment

Basic nonproduction funds: *kolkhoz* clubs, reading rooms, kindergartens and nurseries

Working capital funds: materials and financial means earmarked for development of communal economy: seeds and planting material, fodder, fertilizers, chemical pesticides, spare parts and repair materials, fuel and oil, younger animals and animals for fattening

the state for all the activities of his enterprise. The main organ of a *kolkhoz* is the general meeting of its members, who elect the administration board and the chairman of the collective farm. The *kolkhoz* members make decisions about the problems of the farm's organization and management according to existing laws and the "Regulations for the Collective Farm," adopt plans in the *kolkhoz* interest as well as the state interest, approve reports, establish procedures for income distribution, and so forth.

The socialist state establishes close economic ties with the *kolkhozes*. It supplies them with farm machinery, fertilizers, and high-grade seeds; organizes the training of managerial personnel and farming specialists; provides veterinary supervision; promotes dissemination and application of advanced production experience; grants credits to the *kolkhozes* and purchases their products systematically.

Personal Property

There is personal property as well as social property under socialism. This consists of earned income and savings of the population, houses belonging to individual citizens, household articles, and objects of personal use.

The personal property of a *kolkhoz* homestead is a special type, which may include subsidiary husbandry on a private plot, productive livestock, poultry, farm buildings, etc. Subsidiary private farming by *kolkhoz* members is necessary because the agricultural level there does not permit them to satisfy all their personal needs.

Personal property under socialism has nothing in common with capitalist private property, since it is based on personal labor and may not be used for exploitation.

Only very few objects of personal property may be used for profitmaking purposes. Housing, for example, may be rented at speculative prices; an automobile may be contracted out for private transportation by its owner for payment. In time the possibility of using personal property in this way will be eliminated by the economic situation. Adequate housing (including state summer cottage settlements), for instance, will eliminate the need to rent homes. Until such time the state must use moral and legal means to fight against those who are after easy profit; that is, it must punish them according to law.

As the social wealth increases, an ever greater quantity of commodities produced by society is being made available to satisfy personal needs of the toilers, leading to increase in amount of personal property. However, the state regulates the growth and range of personal property. This is made possible by a system of wage payments according to the quantity and quality of labor, by a price policy for consumer goods, and by increase of social consumption funds, about which we shall speak later.

Soviet laws safeguard social as well as personal property. Theft of state or *kolkhoz* property is punishable by prison terms of up to three years or by corrective labor. In the case of a second offense or of theft committed by a group of accomplices before the fact, the prison term is up to six years. Theft by an individual who has repeatedly been found guilty of committing crime (a recidivist) may be punished by prison terms of five to fifteen years. The death penalty is meted out for especially large-scale embezzlements.

Attempts on a citizen's property entail prison sentences ranging from two to ten years (in especially aggravating circumstances). Robbery, that is, assault combined with violence endangering human life, is punishable by sentences of up to fifteen years.

Goal of Socialist Production

None would hesitate to answer the question, What is the goal of socialist production? It is to create the conditions for a happy human life. This is the age-old popular dream of communism, for the sake of which the socialist revolution was carried out, socialism was built, and communism is being built.

Under socialism all production is subordinate to the task of improving the well-being of the people. And this is not only proof of the humaneness of the socialist system; it is an *economic necessity* as well. After all, should developing production fail to meet an increasing demand for its products, the rate of growth would inevitably slow down. Increasing consumption by the people is continually pushing the production ahead, while the growth of production, in turn, ensures ever-increasing satisfaction of human needs.

For example, sale of commodities for personal use has been marked by rapid growth. Every year Soviet citizens acquire watches, washing machines, refrigerators, television sets in increasing numbers. It is a well-known fact that the demand for certain of these is not being satisfied as yet in our country. In the next few years, however, the production lag will be eliminated. How will things be then? The answer may be found in the example of our watch industry. For the past few years it has been satisfying the demand for its products fully. Watchmakers are now busy creating even more perfect articles with new and more refined design. The watches are improving, and their prices are lower. A similar level has been achieved by industries producing cameras, radios, and a number of other items. [In 1969, Soviet industry produced 38 million wristwatches, 7.3 million radios, 4.4 million bicycles, 6.6 million television sets, and 3.7 million refrigerators.]

How can the goal of socialist production be reached? Obviously, not by simply expanding production. The quality of the goods must be improved, new types of manufacture created, and prices reduced. There is only one way that all this can be achieved at the same time: through *technical progress.* Only technical progress assures steady increase in the productivity of social labor.

Production development on the basis of advanced technology is as indispensable as steady rise in the living standards of the people: one is impossible without the other. Therefore, uninterrupted expansion and quality improvement of production based on modern technology and collective labor, in order to satisfy the constantly growing needs of all members of society to the fullest extent, is the *fundamental economic law of socialism.*

Relying on this fundamental economic law in its productive activities, socialist society is rapidly increasing the quantity of material goods produced by the country's economy every year.

Planning

The Power of the Plan

Every enterprise in our country is a cell within the single economic organism, unified by social ownership of the means of production. All enterprises belong to one owner, the people. And wherever there is a single master, there is a single goal and a single program of action—the plan.

The plan's power is wonderful. For example, a new chemical combine is under construction: as the builders erect the plant structure, equipment for the combine is being manufactured by chemical machinery plants over the country; oil refineries have the assignment of supplying its raw materials; railroads are solving the problem of how to haul the raw materials to the enterprise on time and how to ship the finished product to the consumer; chemical technology institutes are providing additional specialization courses for senior students who will become designers, engineers, and foremen in the plant; schools and technical vocational schools are training the combine's future workers in the knowledge and skills they will need.

This requires exact calculation, coordinated work, and unity of activity at all levels. These are achieved with the help of the plan, a state document that distributes resources among various branches of the economy and sets tasks for expanding production and improving the living standard of the toilers as well as for the development of culture, volume of domestic and foreign trade, and many other indices.

Planning economic development is one of the most important advantages socialism has over capitalism. For the first time in the thousands of years of human history, society is in a position to control the conditions of production and production is carried on in a conscious, rational manner, thus achieving the maximum saving of social labor. The destructive effects of competition, production anarchy, and economic crises are forever eliminated from social production. However, rational management of the economy does not create possibilities for arbitrary action. It is perfectly clear that we cannot, for instance, plan construction of new factories without guaranteeing the supply of raw materials for them. It is impossible to plan for a tenfold increase of footwear production annually for the simple reason that it would be impossible to provide enough raw material.

These and thousands of other examples lead to an important conclusion. Planning reflects the effects of one of the objective economic laws of socialism, *the law of the planned, balanced development of the economy.* In rendering planning possible, this law requires strict observance of certain proportion (correlation) between the various economic branches. (See diagram, p. xx.)

In its use of the law of planned, balanced development, the state consciously establishes and supports proportion in the economy. This, however, does not exclude the possibility of the formation of partial disproportion. The main reasons for this disproportion are miscalculations in planning and inadequacies in the organizational process. Production output plans are not always coordinated with those for supplies of material and technical equipment and for their cooperative deliveries; nor are construction plans always coordinated with financial allocations, material funds, and target dates for equipment schedules and deliveries. All this interferes with normal production development. In practice we are faced frequently by the following situations: plant structures have been completed without proper steps having been taken to order some of the necessary equipment, or production plans for an enterprise have been lowered without regard for real growth possibilities.

Partial disproportion may also occur because of natural causes. When adverse conditions create a sharp drop in yield of certain crops, plants processing these crops may experience shortages in supplies of raw material.

Thus, under socialism disproportion is not caused by the economic system itself, as is the case under capitalism. It results either from human error or natural calamities, is transient, temporary in nature, and does not cause the destruction of productive forces, unemployment, and economic crises.

State reserves are the means of combatting partial disproportion that may occur. Our society forms reserves of raw materials, fuels, consumer goods, financial resources in order to avoid interruptions and dislocations of the production processes and, most important, to save people from privations caused by unexpected natural calamities.

The economic plans embody the policy of our Party and are important instruments for its implementation. V.I. Lenin said: "Our program cannot remain merely the Party's program. It must be converted into the program of our economic construction. Otherwise it would be inadequate even as a Party program. It must be supplemented by a second Party program, a working plan for the reconstruction of the entire economy on the basis of modern technology."

Birth of the Plan

Our plans must reflect the objective law of planned, balanced economic development. The task of the state organs consists in mastering this law, learning how to apply it, and in drawing up plans corresponding with its requirements. The planning may be current or long-range, that is, for several years ahead.

The leading role belongs to long-range planning. This planning fully reveals the capacity of the socialist state not only to foresee the course of economic

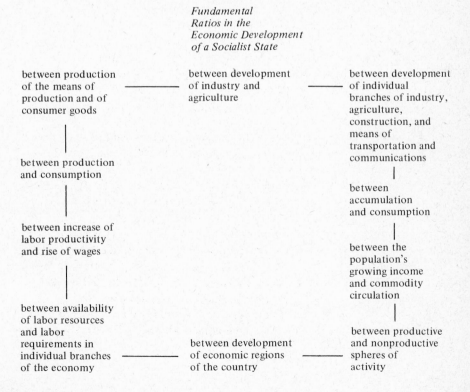

Fundamental Ratios in the Economic Development of a Socialist State

between production of the means of production and of consumer goods ——— between development of industry and agriculture ——— between development of individual branches of industry, agriculture, construction, and means of transportation and communications

between production and consumption

between accumulation and consumption

between increase of labor productivity and rise of wages

between the population's growing income and commodity circulation

between availability of labor resources and labor requirements in individual branches of the economy ——— between development of economic regions of the country ——— between productive and nonproductive spheres of activity development but also to carry out a system of efficient measures that determine paths of development for the entire economy.

What are the indices in a long-range plan? They determine the rate and proportion of production development, volume and direction of capital investment by individual branches of the economy, by republics and economic regions. Construction of new industrial centers, large enterprises, and highways is anticipated, completion of technical reconstruction of various production branches and enterprises is projected, and so forth. In our country the long-range plans are usually five-year plans.

The five-year plans are drafted according to the directives approved by the Party and the government.

All planning organs—from the USSR State Planning Commission (GOSPLAN) to planning departments of enterprises—follow these directives in working out plans for the economy as a whole, its various branches down to industrial associations and enterprises included. The planning process thus operates in two counterdirections, from the bottom up and the top down. Each enterprise's collective works out the production development plan for a given plant or factory and transmits it to the respective ministry or agency. The GOSPLAN then combines the plans of various ministries and agencies and draws up the general economic plan.

Long-range plans are implemented by combining and fulfilling current (annual) plans. These help to control progress of completion of the long-range plan, as well as accuracy in the assignments set down by it.

Preparation of balance sheets plays a major part in substantiating the tasks included in a plan. The concept of balance corresponds directly to the established meaning of the verb "to balance," i.e., to maintain equilibrium. Balances fall into three categories: material, financial, and manpower. Material balances are set up for various important types of industrial and agricultural production in their natural amounts or quantities (tons, unit measure, etc.). There is the coal balance, for example; the cereal crop balance, electric-power balance, meat balance, steel balance, cotton fabric balance, and so on. Balances are also prepared for groups of homogeneous products: fuel balance, industrial equipment balance, and others.

Each balance sheet consists of two parts: income and expense. The first accounts for all resources; the second, for all expenditures in the period under planning.

The material balance sheet is usually accompanied by the "chessboard table" with staggered rows, which on the one hand shows producers of a given commodity and on the other its consumers. At points of intersection is shown the quantity of products to be supplied to each consumer. This permits one to obtain a graphic view of the link between supplier and consumer.

Material balances reflect only one type of proportion, that between production and consumption of various commodities. But in order to balance the

Sample material balance sheet
(Glass)

1. Remainder at suppliers at beginning of year	100	1. Production-operational needs	15,000
2. Production	20,650	2. Capital construction	3,000
3. Import		3. Expense for suppliers' needs	100
4. Received from state reserves		4. For the market	2,000
		5. Export	300
		6. Placed in state reserves	225
		7. Reserves of the USSR Council of Ministers	75
		8. Planned remainder at suppliers at the end of year	50
Total	20,750	Total	20,750

economy as a whole, it is necessary, as you well know, to determine an additional series of proportions: for example, between the population's income—wages, payments to *kolkhoz* members, pensions, scholarships, etc.—and its defrayment—purchases of commodities in stores, payments for services, for transportation, communications, entertainment, communal meals, etc.

When all the balances are made and reconciled, the final plan variant is approved by the USSR Council of Ministers and the USSR Supreme Soviet. After the highest state authorities have approved it, the plan acquires the power of *law*, fulfillment of which is the duty of all. Violation of, or failure to fulfill, the plan in any of the branches damages the whole economy and adversely affects other production branches, transportation, trade, finances, and others.

The central planning organs concentrate their attention on solving the fundamental tasks of communist construction: ensuring basic proportion within the economy; correct distribution of productive forces; comprehensive development of economic regions; technical progress; wage and price policies. Practical ways and means of fulfilling the tasks planned, use of production resources and manpower, use of various forms of material incentives—all are decisions made by the enterprise collective themselves.

The problems of technology, economics, and finance are originally related in the annual plan of each enterprise. This plan, known as the technical-industrial-financial plan, is the year's program for production, technical, and financial activity. It includes: the production program; plan for technological development, material and equipment supply; plans concerning labor force and wages, production cost, finances; and a plan dealing with organizational and technical measures. The basic section of the technical-industrial-financial plan is the production program, which assigns production goals. It establishes the volume, variety, and quality of output.

The Soviet economy's planned development guarantees its high rate of growth, helps to multiply the country's social wealth, and raises the people's living standard materially and culturally.

Commodity-Money Relations Under Socialism

With our wages we go to a store to purchase what we need to live. Plants and factories sell their products; the money received is placed in banks and credited to the respective enterprises. The *kolkhoz* buys farm machinery from the state and sells it grain, milk, and meat. All this tells us that *commodity production* is retained under socialism.

Why Is Commodity Production Retained Under Socialism?

Commodity production originated, as you know, from the social division of labor. This is the general basis of commodity production, and it will continue to be important as long as commodity production exists. Under socialism there is division of labor between industry and agriculture, between various industrial and agricultural branches, between various enterprises responsible for different products, and between employees in different professions.

Division of labor presupposes exchange. But must it take the form of purchase and sale? Under capitalism products become commodities because their producers operate on the market as private owners. Under socialism there is no private ownership, and commodity producers act on behalf of society as owner.

Why, in spite of this, does commodity production continue?

The need to retain commodity production results from the fact that the level of development of productive forces is not high enough. In order to eliminate the commodity form of exchange of products, an abundance of all material and cultural goods must be created to satisfy all the people's needs without charge. This will be achieved under communism. Under socialism, however, society must distribute the products among the people according to the quantity and quality of their labor; the amount of labor and consumption must be measured. Money used for the purchase of commodities is used as the calculation tool.

The second reason for retaining commodity production is the dual form of socialist property. As a result of the need for exchange between the two basic owners, the state and the *kolkhozes* many products acquire the commodity form, and their production thus becomes commodity production.

Commodity production under socialism is essentially different from its capitalist counterpart, however. It is production without private ownership, without capitalists, whether big or small, and without exploitation of man by man.

In our country commodities are not manufactured, distributed, and marketed spontaneously but according to unified economic plans. Commodity production is restricted in its sphere: the land, mineral resources, forests, factories, plants, railroads, and other important elements of society's wealth cannot become commodities, and they are excluded from commodity exchange; neither is manpower a commodity.

The difference between socialist and capitalist commodity production is vividly clear from the different ways the law of value takes effect.

The Law of Value Under Socialism

The law of value is operative wherever there is commodity production. Its function is to dictate the need for production and exchange of commodities in relation to expenditure of socially necessary labor. In establishing commodity prices, the state cannot base its policy upon the individual expenditure by a specific enterprise. It must be guided by what is the socially necessary expenditure of labor, i.e., whatever is necessary at a given level of the development of productive forces and technology, in addition to taking account of the existing average labor skill and intensity.

In capitalist economy prices are shaped in the market spontaneously, whereas in the socialist economy they are fixed as *planned prices*, except those in *kolkhoz* markets.[a] While it takes into account various economic and political considerations, the state nevertheless is guided first of all by the value of the commodities produced.

Each commodity's price should be as close as possible to its value, the labor expended for its production. The more accurately a commodity's price reflects its value, the easier it is to determine how profitable the use of a certain equipment, raw material, and technological production process is.

Let us assume that a machine part may be made from either of two materials, "A" or "B." Their values are 1.50 rubles and 4 rubles, respectively. If "B" material were used, the part would last five years; if made from "A," only a year. Obviously, making the part from "B" is more advantageous. However, should the price of material "A" be set below its value, and that of "B" above its value, then the use of material "A" would be preferable.

Application of the law of value stimulates introduction of new technology and improvements in labor organization. Steady increase in labor productivity and a reduction in the unit cost of production are thus assured.

All the same, when the interests of social production development and of the population so require, the state knowingly allows disparity between price and cost. This is done when it is considered necessary, for example, to divert part of the income earned in some sectors to speed up the development of others of greater economic importance. Also, it is done to control demand, i.e., the nature of consumption. Thus, commodities in children's stores are frequently priced

[a]*Kolkhoz* market prices are not fixed by the state but are based upon supply and demand. However, the socialist state does influence *kolkhoz* market prices, since the great bulk of commodities is sold by state trading enterprises at prices fixed in the plan.

below cost, but others are sold at prices higher than their actual cost (tobacco, vodka, and others).

In sum we can see the law of value under capitalism operates spontaneously, and disparity between commodity price and cost results from the anarchy of capitalist production. In the socialist economy, by contrast, disparity between price and cost is deliberately permitted in the interest of society.

Money Under Socialism

Money fulfills its intrinsic function under the system of socialist commodity production. Money is the *measure of value*, since the value of all other commodities is also expressed in the money commodity under socialism. Gold is the money commodity. Money in the Soviet Union has a gold content. (The gold content of one ruble is 0.987412 gram.)

Money is an indispensable element of trade; it is the *means of exchange:* without it purchase-sale would be impossible.

Money is put into circulation by the State Bank. Accounts of enterprises, agencies, and organizations are settled by clearing operations. Funds are transferred from the account of one enterprise or agency to that of another. The great bulk of cash issued by the State Bank goes for wages and salaries, pensions, grants, scholarships, and for purchase of farm produce. Cash is returned to the Bank through the network of commerce.

Money becomes *means of payment* when it is used for payment of wages and salaries to workers and employees; for repayment of loans to the State Bank by socialist enterprises; in payment of taxes, insurance premiums, and claims; as distribution of income among *kolkhoz* members—whenever money changes hands outside purchase-sale operations.

Money also is a *means of accumulation.* Plants, factories, state farms, and *kolkhozes* keep their cash income and spare cash in banks temporarily. The accumulated funds and savings are used by the state for production expansion, creation of reserve funds, and for credit grants to other enterprises and organizations.

The social function of money is completely different in capitalist and socialist society. Under capitalism money becomes capital, the tool for exploitation of workers, the means to acquire the results of someone else's labor. Under socialism money cannot turn into capital, since one cannot use it to purchase a factory, plant, manpower, land, or an electric-power station. Under the conditions of capitalism, money is the instrument of spontaneous market laws. The socialist state uses money purposefully as a means of general accounting and control over production and distribution of commodities and over the quantity of labor and consumption.

Under socialism money is an indispensable instrument of distribution according to labor. When the toilers purchase commodities for their personal use, they receive that share of the social product that corresponds to the quantity and quality of their work performance.

With the help of money the state can evaluate the results of economic activities by the enterprises, whose financial accounts show the expenditure of labor necessary for production of a commodity; expenses for materials—raw and other—and fuels; depreciation of equipment; administrative expenses; transportation costs; and the cost of product distribution to consumers through the trade network. The ruble control of the performance of socialist enterprises is the most flexible method of economy management.

Socialist countries maintain trade relations with the countries of the world capitalist system. Inasmuch as prices for goods and services in each country are expressed in the state currency, the problem of exchange (the relative value of the monetary unit of each country) inevitably arises. One American dollar, for instance, according to the present currency exchange rate, equals 90 kopecs in Soviet money. This relationship is established on the basis of the gold content of the ruble and the dollar.

System of Economy Management and Control

The planned character of socialist economy favors possibilities for its steady, rapid development. These possibilities are not realized automatically, however, but by means of a system of management and control of the economy.

The management system presupposes application of the most diversified approaches, forms, and methods. To master it requires a lengthy, theoretical study course; neither can one do without practical experience. We should, as a beginning, acquire some knowledge at least of the basic concepts of this system: economization policy, self-support management, prime cost accounting, profit-taking, and "paying concern."

Drive to Economize

Under socialism all of society's wealth is owned by the people. It is in their vital interest that social labor should be expended economically and natural resources used with maximum effectiveness. Less depreciation of equipment, more economical use of raw materials, fuels, electric power, and other means of production means that more products may be obtained at the same expense.

We forget to turn off the hall or kitchen light before going to bed. The cost is just a trifle, a few kopecs. But let us multiply the result of this absentmindedness by similar cases of negligence by all those who do not care about being thrifty with electricity at home or in the factory. Millions of kilowatt hours and hundreds of thousands of rubles are wasted. Figures ending with several zeros do not speak; they shout: Be careful! Observe the drive to economize!

In the case cited, the wastefulness is striking. However, matters are not always that simple. Here is an example: Garment factories have an official, normal amount of waste. It would appear that nothing can be done about it. A suit cannot be made without material left over. Front-rank garment workers cannot become reconciled with this seemingly unavoidable waste. They industriously search and experiment, and finally propose a change in cutting methods. As a result, not ten but eleven suits can be made from the same quantity of fabric. A streamlining idea thus helps to save many thousands of meters of fabric.

Quite understandably, economization may be achieved not only by careful use of raw material but also by increase in labor productivity.

We are trying to economize not in order to sit on our well-stuffed coffers and, like the miserly knight, relish thoughts of our power. We are being thrifty, in the final account, not with money, metal, or fabric but with our most valuable possession, social labor. We do this to increase the people's prosperity. Resources used economically enable society to increase housing, schools, and rest-home construction, to increasingly satisfy the needs of the Soviet people without undue economizing.

Pettiness or pennypinching have nothing in common with the drive to economize. In fact, they are diametrically opposed to it. Any forward step, any technical progress calls for funds, and the Soviet state allocates them without stint. This is the high purpose of the long-range savings of social labor. Of course, any outlay must be justified in order to reassure society that the funds are not being wasted but will bring increased wealth (and not after half a century).

A planned socialist economy makes possible maximum economization of labor. Does this mean that all losses have been eliminated from our economy? Unfortunately, no. Overexpenditure of funds is still occurring in many enterprises, on construction projects, in *kolkhozes* and state farms. Raw and auxiliary material and fuel are often not used sensibly; machines and machine tools are allowed to idle; new equipment is put into use too slowly; the workers' labor is poorly organized. The carelessness, inertia, and conservatism of some leaders prove very costly to the state and cause it actual damage.

The drive to economize cannot succeed without concern for socialist property, steady increase in labor productivity, improved equipment; without systematic reduction in outlays of labor, raw materials, auxiliary material, electric power; reduction in amount of waste and the number of rejects. The drive to economize, in short, is a method of socialist management, the purpose of which is to turn out more and better quality products with less outlay of materials and labor. This is being achieved mainly through *self-support management* by certain enterprises.

Self-support Management

Under the system of self-support management, an enterprise obtains buildings, equipment, raw materials, fuel, and financial means from the state. It is responsible to the state for safekeeping and proper use of the means of production. Once it has received its planned production goals, the enterprise organizes production activity by itself.

Self-support enterprises enter into relations with other enterprises. A cotton-spinning mill, for example, pays a state farm for its cotton deliveries and the railroad for transportation; it sells the finished yarn to another factory producing cotton fabric. This factory, in turn, sells its fabric to trade organizations. In this arrangement contracts are signed with enterprises that supply equipment, fuel, and raw materials, as well as with other enterprises that are customers for the sale of the produce. The contracts specify conditions of delivery, volume, variety, and quality of products; delivery dates; prices; dates and form of payments; and also responsibility for violation of any contract provisions.

These enterprises function according to the principle of self-support: they use funds received from the sale of their commodities to cover all expenditures for raw materials, fuel, and auxiliary materials, and for wages and salaries of their workers and employees. They must make some profit in addition. The higher the production rate and the lower the expenditures of the enterprise, the larger the sum it may retain for its own use. This so-called factory fund consists of money allocated from planned and above-plan accumulations. It is used to acquire new equipment; increase production; construct and repair housing; maintain children's facilities such as nurseries, kindergartens, and pioneer camps; equip rest homes, sanatoria, cafeterias, and clubs; purchase admissions to rest homes and sanatoria for its employees, and award bonuses to the workers. Naturally, such self-supporting enterprises as a whole, as well as each of their workers, are interested in the best possible employment of work time, in thrifty use of material and financial resources, and in improving production quality.

Prime Cost

The socialist enterprises have a special thermometer by which they judge how skillfully they are being managed—the prime cost of production. It shows just how much it is costing a given enterprise (the "prime producer") to manufacture a certain commodity.

Prime cost is calculated by assessing outlay of raw materials and auxiliary materials (lubricants, dyes, etc.), fuel and electric power, depreciation (allowance for wear and tear of work facilities such as buildings, machinery, and equipment), wages, deductions for social security and administrative expenses. After the total amount of expenditures are computed, the sum is divided by the quantity of goods produced, and the result is their per unit cost. *Prime cost is an enterprise's total expenditure for production and sale of its output expressed in money terms.*

If production prime cost in any enterprise is excessively high—if the thermometer indicates fever—the enterprise managers and the entire collective must look for the causes and eliminate the disease. It may be a case of extravagant use of raw materials or unproductive employment of equipment or inflated administrative expenses. When the disease is correctly diagnosed, it is easier to cure the patient.

However, the question arises of how to determine whether the prime cost is high or low and how it can be lowered.

In a well-managed enterprise production prime cost is usually much lower than in one that lags behind. What is the explanation? In well-managed enterprises new, modern equipment is being introduced with consequent rapid increase in labor productivity; materials are used sparingly, and they are the most up-to-date types (plastics are substituted for metal, for example); also, the design of items in production are constantly being improved—all measures permitting cuts in production prime costs. If the management is incompetent, however, labor productivity fails to rise, overexpenditure of raw and auxiliary materials is tolerated, and production prime cost will inevitably be high.

In the capitalist world, the owner who does not manage his enterprise competently is ruined and, sometimes, he puts a bullet through his head. In our country there cannot be such failures, because all enterprises are backed by a single owner, the people. But this does not by any means imply that the people, the Party, and the state can tolerate a violation of the public interest or the breakdown of an enterprise. The Party and state organizations, the people's control organs, the press, and Soviet society check on the activities of enterprises; they help them, note shortcomings, and sound the alarm when things are not going well. If leaders prove to be incompetent and unable to organize production, they are removed to other work. However, if they tolerate criminal negligence and carelessness or even fraud committed against the state, they are punished to the full extent of the law.

Profit and Profitable Management

The prime cost index is useful in examining the condition of an enterprise. However, it does not make it possible to evaluate the enterprise's operation from the viewpoint of the interest of the economy as a whole. This function is best fulfilled by other indices, namely, *profit and profitable management.*

Profit is that part of the surplus product created by the workers of an enterprise which is at the enterprise's disposal immediately upon sale (realization) of its product.

Mathematically, the amount of profit is determined as the difference between the product price at wholesale and its prime cost. If an enterprise sells goods worth 2.2 million rubles after having spent 2 million for their production and distribution, the amount of profit is 200,000 rubles. The amount of profit therefore depends, first of all, upon the level of expenditure for production and sale, the prime cost. The following factors influence amount of profit: quantity of goods produced (if the price of one pair of shoes includes 1 ruble profit, the profit on 10 pair will be 10 rubles); quality (prices for better quality goods are set higher); volume of sales (the profit hidden in the value of shoes stored in the factory warehouse is not a real quantity until sale, becoming tangible only after the money paid by the recipient of the goods is credited to the enterprise's account).

Under the conditions of socialism an enterprise's profit cannot become some sort of gain obtained without work. The objective of socialist production is not to extract profit but to satisfy to the utmost society's constantly increasing needs.

The profit index is superior to the prime cost index in one significant way.

The struggle to lower prime cost at times is found to be in contradiction with the task of improving product quality. Occasionally, additional investments by the producer enterprise result in great economy in operational cost of its product (because of quality improvement in aircraft engines, for example, our economy has gained several billion rubles). But these additional expenditures lead to increased prime cost.

If an enterprise's work is judged solely by prime cost, it may look as if its performance is deteriorating (the prime cost, after all, increased). If performance is judged by the enterprise's profit, however, we arrive at the correct conclusion: its performance is improving (its profit increases inasmuch as higher quality product is being sold for a higher price). Profit, therefore, favors quality improvement advantageous both to the producer enterprise and the consumer.

Understandably enough, setting profit targets does not diminish the importance of lowering prime cost.

However, the sum total of profits does not give a sufficiently exhaustive description of an enterprise's work performance. To evaluate quality of performance it is necessary to use the index of profitable management, which reflects the ratio of profit obtained to the amount of basic and working funds. The more profit an enterprise makes from each ruble of its production funds, the better its profitable management. Calculating according to the index of profitable management, therefore, stimulates an enterprise to use its equipment, materials, and other production funds with utmost efficiency.

Prime cost, profit, profitable management, and other economic indices, when used correctly, facilitate achieving the main goal—increased effectiveness of social production.

Managing the Economy

Managing socialist production requires the combination of centralized control with far-reaching independence of individual enterprises and economic associations. Actual management methods have differed in various stages of development of the country's economy.

At first, in 1918 and 1919, management took the form of local (provincial and district) economic councils subordinated to the executive committees of local soviets. During the years of "war communism" (1919-21) economic management was rigidly centralized. Management functions were performed by forty central boards and the Supreme Economic Council, to which all plants were subordinated. After transition to the "new economic policy" (1921-28) a management form was introduced whose main components were trusts, organized locally, as a rule, and enjoying a great deal of independence. A departmental form of management functioned from 1929 through 1957. Industry was supervised by the people's commissariats (ministries). In 1932 four industrial people's commissariats were organized; before the war there were nineteen; and by 1957, as many as thirty-three.

In 1957 it was decided to restore the territorial system of management through the economic councils functioning in administrative territorial regions. This reorganization was definitely a positive change, in that it favored development of interbranch specialization, mergers of smaller enterprises, and curtailment of inefficient freight hauling. However, as time went by, this system's serious negative aspects became apparent: the territorial fragmentation of management by economic councils began to hinder development of branch specialization and infringed upon the single technological policy.

Contemporary large-scale production, with its extremely complex technological processes and equipment, calls for production-branch management, which takes fully into account each branch's specific developmental potential and solves the task of production improvement effectively, closely tying it up with the latest scientific achievements.

Yet separate production branches cannot develop independently. The whole economy is not merely the sum total of all its branches. It constitutes a single complex. The branch management principle must therefore be combined with the territorial, with development of initiative on the part of the union republics and local administrative organs.

The management system functioning at present in the USSR has absorbed what is positive in experience previously accumulated, thus overcoming the inadequacies of preceding management forms. At present the economic branches of our country are directed by ministries of three types: all-union, union republic, and republic. Local industry enterprises are subordinated to the republic ministries.

This management system differs from the territorial and departmental systems existing until 1957. First, establishment of ministries has been combined with considerable broadening of the rights of the union republics in the area of planning and management, capital construction, and financing. Second, the territorial supply system organized by the economic councils has been preserved. The third and chief difference lies in the fact that the ministries rely in their work upon enterprises that enjoy broader rights and more independence.

The management system now functioning, in other words, has been determined in many respects by those great transformations connected with the radical improvement of the entire economic system of our country.

Labor and Distribution of Material Goods

Working Conditions

The source of all well-being and man's ultimate satisfaction in life—the joy of creating—labor was considered to be a heavy burden for thousands of years under the exploiter system. It could hardly have been anything else for those who grew abundant crops and yet were half starved, made fine fabrics and wore rags, built beautiful palaces and lived in hovels.

Under socialism the toilers have become full-fledged owners of the country's total wealth. They do not work for the enrichment of a few parasites but for themselves, for their own society. The conversion of labor from forced to free is socialism's greatest accomplishment.

There are fundamental changes in working conditions connected with this conversion.

One of the most important is the guarantee under socialism of *full employment* in our country. In 1930 the door to the last labor exchange office in the USSR was closed, and ever since the young generations in the Land of the Soviets have known unemployment only from books and newspaper reports about capitalist countries. Moreover, the Soviet people may choose professions according to their inclinations and obtain corresponding vocational education.

Bourgeois ideologists predicted that with production growth socialist countries would find it impossible to avoid unemployment. Now it is obvious that their calculations were built on sand. Production is growing at a gigantic rate in our country, mechanization and automation are steadily developing, and still there is enough work for everyone. The number of workers and employees in the economy has been continually increasing, and in 1968 it reached 86.1 million persons.

As productive forces develop, *work time is reduced*. The worker has enough time left for rest, education, and his personal life. Overtime work has been strictly limited in our country. In 1967 workers and employees went on a five-day work schedule, with two days off each week.

Particular attention is given to *industrial safety* under socialism. It is well known that accidents resulting in severe injury and even death occur in many branches of contemporary industry. While improving industrial safety, the socialist society tries to bring the number of accidents down to a minimum.

Finally, socialism gives everyone an equal *right to obtain material goods according to his labor.*

To Each According to His Labor

The level of development of productive forces that has been achieved is still inadequate to introduce the communist principles of distribution, to satisfy all the people's needs free of charge, regardless of their personal contribution to the common treasury. On what basis should material goods be distributed now, under socialism?

Let us imagine that together we have been given the right to decide this question. Should not everyone be paid at the same rate: a lathe operator of the first class, a beginner, and an experienced one of the sixth class; a qualified specialist with higher education and a trainee at a plant?

This method of distribution is called *wage leveling*, and it expresses the petty-bourgeois idea of socialism. The consequences of wage-leveling may be easily imagined. Workers would lose interest in improving their skills and the productiveness of their labor. Why would anyone attempt to improve his skills and work habits to achieve greater productivity if he knew he would receive standard leveled wages? Work remuneration under this system would necessarily be meager; instead of growing, it would tend to decrease because the less work people do, the poorer society as a whole becomes.

Wage leveling would therefore lead not to real equality but to its sad parody. Can the have-nots be made happy with the idea that all are equal because no one has more than another person? This situation would mean gradual erosion of social wealth. For that reason Marxist-Leninist theory firmly rejects wage leveling. Both Marx and Lenin emphasized that distribution is subordinated to production and regulated by it. Society cannot choose any form of distribution at will. To each mode of production there is a corresponding mode of distributing products.

Under socialism distribution must promote a constant growth of social wealth, assuring at the same time a steady rise in the living standard for all toilers. Only under this condition can material goods be produced in abundance and true equality be achieved, that is, the satisfaction of all according to their needs. The socialist principle, *to each according to his labor*, or remuneration according to quantity and quality of labor, accords fully with these prerequisites.

The second (negative) way of expressing the same principle is the socialist rule *he who does not work does not eat.* To be sure, we are not talking here about children, students, housewives, who are engaged in the useful and socially necessary activity of bringing up the new generation, or about old or sick persons. This socialist rule is directed to persons who do not want to work, to the most despicable vestige of the past—parasitism.

The principle of distribution according to labor ends the greatest injustice inherent in the exploiter society, where the exploiters appropriate to themselves the bulk of the material goods produced. Under socialism, as has been stated, labor and labor only is the legal source of the means of existence, and it determines a man's position in society.

Who has not laughed over the misadventures of Ostap Bender, the main character in the satirical novels by I. Il'f and Ye. Petrov! Having acquired one million rubles through extortion, the swindler imagines that because of his wealth people around him would consider him an eminent person, flatter him and fawn on him. It turned out, though, that in the Land of the Soviets people no longer worship the golden calf. The ill-starred millionaire was laughed at and driven away ignominiously wherever he went.

Besides being humorous the story is also instructive. Under socialism money—even a great deal of it—has ceased to be a tool of power, an object of worship. Notions of the past such as "rich inheritance" and "profitable marriage" have lost their meaning and are gradually disappearing from life. In a socialist society one cannot buy a plant in order to exploit workers or buy a seat in parliament or a cabinet post. Each person's value under the socialist system is measured only by his capability and his labor for the good of society.

Remuneration according to labor makes possible systematic implementation of another economic principle of socialism: *material incentives to make people take an interest in the results of their labor.* The better a man works, the more he produces for society, the higher his remuneration. This motivates men to work to the full measure of their capacity to attain higher labor productivity.

Material incentives spur men to work according to their ability. They also help develop moral, or more exactly, *ideological stimuli for labor.*

These stimuli appeared immediately after the October Revolution. The liberation of labor from exploitation led to great enthusiasm and a desire to build a new society as rapidly as possible and create a better life for all. Can the exploits of those who built Dneproges, Magnitka, Komsomol'sk be explained only in terms of a desire for material gain? Men suffered privations for the sake of a great ideal, because of their belief in a radiant future and their desire to hasten it by their work, and not because of greed. The same attitude motivated hundreds of thousands of young Soviet people of both sexes who took part in settling the virgin lands and built new industrial centers in Siberia and the Far East.

The combination of material and ideological stimuli of labor is clearly reflected in one of the most powerful motive forces in socialist production— *socialist emulation.*

Socialist Emulation

Socialist emulation is the expression of new, socialist relations within the production process; an effect of free, creative labor; a manifestation of the ideological stimuli of work called forth by the revolution. In short, it embodies the concern of the toilers to improve production and increase society's wealth. The workers are competing among themselves for successful fulfillment and overfulfillment of plans; for improvement of product quality and reduction of production cost; economization of raw materials; auxiliary materials, fuel, and electric energy; strengthening labor discipline; and for improved professional skills.

Communist Saturday volunteer workers during the Civil War period were the forerunners of socialist emulation.

In the spring of 1919 the workers at the Moscow sorting yard, led by the communists, decided on their own initiative to repair a locomotive engine in their spare time and free of charge. This old-fashioned steam engine is now in a museum, material proof of the birth of a new, communist attitude toward work.

During the period of socialist industrialization and of the collectivization of agriculture, a widespread movement of shock workers developed, followed later by the *stakhanovite* movement. During the Great Patriotic War shock brigades were organized at industrial enterprises to complete orders from the front ahead of schedule. After the war arose a mass movement of innovators, efficiency experts, and inventors. At present socialist emulation is at a new, higher level in the movement of communist labor.

The basic tenet of socialist emulation is help by progressive workers to those who fall behind, an effort to encourage the laggards and achieve overall production increase.

The main feature of emulation is dissemination of work experience. Whereas in capitalist production all manufacturing improvements are concealed from competitors like the apple of one's eye, under socialism the very idea of emulation promotes rapid and far-reaching application of the experience of production innovators. Socialist emulation is inseparable from broad dissemination of new work experience.

Socialist emulation is radically different from capitalist competition, where the motto is defeat and extinction to some and domination to others. By its very nature socialist emulation rejects the wolfish laws of competition. This, however, does not mean that the concept of "competition" is emasculated: those who achieve the best results are especially honored and respected by all. Those who have been instrumental in imparting their knowledge about their achievements to their comrades obtain even higher honors and respect. In other words, there are winners in emulation but there are no losers; everyone gains from it.

Reproducing the Means of Production

Our Growth Rate

Day after day, year after year men must produce food, clothing, footwear, and construct housing. The means of production must be renewed; raw materials and fuel must be excavated; worn-out machine tools and machinery must be replaced. It follows that the most important condition for society's existence is constant renewal of the process of production, or *reproduction.*

If the social production does not increase annually but instead is maintained at a constant level, *simple reproduction* takes place. In this case, the material goods consumed are only restored to their previous quantities. If, however, the volume of production increases, there is *expanded reproduction*, where society not only replaces material goods consumed but also produces additional means of production and more consumer goods.

Not only may material goods be reproduced and renewed, but production relations as well. For example, a typical configuration of capitalist production is the capitalist on one side and the hired worker on the other. And what happens? Capitalist reproduction engenders and consolidates conditions for the exploitation of the worker by constantly compelling him to sell his manpower for the enrichment of the capitalist.

Socialist reproduction, quite naturally, renews the relations of comradely cooperation and mutual aid. These are not just repeated but are being perfected inasmuch as socialism is developing into communism.

Socialism's economic laws make possible accelerated rates of reproduction expansion.

Our country's share of world production has been growing without interruption. The Soviet Union accounts for nearly one-fifth of the world industrial output, whereas her population barely amounts to 7 percent of the earth's inhabitants. The gap in level of industrial production between the USSR and the USA, the most powerful capitalist country, is steadily narrowing.

Let us consider the laws by which socialist reproduction is governed and how newly created material goods are distributed.

The sum total of material goods produced in a society within a given period of time constitutes the *total (gross) social product.*

The total product, by its very nature, may be divided into means of production and consumer goods. There are two large subdivisions of social production, therefore: *subdivision I: production of the means of production*; and *subdivision II: production of consumer goods.*

Because of the nature of the products under subdivision I, they are unsuitable for personal consumption. This production is limited to the elementary means of production such as coal, cement, steel, heavy machinery, electric locomotives, and various types of raw materials earmarked to re-enter the production process as labor tools and objects.

Products of subdivision II are foodstuffs, footwear, clothing, furniture, household utensils, and the like. These are used only for personal consumption.

What are conditions necessary for all enterprises to satisfy their demand for raw materials, fuel, and equipment; for all workers to find the consumer goods they need in the stores; and, as a result, to continue the process of reproduction in a steady manner?

Obviously, in subdivision I the output should suffice not only to replace the means of production expended (depreciated machinery and buildings, consumed raw materials and fuel, etc.) but also to ensure further expansion of social production as a whole.

In subdivision II consumer goods must be produced in quantities sufficient to satisfy fully the needs of all the workers. Rates of production expansion and technical progress in the branches of subdivision II are primarily determined by the quantity and quality of the means of production which these branches receive from subdivision I. Thus, the economic laws call for *preferential development of the production of the means of production over the production of consumer goods.*

The law of preferential production growth of the means of production signifies that, with correct economic planning, the branches that expedite technical progress and ensure increased productivity of social labor in all other production branches are developed on a priority basis.

However, production of the means of production is not an end in itself. In the final analysis, the means of production are indispensable for increased output of consumer goods and improvement of life for the people. This is the reason why we can and shall expand consumer-goods production along with heavy-industry development.

During the prewar five-year plans (1929-40), the average annual rate of industrial production increase in subdivision I exceeded by 1.7 that of consumer goods production increase. This means that production of the means of production increased nearly twice as fast as that of consumer goods. Since the war the rates have drawn somewhat closer. From 1960 to 1969 production in subdivision I rose 58 percent; and that in subdivision II, 36 percent. From 1968 to 1969 the output of consumer goods slightly exceeded that of the means of production.

If we consider the gross social product from the point of view of its value, it equals the sum total of values produced in all branches of material goods production. The gross social product, as evaluated, consists of the initial value preserved and transferred to the finished product, and the newly created value. One portion of it is used for reimbursement of expenditures made for the means of production in both subdivisions I and II. The second portion is earmarked for personal consumption and expansion of production, maintenance of nonproductive spheres of activity, accumulation of reserves, and so forth. This new value constitutes the *national income.*

National Income and State Budget

The national income is created in the process of material-goods production; its substance consists of the means of production and consumer goods: raw materials, auxiliary materials, machinery, machine tools, grain, sugar, clothing, footwear, books, and so forth. Since there is commodity production under socialism, the national income, in addition to its material form, has monetary value as well.

The entire national income is divided into a *consumption fund* and an *accumulation fund.*

The consumption fund is used to satisfy personal and social needs. It is subdivided into a wage fund for toilers in the field of material-goods production and a social consumption fund earmarked for salaries of persons employed in science, education, culture, public health; and a fund covering social-security cost and maintenance of the state administration and the army. The consumption fund accounts for approximately three quarters of the entire national income.

The accumulation fund is divided into three parts: the first, for expanding production; the second, for capital construction in the field of cultural-social services and public amenities (schools, hospitals, nurseries, kindergartens, housing, and the like); the third part is the reserve and insurance fund. The accumulation fund is of utmost importance: expanded reproduction is impossible without it.

All funds, except for the part left at the direct disposal of socialist enterprises, must be centrally collected. This is achieved by means of the *state budget.*

The revenue and expenditure budget plan is the basic financial plan of the socialist state. It shows the origin of funds and the objectives for which they will be used. The budget is drawn up by the government for one year and submitted for discussion and approval to the current session of the Supreme Soviet of the USSR.

Funds go into the state budget from the net profit of the socialist enterprises and from the *kolkhozes* in the form of income taxes. Only an insignificant part of budget funds comes from personal taxes.

Let us see where the budget funds go.

In the December 1969 session, the Supreme Soviet approved the budget of the USSR for the year 1970 as follows: 144.9 billion rubles in revenue; 144.6 rubles expenditure, of which 63.5 billion rubles were allocated for economic development; 54.8 billion for development of science, education, public health, physical fitness, pensions, grants, scholarships, i.e., for social and cultural needs. Part of the state budget is earmarked for the country's defense (17.8 billion rubles) and for maintaining the state administration (1.7 billion rubles).

Total (Gross) Product of Socialist Society

Replacement of Used Means of Production

National Income

Accumulation Fund

Consumption Fund

| Production Expansion Fund | Capital Construction, Cultural and Social Services Fund | Social Reserves and Insurance Fund | Labor Fund of Wages to Workers Engaged in Material Goods Production | Science, Education, Health, and Art Fund | Social Security Fund | State Administration and Defense Fund |

Contemporary Stage of Economic Policy of the Party and Soviet State

The aims of communit construction and the growth and increasingly complex nature of social production commit society to the task of continuous improvement of the entire system of management and control of the economy. To solve this task is the essence of the Party's *economic policy.*

After the CPSU October (1964) Plenum, the Party did a great amount of preparatory work for an economic reform. The results of the fulfillment of the Seven-Year Plan were thoroughly analyzed; causes of difficulties and shortcomings that had come to light were discovered. The press presented a far-ranging scientific discussion, including suggestions for future economic management. Economic experiments were undertaken: as a number of enterprises changed over to a new system, their operations were closely observed in order to test them in practice and reject whatever proved of no value. Much attention was given to the experience of European socialist countries that have also been introducing economic reforms.

As a result, an entire system has been outlined of measures aiming at radical improvement in the effectiveness of social production. These were reflected in the decisions taken by the CPSU Central Committee March and September (1965) Plenums and in the directives for the Five-Year Plan (1966-1970) of development of the country's economy issued by the Twenty-third Party Congress.

What is the main trend of the economic policy of the Party and of the Soviet state? The policy's goal is to increase the importance within the planned management of the economy of economic methods of stimulating production.

To Economic Methods, the Decisive Role

Under socialism every worker is vitally interested in the development of social production: the more efficient the operation of our industrial enterprises and collective and state farms, the higher the country's national income and the faster the growth in the people's material and cultural well-being.

But the general coincidence of interest of individual persons and of society as a whole is hardly sufficient. It is imperative that every enterprise (in other words, each working collective and all its members) be directly interested in turning out more products of higher quality, in economizing on raw and auxiliary materials, and in efficient use and updating of its equipment. If interest in work results at any one enterprise is added to the general interest in the country's economic success, then there is real assurance that that enterprise will carry on production with zeal and maximum efficiency.

Planning and management methods in the past very seldom ensured this coincidence of society's interests with those of individual enterprises. Often, they shackled the initiative and independence of enterprises. They also failed to create sufficient incentives for the maximum use of the socialist economy's rich resources.

Collectives at enterprises attempted to satisfy the country's needs with various new products, but their possibilities were limited. In order to streamline their production, the enterprises must be free to experiment: they should be able to attract designers and artists who would create new models, find suppliers of new materials, reorganize production procedure, and reassign personnel and crews. Enterprise directors had no such leeway, since they were restricted by thirty-five to forty plan indices, which they were obliged to observe strictly. The enterprise was assigned not only a specific quantity of goods for production but also the cost per unit in addition to the total output cost. In addition to the total expenditure for wage payments, the average wage per worker, number of workers, engineering and technical personnel, and auxiliary labor force were predetermined by a schedule.

The enterprise collective's interest in streamlining the production process and improving quality is increasing also because not the volume of gross production, as formerly, but the value of goods actually sold must be reported. This index shows the value of produce received by customers and paid for, and not simply the value of the goods produced. Enterprises therefore now strive to produce goods the customers need, for which there is demand.

For instance, the director of the Moscow "Borets" compressor plant wrote:

Formerly when a compressor was assembled, we would tick it off and send it to the warehouse with a feeling of accomplishment. Even if that's where it remained, the plant would make neither gain nor loss, since the compressor was included in the fulfillment of the annual production plan. Naturally, we didn't deliberately act this way, but, on the other hand, we didn't worry too much if through our fault or someone else's similar cases occurred.

Now the plant is not interested in producing "for the warehouse." It is more profitable to sell the finished product quickly. And it is considered sold when the customer receives it, pays for his order, and the money is credited to our account at the State Bank. Therefore, now the plant has to expedite compressor shipments, follow their routing, check whether the customer received and paid for his shipment. And if our compressor has imperfections, who is going to spend money for a low-quality product?

You have now become familiar with the self-support accounting system, one of the basic methods of socialist management. At its present stage, the Party's economic policy anticipates further development of this method: broadening of independence for the enterprises, strengthening the system of material incentives for the entire working collective, so as to give the country increased and unfailingly high-quality production.

Now the main indices of an enterprise's work quality are its net gain and profitable management. Deductions from plant profits added to the material incentive fund for worker bonuses have been increased considerably. Enterprises have been given the right to decide their labor force strength, as well as the right to introduce the forms of wage payment and bonus awards best adapted to the concrete conditions and needs of their operation.

The essence of the economic reform, in the final analysis, may be summed up as *strengthening economic levers and stimuli for production development* on the basis of an effective combination of centralized, planned control with initiative and independence of individual enterprises.

Misinterpreting the content of the economic reform, bourgeois propagandists attempt to prove that the new methods of economic management repudiate single, centralized state planning. Such allegations are entirely groundless. Centralized planning is one of the advantages of socialism over capitalism. Not only the socialist countries but also many developing countries which have recently won their independence are making far-reaching application of the USSR experience in organizing economic planning. And what of the attempts to program economic development in several capitalist countries? Are they not an indirect recognition of the great superiority of a planned economy as compared with the spontaneously developing capitalist economy?

By no means does economic reform require abandoning centralized planning; on the contrary, it proceeds from the necessity to preserve and increase the leading role of this planning.

This is reflected in the fact that centralized planning is now focused on deciding key strategic problems of economic development. The central planning organs, now freed from the task of excessive regulation and detailed supervision of enterprise operation, are improving long-range planning and upgrading the scientific validity of planning by applying modern methods of econometrics.

Most Important Economic Task

New management forms are being introduced in agriculture as well as in industry. The Party has made a number of important decisions in order to achieve steady growth of agricultural production. Over 70 billion rubles were invested in agriculture during the 1966-70 Five-Year Plan. Agriculture has never received such abundant funds before. But the problem is not limited to money. First and most important, it is imperative correctly to balance social and personal interests at the collective and state farms, and raise the interest of the toilers in agriculture in work results by offering material incentives.

Not so long ago purchase prices of many farm products (for example, grain, meat, and cereals) were often below production costs. This infringed upon the main requirement of the law of value: equal value for goods exchanged, calculated on the basis of socially indispensable production time. At times there were paradoxical situations: the greater the quantity of products indispensable to the country (grain, meat, cereals) produced by a collective farm, the larger the losses by the farm and the fewer the funds left for allocation to the toilers according to their labor. Because of lack of material incentives, the collective farm members lost interest in production. It was only natural that the output of these foodstuffs decreased and the public experienced shortages.

These are some of the most significant measures taken by the Party and the government. The system of state purchase of farm produce has been improved: for each collective and state farm a fixed plan of state-purchased deliveries of agricultural and animal husbandry products has been established for a five-year period. Therefore, if a collective farm increases its grain harvest or produces more milk and meat, all this surplus production remains at its disposal and may be sold to the state over and above the delivery plan, or on the *kolkhoz* market. Basic state purchase prices for wheat, rye, and certain other cereal crops have been increased (price for wheat and rye sold over and above the plan has increased 50 percent); prices paid for long-horned cattle, hogs, and sheep have also been raised. Many items needed in production and sold to collective and state farms have dropped in price. Price adjustments of widely used consumer goods sold in the countryside have been downward. Income tax paid by the collective farms has been cut.

In the final analysis, we are describing forms and methods of management similar to those now being applied in industrial production: increasing independence of agricultural enterprises, wide application of economic methods, and material stimulation of production. In these measures is reflected the Party's consistent economic policy: concern for development of all branches of the economy and for uplifting the well-being of all classes and strata of Soviet society.

A far-reaching work program must be carried out in order to ensure stable growth of agricultural production.

It is imperative, first, to improve soil conditions, the principal means of agricultural production. With this objective in view, the CPSU Central Committee and the USSR Council of Ministers passed a resolution "On Urgent Measures to Protect the Soil from Wind and Water Erosion." Second, power supplies for production on collective and state farms must be greatly increased and their technical equipment improved. Third, specialization by collective and state farms must be intensified; all organizational and managerial activity must be improved, based on transition to full, effective self-support. Fourth, democratic principles in the management of collective farm production must be developed in every possible way.

Understandably, implementing the Party's economic policy is not a simple task. We cannot stop production even for a day; we must reorganize while the wheels continue turning. There is need for large-scale material preparation, calculations, experiments. Experience accumulated from the new type of labor and time to set up a genuinely scientific labor organization are also needed. Most important, however, mastery of economic know-how and skill in management according to a new way are indispensable for our economic administrators, engineers, agronomists, and all those working in industry, agriculture, and other productive branches.

This is why the Party is introducing the new management forms and methods gradually. It is only natural that their practical application indicate many new solutions. And this is understandable. We are constantly moving, and this necessitates seeking the most effective forms and methods of economic construction.

Review Questions

1. What are the fundamental differences between the socialist and capitalist economic systems? What is the decisive advantage of the socialist system?
2. What is the objective of socialist production? How is it attained?
3. In what way does labor differ under socialism and under capitalism?
4. What is the advantage of planned economic management? Familiarize yourself with the planning procedures and labor organization and compensation in an enterprise or at a collective farm.
5. What is the meaning of the indices of production cost, profit, and profit management?
6. What part does socialist labor discipline have in production development?

7. Why is it necessary to interest a worker in the results of his labor by offering him material incentives?
8. What is the essence of the Party's economic policy in its present stage? Familiarize yourself with the resolution of the CPSU Twenty-third Party Congress. Ask the director of an enterprise that adopted the new management system to tell you about the experience he has gained.

Points to Consider and Discuss

1. Bourgeois ideologists maintain that social ownership restricts the workers' initiative, hinders the growth of labor productivity, and even "contradicts human nature." Refute these assertions.
2. In a discussion of the subject of "planning," a heated argument develops about the best way to organize planning. One point of view is that plans should be drawn up centrally and then "channeled downward" to the regions, districts, and enterprises. According to another point of view, plans should be prepared at the enterprises, and the task of the higher planning organs should be to integrate them. What is your opinion?
3. Imagine you are an enterprise director. Your task is to increase profits. What will you direct your attention to, first of all?
4. Let us continue with all students imagining they are directors or financial administration staff at various enterprises. The first enterprise supplies raw materials; the second produces certain goods; the third takes responsibility for their transport; and the fourth distributes them to consumers. Do not forget to "appoint" a bank director. Now try to enter into economic relations among yourselves, and then let the whole class sum up the results of your economic activities.

5

Sociopolitical System of Socialism

Society of Toilers

As a result of building socialism, the character of Soviet society has undergone radical change. Exploiter classes have been eliminated once and for all. Great changes have taken place within the working class, peasantry, and intelligentsia. Comradely cooperation, solidarity, and mutual support among toilers of various nations and peoples have been established.

Toilers of Socialist Society

At the beginning of 1970 the population of the Soviet Union was 241.7 million. Over three-fourths were blue-and-white-collar workers (including their families) and slightly less than one-fourth were collective farm peasants.

The *working class* is employed primarily in socialist industry, the leading sector of the economy. Its labor creates the means of production and industrial consumer goods. Workers are also employed on state farms.

Transformation of the Soviet Union into one of the most advanced countries of the world and creation of modern branches of industry have led not only to rapid increase in the working-class numbers but also to qualitative change in its structure. Prior to the revolution most workers were employed in light industry and in the food-processing industry. Now the majority are engaged in machine building and metal processing, ferrous metallurgy, and the chemical and oil industries.

The working class supplies the peasantry with the basic agricultural tools and chemical fertilizers. Workers process agricultural products in state industrial enterprises. According to the calculations of the prominent economist Academician S.G. Strumilin, the working class provides 50 percent of the labor expended to grow one ton of wheat.

Technical progress has led to improvement in the productive qualifications of workers; many new professions have emerged. The cultural and general educational level of the working class has risen. Prior to the revolution more than one-third of the workers employed in factories and plants were completely illiterate. At present 59 percent of industrial workers have some secondary-school education. Many study in night schools, technical schools, and institutions of higher learning without giving up their jobs. Workers, especially the innovators among them, are approaching the level of technical engineering staffs as to education and type of work.

"The worker-innovator," wrote L.K. Laletin, a turning-lathe operator at the Kirov plant, in his book *Trudit'sya znachit derzat'* (*To Toil Means to Dare*), "is a man with broad statesmanlike views. He combines the remarkable qualities of a master worker with the thorough knowledge of a good engineer. His aim is constantly to improve production technology and struggle for what is new, progressive."

The leading part it assumes in production, its rich political experience, and its high degree of discipline and self-denial guarantee to the working class its directing role in society. The Communist party created by the working class organizes and directs the development of society.

Socialism has also changed the character of the other main class of Soviet society, the *peasantry*, the large mass of which entered upon the path of socialist development in the thirties. (Collectivization in the socialist republics of the Baltic Region, Western Ukraine, Western Belorussia, and Moldavia was carried out during the postwar years.)

During the collectivization years the working class sent tens of thousands of its best sons and daughters to work among the peasantry. They helped to form the first cooperative farms, organize their production, and change the culture and living habits in the rural areas. We can read about the heroism of those times in the famous novel by M.A. Sholokhov, *Podnyataya tselina* (*Virgin Soil Upturned*), which vividly describes the work of a communist at the Putilov plant, Semyon Davydov, who was put in charge of the collectivization. Later, too, in every crucial period of every campaign to boost the production of agriculture, working-class "envoys" went to the aid of the peasantry. In the spring of 1955 about twenty-five thousand workers and employees answered the call of the Party and assumed leadership of the collective farms.

The collective-farm peasantry is gradually approaching the working conditions and culture of the working class. The *kolkhoz* members work on large-scale socialist farms established on the basis of collective labor and use of mechanized equipment. Completely new professions have emerged in the villages; a large group of machine operators has been trained. In 1967 they reached the total of 3,293,000 persons, including 2,358,000 tractor and combine operators and mechanics and nearly a million truck drivers. More than one-third of collective farm members have either seven-year or secondary-school education.

Nearly 100 percent of the state farms and over 98 percent of the collective farms have been supplied with electric power. Because of the construction of schools, clubs, motion-picture theaters, and health and sports facilities in the villages and thanks to wider use of television and other information media, life in the Soviet countryside has been transformed; the rural population has gained access to the riches of contemporary culture.

Industrial development, the growth of cities, and gradual transformation of agricultural labor into mechanized labor have continually decreased the proportion of peasants in the country's total population. As may be readily seen, this is an entirely different process from the ruin and fractioning of the peasantry under capitalism.

The *intelligentsia* is a fast-growing group in Soviet society.

Mostly, they are qualified specialists engaged in the production of material goods; in science, technology, culture, health, and in state and public administration.

In 1926 there were 2.9 million persons engaged in intellectual work; in 1937, nearly 10 million; by the beginning of 1969, their number reached 29.9 million. Specialists with university and specialized secondary-school education employed in the economy grew in number from 500,000 in 1928 to 14.9 million by the end of 1968. The percentage of production-oriented, technical, and scientific intelligentsia, at the same time, is growing particularly rapidly. The intelligentsia will continue to increase in number in the future, since this is what the development of our domestic economy and culture and the educational interests of the people as a whole require.

The intelligentsia in the capitalist world is compelled to sell its knowledge and talent to the owners of capital. Along with those who hold progressive views and have joined the struggle for society's renewal on the basis of socialist principles, there is a large group of specialists who, while having adapted to the capitalist order, consider themselves nevertheless to be a "spiritual elite." Under socialist conditions the intelligentsia builds the new world hand in hand with the workers and peasants, considering serving the people's interests its higher obligation. The Soviet intelligentsia, originating in all classes and social groups, plays an important part in solving the diverse and complex tasks of communist construction in our country.

New Social Relations

What is the picture of social relations within Soviet society?

Let us take the decisive area of human activity, material goods *production*. As has been said, social ownership has abolished domination of some classes by others. Workers, peasants, and intelligentsia have equal opportunity to work for socialist society, and for themselves; they are equally interested in seeing the economy and culture flower. A person's material well-being and position do not depend upon class membership but upon his labor, ability, and knowledge.

No *political* privileges are attached to belonging to the working class or the collective farm peasantry: all citizens of the Soviet state, regardless of class or stratum, enjoy identical rights to participate in the management of state affairs. Soviet society has no clear-cut lines between classes: the workers, if they so desire, may become peasants; the peasants may become workers. Young men and women in worker or peasant families, once properly qualified, join the ranks of the intellectual workers. This mobility is proof that the classes are increasingly drawing together.

Neither are any cultural privileges connected with belonging to the working class, peasantry, or intelligentsia. Socialism has made education available to all citizens and created conditions favoring development of people's talent. Understandably enough, the level of spiritual culture cannot be identical among all strata of the population, especially since cultural pursuits constitute the profession of a certain segment of society. This specialization, however, does not change the fact that every person, irrespective of the work he does, has the opportunity to acquire knowledge, gain access to science and the arts, and be civilized and intelligent in the fullest sense.

For thousands of years humanity has been torn apart by irreconcilable class contradictions, and at present a most acute class struggle is taking place in the capitalist world. Under socialism, by contrast, *the sociopolitical and ideological unity of the entire people* is being established. This unity is based upon the fact that all the toilers in a socialist society are equal in social relations, united by the community of their fundamental interests. With regard to political matters, all toilers are united by their common objective: building communism under the leadership of the Communist party. With regard to ideology, the working class, the collective farm peasantry, and the people's intelligentsia are united by their common ideology—Marxism-Leninism.

The alliance of workers and peasants, in which the directing role belongs to the working class, is especially important for the friendly cooperation of the whole people. The working class does not claim any special privileges; its leadership is based entirely on its directing role in social production and on its great political and moral prestige.

Sociopolitical and ideological unity does not simply mean identity of interests of all strata in society. In addition to common fundamental interests, each stratum may have specific demands and needs of its own. Thus, for example, all Soviet people are equally interested in continued economic expansion, in consolidation of the country's economic and political power, improved living standards, and the flowering of culture. But in addition specific needs exist: those of rural mechanization specialists, let us say; or schoolteachers, or persons toiling under the harsh conditions of Siberia, or inhabitants of the country's southern regions.

The organs of power and administration, therefore, often are faced with complex tasks: Which social needs should have priority? Where should the resources be directed? In other words, it is always necessary to reconcile specific interests of society's different strata in a satisfactory and just way. These tasks are solved by the Communist party policy, which expresses the interests of all the toilers.

As well as establishing the sociopolitical and ideological unity of the people, the victory of socialism brought about other important changes in social relations. Socialism forever eliminated that ugly heritage of exploiter formations, the *opposition* between intellectual and physical labor and between town and country. Social conditions were abolished under which the owner classes had special privileges because of their intellectual occupations and town could exploit country.

At the same time it is incorrect to think that under socialism all problems in the area of social relations have already been solved. In the course of building the classless communist society, such differences as still exist between the working class and peasantry, the town and country, and others must be overcome.

Chapter 6 discusses this problem in greater detail.

Nations and National Relations

Solution of the National Problem

The first victorious socialist revolution was achieved in the most multinational country in the world, where there are over one hundred nations and nationalities. All forms of national oppression existed in Czarist Russia, from complete absence of political rights to colonial exploitation of backward peoples. For decades the ruling classes propagated great-power chauvinism and local nationalism, planted quarrels and suspicion among people of different nations, and set them against each other in order to prevent the toilers from achieving unity. Bloody clashes caused by national antagonisms, slaughters, and pogroms were normal occurrences.

But all that could not prevent proletarian solidarity. The socialist revolution developed and succeeded, because it is the common cause of the toilers under the leadership of Lenin's party; leading representatives of the working class of the various peoples in the country fought in its ranks. Upon assuming power, the Party began to put into practice with consistency its program to solve the multinational problem. The essence of this plan was to establish political equality of all nations, liquidate all forms and types of national oppression, afford each nation the right to make independent decisions about its fate (the right of self-determination) and about its voluntary union with equal national republics into the Soviet Federation; and to guarantee, as well, equal conditions for each nation's maximum development, with practical equality among peoples as the objective.

Lenin's program of solving the multinational problem has been fully carried out as a result of building socialism.

On December 30, 1922, the First Congress of Soviets unanimously approved the Declaration and Treaty establishing the Union of Soviet Socialist Republics.

The *Soviet Federation* makes possible a harmonious combination of the rights of each national state formation with the all-union interests, the interests of the entire people.

The all-union organs of state power administer the economic and cultural development in the country's entire territory. We have a single Soviet citizenship, budget, monetary system, and armed forces.

At the same time each *union republic* has its own constitution and may enter into direct relations with other states and exchange diplomatic representatives with them. A union republic works out its own plan of economic development and its own budget, operates industrial enterprises under union republic jurisdiction, manages housing and communal services, administers public health services, social-security insurance, and education on the elementary, secondary, and higher levels.

Many different nationalities reside on the territory of a number of union republics. If a certain nation or nationality lives as a relatively compact group, its government structure takes the form of an *autonomous republic, autonomous oblast'* [region], or *national okrug* [district]. Within its own territory an autonomous republic also directs its domestic economy and culture and has organs of power and a constitution.

Soviet federation embodies the fraternal collaboration of socialist nations and nationalities. The remarkable motive force of Soviet society—friendship among the peoples in the USSR—is the result of the formation of the union of the socialist republics. The peoples' friendship is the paramount source of the strength and invincibility of socialism.

The most complex task in solving the multinational problem was to achieve de facto equality among the nations, inasmuch as the country's different peoples were at so widely divergent levels of social development. Alongside advanced nations were backward nationalities and tiny ethnic groups. In most areas of Central Asia, for instance, feudal relations prevailed. In the Far North, in numerous regions of Siberia and the Far East, the patriarchal tribal order was preserved. Accelerated economic and cultural development was required to raise the backward peoples to the level of the more progressive. And this was the course of action the Party took. While the gross output of large-scale industry in the USSR taken as a whole increased 73 times in 1967 as compared with the year 1913, in the Kazakh SSR the increase was 114 times; in the Kirgiz SSR it was 138 times. Teams of skilled specialists have been trained in all production branches in the national regions.

Socialism has secured the revival of previously backward peoples. In the years of Soviet power about fifty nationalities have created their own script and developed a literature. Classroom instruction is given in sixty-five languages of the country's nations and nationalities. Union republics have their Academies of Sciences, numerous scientific research institutes, national theaters, and motion-picture studios.

Relying on the mutual fraternal assistance of all peoples—of the Great Russian people, first of all—many formerly backward peoples have achieved transition from the Middle Ages to socialism in three to four decades, avoiding the agony of capitalist development; certain ones have literally been saved from physical extinction. As a French correspondent has said, "Ten centuries were traversed in less than forty years."

Progressive forces in the young independent states in Asia, Africa, and Latin America are watching the Soviet experience with growing interest. Many of their leaders say that humanity owes socialism great respect for its justice and humanism, if only because it has eliminated national oppression and lifted formerly backward peoples to prosperity. The Indian writer Pandit Sunderlal, giving his impressions of Soviet Uzbekistan, has said, "If Uzbekistan has become a highly developed country under the Soviet system—and it has—then the Soviet system is the best in the world."

Two Trends in the Development of National Relations

There are two trends under socialism: nations are simultaneously developing and drawing together. Both trends are progressive and indissolubly related.

In fact, on account of the friendship among peoples and their mutual assistance, former backward nations of the border areas of the Russian Empire have succeeded in rising to the level of the country's developed central regions. Now all the national republics of the USSR possess highly developed industry and mechanized agriculture and, in addition, highly qualified specialists in all branches of the economy and culture.

How rapidly the Soviet republics are developing may be seen from the following examples:

In per capita production of electric power Azerbaydzhan leads Japan, France, and Italy. In Turkmenia, where prior to the revolution there were no literate persons, there are now twenty-four students per each ten thousand of the population. In Kirghizia, one out of twenty-five inhabitants is a specialist with secondary-school education or higher. Kirghizia, once completely devoid of industry, now delivers modern industrial equipment to fifty foreign countries. Formerly, a literate Chukchee was rare. Now there are native miners, geologists, seamen, flyers, teachers, writers, and scientists on the Chukotskiy Peninsula.

Despite the fact that USSR national member republics individually render assistance to other peoples and states, the CPSU Program emphasizes that the Party "shall, as heretofore, continue the policy guaranteeing factual equality of all nations and nationalities, taking their interests fully into consideration and giving special attention to regions in need of more rapid development."

It is precisely this national development that calls for increasingly closer cooperation. Expansion of industrial and agricultural production and economic specialization of the national republics are without fail accompanied by broadening cooperation among them. Not a single large-scale construction project at the present time could function without participation by plants and factories in numerous Soviet republics; nor could such gigantic undertakings as the "opening up" of virgin territory nor the creation of new industrial bases in the eastern part of the country have been realized without the common effort of all the Soviet peoples.

In recent years, on our Party's initiative, the rights of the union republics have been considerably broadened and administration of the overwhelming majority of industrial enterprises located in republic territory has been transferred to them. As a result, need for even closer coordination of economic construction in the union republics is great.

Some three or four decades ago the country's entire scientific life was concentrated in Moscow, Leningrad, Kiev, and a few other larger centers. Now, since a base for scientific research has been organized and talented scientists trained in each national republic, the development of science is unthinkable without their cooperation.

Astronomers at the Pulkovo Observatory cooperate with their colleagues in Byurakan. Mathematicians in the capital are in constant contact with their "comrades in arms" in Tbilisi. Metallurgists from all ends of the country travel to Kiev to acquire professional experience. The common front of Soviet science is being strengthened.

When we read books, watch motion pictures, listen to music created by the cultural leaders of any one of our nations, we are enriching our spiritual world, finding new life horizons and new sources of aesthetic enjoyment. This encourages us to know the culture of our fraternal peoples more deeply, understand it better, and appreciate it.

Thus, all of society greatly profits from each nation's further development, which generates mutual respect and strengthens friendship among the peoples. *The prosperity of nations made possible by drawing closer and their drawing closer because of their prosperity is the dialectic of the development of national relations in the Soviet Union.*

One must not, however, overlook a most important factor. When we speak of a nation prospering, we refer to the better, the progressive aspects of national culture, healthy national customs and traditions that truly serve the cause of enriching the culture of all nations. But in every nation vestiges of the old way of life linger on, and harmful traditions have their effect. Obviously, it would be absurd to speak about promoting the tradition of paying bride-money or clinging to the outdated extended family structure. Such traditions, on the contrary, must be fought with utmost severity. In the first place, to eliminate them is a matter of honor for the very nations that still practice them.

Particularly tenacious and harmful are the remnants of the nationalistic attitude. Nothing is more repulsive and contrary to the spirit of our society than nationalistic conceit, contempt for people of other nationalities. Our laws severely punish any signs of discrimination or violation of people's rights prompted by nationalistic or racial motives. The Party educates the Soviet people in the spirit of internationalism, equality, and friendship of peoples. Each Soviet man has a sacred duty to remain faithful to these ideas in all his thoughts and deeds. One cannot be a conscious builder of communism without being an internationalist.

Common Features of Spiritual Makeup

Because nations are increasingly drawing together and are mutually enriched, *features of spiritual makeup common to all people* are emerging as a result of the new social system, combining the best traditions of the peoples of the USSR.

Those who have had an opportunity to travel across the Soviet land could not but notice everywhere distinctive marks of the Soviet life, whether in Central Asia or the Baltic Region, Transcaucasia or Moldavia. In outward appearance, manner of dress, speech, even in their gesticulations, there is great variety among people. But for all that, they have certain common traits by which one cannot fail to identify a Soviet man. It cannot be otherwise: after all, community of convictions and identical conditions of social life cannot but find their reflection in the people's spiritual makeup.

National character is unusually stable; its formation is influenced by all the aspects of a nation's life. Without doubt, certain traits connected with differences in temperament clearly stand out in the people of each nation or group of kindred nations. This does not prevent development of new common traits in the *Soviet man*, however: efficiency and enthusiasm, magnanimity and generosity, directness and adherence to principles, and many other qualities have become widespread since the affirmation of the new, communist morality.

In the process of building communism a culture common to all Soviet people is successfully developing as a prototype of the communist culture that all men will share. Though a truly great variety of styles and forms appear in their creative work, Soviet writers, composers, or painters are all equipped with one method of artistic creation—socialist realism.

Contemporary architecture is typical in this respect. Architects in every nation use the best features of national building traditions. At the same time they strive to create structures corresponding to the aesthetic ideals of our epoch. They seek the simplest and most telling forms and erect economical buildings that are comfortable at the same time. The features of economy and comfort are also necessitated by the use of new materials: concrete, plastic, and glass. Thus, a new architectural style is emerging that reflects the best national traditions. Not an eclectic conglomeration of styles and methods, which itself would be poor taste, it is, in fact, the synthesis of the universal and national styles in architecture.

An important problem, *development of national languages*, is being solved in our country from a consistently internationalist position.

Each nation in our country has every possibility to develop and enrich its own language, creating a powerful tool of national culture. At the same time, it is imperative to have a means of communication within the family of fraternal peoples. The Russian language has become this means, and not by any decree. All Soviet peoples have freely adopted the Russian language as their means of communication. And this is only natural, inasmuch as Russian is the language of the largest nation inhabiting the USSR (Russians account for one half of the country's entire population). Also, the Russian language possesses an exceptionally rich vocabulary, making it possible to express the most subtle nuances of human thought. A very rich literature exists in Russian, both original and translated. Whatever Soviet nation we belong to, we love the Russian language because it is the language of Lenin and Chernyshevsky, Tolstoy and Chekhov, Pushkin and Gogol, Gorky and Mayakovsky.

Clearly, the Soviet people will continue studying the Russian language and using it widely for communication among themselves. This progressive trend by no means excludes further development and enrichment of other national languages. The Communist Party Program, while mentioning the positive importance of learning the Russian language along with a given nation's native language, forcefully stresses that "no privilege, limitation, or compulsion in the use of one or another language" should be permitted.

With the worldwide victory of communism, national differences will ultimately be erased and one common language, one common culture will become firmly established. But this process will be exceptionally long, and now it is impossible to predict, even approximately, when it will be completed.

Soviet Socialist State

The concept "state" enters our lives at an early age. We all study in state schools and upon completing our education go to work in state enterprises or institutions. When we reach draft age we serve in the state's armed forces. We participate in elections for the organs of state power, and we go to them for help for a great variety of reasons. Even when we take a Soviet ship to go overseas, we are on our state territory. When we are abroad on an official assignment or a tourist trip, as Soviet citizens we are under the state's protection.

Every Soviet person is proud of belonging, as a full-fledged citizen, to the powerful force that is the first *socialist state of toilers* in the world.

Functions of the Soviet State

What are the basic types of activity of the Soviet state, its basic functions? From the moment it emerged, the new Soviet state was faced with the task of consolidating the transition of power into the hands of the working class and suppressing resistance by the exploiters. With the liquidation of the exploiter classes, however, the function of suppression has become unnecessary.

As with any other socialist state, the principal functions of the Soviet state are determined by the great creative task of building socialism and communism.

First of all, there is the *economic-organizational function*. Our state is the collective owner of the basic means of production. It coordinates the planned development of all branches of the economy, organizes the people's labor, and sees to the improvement of the living standard. As long as the principle of distribution according to labor operates in society, the state controls the amount of labor and consumption, keeps strict account of all social wealth, and protects social property from thieves and plunderers.

The *cultural-educational function* is closely connected with the economic-organizational one. The Soviet state administers public education and organizes the activities of scientific institutions. Museums, motion-picture studios, publishing houses, and so forth are under its control. While it satisfies the people's intellectual and cultural needs, the state makes a great effort at the same time to educate the toilers in the spirit of communism.

An important function of a socialist state, also, is *protection of public order and the citizens' rights and freedom*.

In addition to internal functions, the Soviet state has a number of important external ones. These are determined by the objective of securing the most advantageous international conditions for constructing communism in the USSR and by our international obligation toward the toilers of the whole world.

As long as danger of military attack by imperialism remains, the Soviet state has the responsible function of *the country's defense*. It fights for *strengthening of world peace*, for consolidation of the principle of peaceful coexistence of states with different sociopolitical systems. Also among its important functions are the *strengthening of fraternal collaboration of the USSR with other states of the world socialist system, support of the national liberation struggle of peoples, and the development of economic and cultural ties with all countries*.

Merely enumerating the functions of the socialist state shows that it represents a political organization acting in the people's name, in the people's interest, and with its direct participation.

Socialism restores to the concept "democracy" its true meaning by making the state an instrument of genuine popular rule. Of course, this does not mean that socialist democracy emerges in a ready-made, final form. The system of popular rule develops and is perfected along with society's development. Theory and practice are always advancing new democratic forms, new political institutions that make it possible to enlist broader and broader participation by the masses in solving state affairs, improve the structure of government apparatus, and eliminate vestiges of bureaucracy and formalism.

The Soviets of Toilers' Deputies

All power in the USSR belongs to the toilers and is exercised through their representative organs—*the Soviets of Toilers' Deputies*. They function every-where, in every city, workers' settlement, village, Cossack *stanitsa* [village], Caucasian village and *kishlak* [village in Soviet Central Asia]; in every *oblast* [region], *kray* [territory], and republic. The Soviets constitute the state's political basis: all state agencies derive from the Soviets, receive power from them, and are under their control.

As organs of genuinely popular power, the Soviets differ in a number of fundamental ways from the representative institutions of the bourgeois state.

The Soviets, first of all, are *all-inclusive* organs, since they represent almost the total adult population. They enlist the participation of the broad popular masses in administration of public affairs.

Secondly, the Soviets are not only legislative but also executive organs: the deputies adopt resolutions in sessions and committees and carry them out in person or through each Soviet's executive committee.

Finally, the Soviets are *sovereign* organs: they decide all key political problems, manage the total social wealth, direct the economy and cultural development. Also, by combining the features of state and social organizations, they function as agencies of local self-government.

A democratic *electoral system* assures complete representation of the people's interests in the Soviets.

That *suffrage is universal* is the chief indication of the democratic nature of the electoral system. All citizens who have reached the age of eighteen have the right to vote, regardless of social and ethnic origin, sex, education, religious belief, place of residence, property status, and past activities. The only exceptions are the mentally ill.

Eighteen-year-olds have the right to be elected to the local Soviets of Toilers' Deputies; twenty-one-year-olds have the right to be elected to the Supreme Soviets of the union and autonomous republics; twenty-three-year-olds may be elected to the Supreme Soviet of the USSR. Soviet citizens may be active in governmental affairs from early youth.

In the USSR the *electoral right is equal and direct*. All citizens take part in elections on an equal basis. Every person has one vote. The deputies of both local and Supreme Soviets are elected directly, without intermediaries.

No one in the Soviet Union can influence the free expression of the voters' will: voting is by *secret ballot*.

In elections the Communist party acts in close association with non-party people who are organized in labor unions, cooperative organizations, the *Komsomol* [League of Communist Youth], and cultural and other mass organizations of toilers. Candidates for deputies are nominated by the people. The broad public exercises control over the entire procedure of the electoral campaign; more than twenty-five million persons participate in organizing these campaigns, acting as voters' proxies, members of electoral commissions, and canvassers.

The Soviets' deputies are not professional politicians. By far the majority are workers in factories, *kolhozes*, institutes, and research laboratories. They must report regularly to the Soviet and directly to the voters. They are under constant supervision by the voters, and in the event of poor performance or improper conduct they can be recalled.

The membership of the Soviets is regularly renewed with every election. Not only does this help to improve the work of the Soviets themselves, it also ensures an influx of new forces and the training in state administration of new hundreds of thousands, even millions, of toilers.

The USSR Supreme Soviet

The supreme organ of state power in the USSR is the *USSR Supreme Soviet*, elected for a four-year term by the citizens of the USSR on the basis of universal, equal, and direct suffrage by secret ballot.

The USSR Supreme Soviet is invested with all the sovereign power that the people possess and delegate. It considers and decides the most general and important problems of the Soviet Union's domestic and foreign policy. It approves the state plan for the development of the economy and the budget, passes all-union laws binding on all citizens and institutions. It adopts the USSR constitution and when necessary introduces amendments to it; it controls the observance of the constitution; it chooses the government and changes its composition; it elects the USSR Supreme Court and appoints the Procurator General. It represents the Soviet Union in international relations and enters into relations with other parliaments. It ratifies the most important treaties with foreign countries and exercises supreme control over the activity of state organs and officials.

The deputies of the USSR Supreme Soviet are envoys of the workers, the collective farm peasantry, and the intelligentsia. Nearly one-half of them are workers and peasants who come directly from the plants and the fields. Almost one-third of the Supreme Soviet are women, and its membership is younger than that of any bourgeois parliament.

Compare the membership of the USSR Supreme Soviet with that of the Fourth State Duma in Imperial Russia (1912 elections). Of its 439 deputies, 354 were representatives of the landed gentry, the city bourgeoisie, tradespeople, and *kulaks* [well-to-do peasants]. Bourgeois parliaments today are similar; they are mostly composed of industrialists, bankers, high government officials, managers, and lawyers of monopolistic corporations. For instance, there is not a single worker in the Congress of the United States, not one small farmer; the

Bundestag of the Federal German Republic does not have one deputy who is a worker. Women have insignificant representation in the parliaments of capitalist countries.

The USSR Supreme Soviet has two houses: the Soviet of the Union, representing the common interest of all citizens irrespective of nationality; and the Soviet of Nationalities, which expresses the specific needs and interests of numerous nations and nationalities united in the Union of Soviet Socialist Republics. The organizational principle of the two houses therefore differs somewhat. A deputy to the Soviet of the Union is elected by a fixed number (300,000) of the population. In elections for the Soviet of Nationalities the number of voters does not matter: each union republic elects thirty-two deputies; each autonomous republic, eleven; each autonomous *oblast* [region], five; and each national *okrug* [district], one. Each house has an almost equal number of deputies: 767 in the Soviet of the Union, and 750 in the Soviet of Nationalities.

Both houses have equal rights. A law is considered passed when it is adopted by both houses. Each house organizes permanent commissions to handle basic problems of state, economic, and sociocultural construction, as well as commissions for specific functional problems of the USSR Supreme Soviet. The commissions prepare questions for discussion by the Supreme Soviet and control the execution of the laws and statutes that the Supreme Soviet adopts.

The Supreme Soviet meets in regular sessions to decide important state questions. To take care of current business at the highest state administrative level, both houses elect the *Presidium of the USSR Supreme Soviet* in joint session at the first meeting of each term.

The Presidium consists of a chairman, deputy chairman from each union republic, a secretary, and members. Also, it functions as the highest organ of the Soviet state, since it represents the Supreme Soviet and discharges some of its duties between Supreme Soviet sessions. The Presidium's most important decrees must be approved by the Supreme Soviet in regular session.

The USSR Council of Ministers

The USSR Council of Ministers, the government of the Soviet Union, is formed at a joint session of the Soviet of the Union and the Soviet of Nationalities. In order to secure the participation of the national republics in the solution of all-union problems, the chairman of the Council of Ministers of each union republic belongs to it exofficio. The USSR Council of Ministers is responsible and accountable to the Supreme Soviet and, between its sessions, to the Presidium. It is the highest executive and administrative body of state authority in the USSR.

The Council of Ministers directs the development of the economy and culture, organizes implementation of the state budget, puts into effect the laws of the Supreme Soviet, ensures public order, and defends the state's interests and citizens' rights. General overall management of relations with foreign countries is one of its prerogatives. It builds and controls the country's armed forces. It issues its decisions in the form of resolutions and decrees. On an especially important topic, the CPSU Central Committee and the USSR Council of Ministers issue joint resolutions binding on all state and Party organs.

It coordinates and guides the operations of the ministries and subordinate institutions, organs that administer individual branches of the economy and culture.

Union Republic and Local Organs of Political Power and Administration

The highest organ of political power in a union republic is the Supreme Soviet. It passes laws binding within a republic's territory, approves its budget, and so forth. It differs in structure from the USSR Supreme Soviet in that it has only one chamber. It also elects its Presidium, the limits of whose competence are defined by the union republic's constitution. The highest executive and administrative organ is the Council of Ministers.

In an autonomous republic the foremost political organ is the Supreme Soviet, which elects a Presidium, forms a Council of Ministers, and elects a Supreme Court.

The local Soviets occupy an important place in the system of organs of governmental power. Soviets of Toilers' Deputies in *kray* [territory], *oblast* [region], autonomous *oblast*, *okrug* [district], *rayon* [county], city, village, and settlement are elected for a two-year term. They direct cultural-political and economic construction—enterprises, institutions, and organizations—within their competence; they fix the local budget, direct the activities of subordinate administrative organs, ensure public order and observance of laws, and protect citizens' rights. An important task of the local Soviets is improving services to the public.

The local Soviets elect executive and administrative organs called executive committees. For day-to-day direction of the economy and culture, local Soviets usually form a planning commission with sections for various branches of economic and cultural construction. The broad masses of the people are enlisted in regular and effective participation in state affairs by means of the Soviets of Toilers' Deputies.

The increasing role and rights of local organizations facilitate the successful construction of communism.

The Communist party is seeking to improve and democratize to the maximum the activities of the Soviets. Their sessions are being upgraded in function and importance: they have increased independence to solve economic, financial, agricultural, and other problems; to direct enterprises of local industry; and to provide for sociocultural needs and public services. The activity of permanent commissions is being expanded, and the deputies are obliged to report regularly to the voters.

The Judiciary and the Procurator's Office

Supervision of the strict observance of Soviet law and protection of public order and the rights and interests of citizens are the duty of all state organs. But there are organs that deal exclusively with these problems, the *courts* and the *Procurator's Office*.

The Soviet courts are based on democratic principles.

The basic link of the court system is the *rayon [county] and city people's court*. There is one in every *rayon* and city. The people's judges are elected for a five-year term by universal, equal, and direct suffrage by secret ballot. The judges are accountable to the voters and can be recalled. Together with the professional judges, people's assessors voluntarily share the court's work without compensation. They are elected at general meetings of the toilers by show of hands for a two-year term. All civil and criminal law cases are decided by the court jointly.

Appropriate Soviets elect the courts for a five-year term for *okrug*, autonomous *oblast, kray, oblast*, and autonomous and union republics. The highest judicial body of the country is the USSR Supreme Court, elected for a five-year term by the USSR Supreme Soviet.

The judges are independent and subject only to the law. Legal proceedings are conducted in the languages of the union and autonomous republics and the autonomous *oblasts*. Any party to a court case may speak his native tongue. The public nature of the procedure in court cases (with the exception of a very few instances specified by law) assures publicity and objectivity. The accused is entitled to defense counsel.

The Procurator's Office, a special organ supervising the strict observance of the law, deals with the problem by different methods.

The Procurator's Office initiates legal proceedings and conducts inquiries about criminal cases, collects evidence against criminals and their accomplices, checks on the legality of the actions of other investigative organs. The court examines cases submitted by the Procurator's Office, with the Procurator appearing before the court as state prosecutor.

The Procurator's Office attends to the uniform interpretation of law throughout the country regardless of local differences and despite local influences.

The Procurator's Office supervision is exercised differently from ordinary state supervision. In the course of their supervisory activities and departmental control, state organs are entitled to intervene in the operational and administrative activities of the organizations under control. In a number of instances they have the right to apply disciplinary and administrative sanctions. In the event of a violation of the law, the Procurator's Office has both the right and the duty to lodge a protest according to established procedures against any executive and administrative organ of the local Soviets or agencies. It has the further right and duty to initiate criminal disciplinary or administrative action against officials or citizens, depending on the specific circumstances.

The Procurator's Office protects the personal inviolability of the Soviet citizen. In our country no one may be arrested except by court order or by approval of the Procurator.

The organs of the Soviet Procurator's Office constitute a unified, strictly centralized system, independent of local governmental and administrative agencies. The Procurator's Office is headed by the Procurator General of the USSR, appointed for a seven-year term by the USSR Supreme Soviet. The USSR Procurator General appoints his counterparts in the union republics, *krays*, and *oblasts. Okrug, rayon*, and city procurators are appointed by union republic procurators and confirmed by the Procurator General of the USSR. Low-ranking procurators are subordinate to those of higher rank.

Soviet Legal Order

Socialist Legality

Soviet laws express the will of the entire people. They regulate economic and other social relations, protect the socialist order, establish the rights and obligations of citizens and officials, and safeguard the social and personal property of the toilers.

The system of all these laws constitutes *socialist law*, which has several branches.

Civil law plays an enormous role in everyday life. The individual enters daily into a multitude of what are called, in legal language, civil legal relationships. To reach school or factory he travels in a streetcar or bus. When he buys a ticket, he enters into a transport contract relationship, even if he is not aware of it at the time. When he hands his coat to a coatroom attendant, he has just entered into a storage contract relationship. When he buys groceries or goods in a store, he enters into a buying-selling contract relationship. By taking out books on a library card he enters into a loan contract. Of course, people usually do not even think of the legal nature of these relationships. But if one does not take a ticket in a streetcar or loses the library book, he comes into conflict with the provisions of the law and begins to understand the need of fulfilling the law's requirements.

There are still more complex relationships. For example, one obtains new living quarters. To acquire a right to them he must get a permit from the local Soviet. The law establishes the rights and obligations of a tenant and his mutual relations with the housing management. There are regulations governing the use of living quarters and their equitable division in case of dispute.

Civil law is of special importance in regulating relations between socialist enterprises and organizations. It specifies the economic rights of each enterprise, defines the procedure for delivering supplies, marketing the finished products, transport, and so forth.

Civil law protects the rights of authors of literary, scientific, and artistic works; and of inventors and efficiency experts. This group of civil-law norms is usually called *copyright law* and *patent law*. The person who has made a scientific discovery has the right to demand recognition of his authorship and priority in the discovery. The right to a discovery is acknowledged by a certificate, which authorizes appropriate award to the discoverer. All these points are regulated by special law on discoveries, inventions, and suggestions for improving efficiency.

The area of familial-marital relations is regulated by *family law*.

Registration of marriage is required by law and aims at enforcing a serious attitude toward the family. Society is vitally interested in having the relation between husband and wife based from the very beginning upon solid foundations of mutual love and esteem, and on common moral ideals. The law provides that both partners to the marriage shall have equal rights in the choice of family name, selection of profession, occupation, and place of residence; mutual material support, and mutual ownership of jointly acquired property. The most important civic duty of married couples who have become parents is the care and training of the children. The state protects the interests of mother and child. Failure to discharge parental obligations is in certain cases punishable by law. The children, in their turn, are obliged when adults to look after parents who are unable to work and to extend them material assistance.

Various violations of socialist order still do occur. In order to counteract these, the law sets standards of proper behavior, defining what actions are criminal and establishing appropriate punishment. This law is called *criminal law*. In ancient times serious crimes such as robbery, arson, and murder were punished by the death penalty or, as they said in those days, by "decapitation." Hence the term "capital" crime.

Soviet laws fix the age of sixteen as the beginning of general criminal responsibility for committing any crime; in certain instances this age limit is reduced to fourteen years. Severe punishment is handed down for theft, embezzlement, and various abuses of position and crimes of office (for example, taking bribes), infliction of bodily injury, hooliganism, personal insult, slander, and poaching. The severest penalties, including the firing squad, are imposed on traitors, spies, saboteurs, and on especially malicious embezzlers of social property, counterfeiters, foreign currency black-marketeers, murderers, and rapists.

Soviet law is imbued with consistent humanism. Its chief aim is establishment of an unshakable, just social order; the training and general improvement of people; and creation of social conditions that increase resistance to antisocial behavior.

Socialist legality and law not only consolidate relationships already formed but they also promote development of new mutual relations. The law trains citizens in a spirit of understanding the requirements of the socialist order and in respect for the interests of the state and society; it requires a conscious and deliberate observance of legal norms. In other words, it inculcates *legal consciousness*. The law is not addressed to the people as a whole; it is addressed to each and every individual person. This is why it is a mistake to think that the legal field is of interest only to jurists and attorneys. Everyone should act within the framework of the law, respect its demands, and fulfill them to the letter. In the struggle for the communist way of life and its new conditions, we must make use of both the force of law and the force of public opinion, which is the collective's influence.

Socialist legal consciousness is closely bound up with morality. While serving to carry out Party and state policy, it evaluates people's behavior as legal or illegal, just or unjust; it provides a moral standard. On the other hand, participation by the broad masses in the struggle to strengthen socialist legality and protect the socialist legal order leads to close association between law and morality. Moral aspects of legal control increase in importance, and violation of law is judged to be amoral behavior.

The entire socialist legal order has the purpose of ensuring the conditions for free development of the human personality. The rights and duties of the Soviet citizen very directly reflect this purpose.

Unity of Rights and Duties

The majority of our country's citizens were born and grew up under the Soviet regime. We are accustomed to enjoying broad social rights that express society's concern for the individual throughout his life.

When the young Soviet citizen reaches seven years of age, the school doors open to him hospitably. With elementary school completed, millions of young boys and girls continue their studies in secondary specialized schools and institutions of higher education. The Soviet citizen is assured the *right to an education*.

All of the children in the country attend school, whereas prior to the revolution almost four-fifths of them did not have that chance. We are now in the process of transition to universal secondary education; broad possibilities have been created for obtaining higher and special secondary education. The USSR holds first place in the world in student enrollment. The state has assumed the total outlay for education, with a considerable number of students receiving scholarships and other subsidies. At boarding schools, living expenses as well as education are paid from state funds.

When he has acquired skills and chosen a profession, every Soviet citizen has the opportunity to utilize his energy and ability. The *right to work*, the most important of all social rights, is guaranteed by the economic system of socialism, which precludes crises and unemployment. The Soviet people have complete freedom of choice in the matter of profession and specialization, and they have freedom of personal creativity if it does not conflict with the interests of society, of the people.

The toilers in our country enjoy paid vacations. They are provided with sanatoria, vacation facilities, numerous tourist centers, stadiums and sports fields, parks and clubs. In case of illness workers receive material assistance (up to 100 percent of their wages) from social insurance funds. They also get free medical care. In the USSR the *right to leisure and medical care* is guaranteed. Each family and citizen in our country have the right to well-appointed living quarters, which are provided from social funds as well as by cooperative or individual construction.

Everyone who has worked hard during his life and reached advanced age receives a pension. Workers and government employees as well as disabled veterans receive their pensions from the state; the *kolkhoz* peasants receive part of theirs from the agricultural cooperatives. In the past few years the state has considerably increased the amount of pensions for disability and for cases of loss of the breadwinner. The *right to material security in old age and in sickness* is guaranteed in our country.

Soviet democracy assures legal equality to men and women in all areas of state, economic, sociopolitical, and spiritual life. The Soviet woman is an active builder of communist society.

Women represent almost half of all those working in the economy. Three quarters of the physicians in the USSR are women. About four thousand *kolkhoz* peasant women have been awarded the title Hero of Socialist Labor, of whom twenty-four received a second gold medal, the Sickle and Hammer.

The Soviet citizen's social rights are protected by the state and the social organization. Any attempt to restrict them for reasons of nationality or race is considered a criminal offense, punishable by law. The law guarantees the inviolability of the person.

In addition to social rights, Soviet citizens enjoy broad *political rights and freedoms: freedom of speech, the press, association, assembly, and demonstration*. Political freedoms are guaranteed not only by law but also by availability of material resources. The toilers and their organizations are furnished with printing presses, supplies of paper, publishing houses, and newspapers, radio, motion pictures, and television. In fact, under socialism these freedoms are guaranteed by the very nature of the social order. In exercising their right to free expression of opinion, USSR citizens discuss the most important legislative bills and Party and government decrees in a wide-ranging and practical manner, submitting valuable proposals that considerably hasten our development and construction of a new life.

Are political liberties restricted in any way? Yes. That is unavoidable. The Soviet press, for example, never gives space to advocates of war, violence, and moral depravity. Promotion of national enmity and hatred between men is prohibited in our country. This is quite natural: everything is prohibited which conflicts with the interest of the people and is detrimental to socialism.

Equal rights involve equal obligations. What are the obligations which society and the state impose on their citizens?

First of all, the *duty to work*, and to work conscientiously and honestly, since labor strengthens our society and helps it move forward.

Understandably, the hard-working person is at pains to safeguard in every possible way the fruits of his labor. Society imposes upon each citizen the *duty to safeguard and strengthen socialist property*, which is the basis of our well-being. At the same time society takes measures against those who try to take more than they give. It does not tolerate parasitism, thievery, hooliganism, and the like.

Soviet citizens have the *duty to strictly observe the laws of the land and of public order*, to behave according to the norms of socialist community life.

A sacred duty of Soviet citizens is to defend the fatherland. Every young man who has reached the age of eighteen is obliged to serve in the Soviet army.

Girls nineteen and over who have medical or other special training may also volunteer for military service.

The law on universal military service passed by the USSR Supreme Soviet in October 1967 establishes a system of training for young boys prior to military service. All young men of preinduction and induction age are obliged to receive required initial military training, including that of civil defense. In addition, preparation for the army and navy of a number of young specialists who have reached the age of seventeen is arranged in educational organizations of the DOSAAF [All-Union Voluntary Society for Assistance to the Army, Navy, and Air Force of the USSR] and in the school system for professional and technical training.

Rights of citizens are inseparable from their duties. There are no rights without obligations, no obligations without rights. If each of us individually or all of us together fail to fulfill our obligations or fulfill them only halfheartedly, there will be no one and nothing to look after our rights, which are always expanding. The character of labor is changing, the work week is being shortened, vacation facilities and sanatoria are multiplying, the size of pensions is growing, and more. All this is possible only thanks to increased labor productivity, and also because people have an ever more conscientious and responsible attitude toward work.

But there is more to it than that. There is organic unity between rights and duties because without duties there are no rights but also because a right itself is an obligation, and an obligation a right. Work in our country is a right and a duty. So is education: in the USSR we have *compulsory* eighth-grade education. And who but miserable cowards and renegades would consider the duty to defend their country a burden? The overwhelming majority of our people consider military service to be a citizen's sacred right to defend his fatherland, weapons in hand. Young soldiers are serving in the ranks of our glorious armed forces with pride, and they protect the peaceful creative work of the Soviet people with vigilance.

That is why we do not oppose duties to rights, why we fulfill our obligations not under coercion but out of a deep-rooted inner conviction. The unity of rights and obligations creates the most favorable conditions for the development of the human personality, talents, and gifts, and also for the development of collectivist social principles in our life.

Labor Relations

In considering labor relations let us start with employment procedures. Before beginning a job every new worker signs a bilateral agreement known as a *labor contract* with the enterprise administration.

The agreement defines the obligations of both parties. The worker is obliged to perform work according to special skill requirements (as a fitter, electrician, etc.) and according to special qualifications (e.g., fourth-grade specialist), or according to position (e.g., engineer-economist). He must observe the internal work regulations of the enterprise. The management is committed to assuring normal, healthy labor conditions and to paying wages at the rate established for the work completed. The length of the work day and amount of leave are regulated by law and therefore are not subject to agreement by the two parties. In special cases additional conditions may be set down in the contract (work during the day shift only, because the worker attends evening school; length of the probationary period).

In some cases a probationary period is required, not to exceed six days for a worker; two weeks for an employee; and one month for an employee hired for an especially difficult job and for engineering-technical personnel. Graduates of vocational-technical schools and institutes, secondary specialized schools, and institutions of higher education are hired without preliminary testing, according to the requirements of the economic plan, and only in the specialized field, grade, or position indicated in the graduate's assignment papers.

The factory management issues a service-record book to the new worker. All information (family name, first name and patronymic, age, education, date of employment, profession selected, position held) is entered in the book in the presence of its owner, who witnesses to its correctness by his signature. He is not allowed to make any alterations or additions. Members of collective farms also have service-record books. The book confirms its owner's participation in the collective farm's productive activity and entitles him to receive an appropriate percentage of the farm income.

The service record shows every stage in the worker's labor activities: new grades, transfers, bonuses, and awards. The service-record book is the individual's chronicle of his working life, his employment biography, and it is therefore important for each man to keep his service record in order. Reasons for dismissal must be registered exactly as formulated in the pertinent laws. Correct entries are also important in determining the worker's *seniority*. Seniority is taken into account when old-age pensions, disability caused by work, sickness not related to the job, and other circumstances are under consideration.

Soviet legislation protects workers and employees from illegal dismissal from their jobs. Management may dismiss a worker in a very few cases specified by law, and dismissal also requires concurrence of the trade-union committee. If the worker resigns his position, he is expected to give the administration two weeks' notice. Young workers and specialists graduated from schools and courses in the vocational-technical education system, from secondary specialized schools, or from institutions of higher learning may not leave their jobs until they have completed the required legal period of work in production (three years after graduation from institutions of higher learning).

Relations between an enterprise's personnel and management are strictly regulated. The local trade-union committee speaks on behalf of the workers, the engineering and technical personnel, and administrative employees. Every year the local trade-union committee and the management sign a bilateral agreement, or *collective contract*.

The collective contract details the measures to be taken to mobilize the workers and employees to fulfill and surpass the plan quotas. It requires the management to provide such working conditions as to enable every worker to fulfill his output norms as well as the commitments he assumed in the interest of social emulation. It contains provisions permitting all toilers to raise their general educational and technical levels. Provisions for industrial safety and for the introduction of the advanced experience of innovators in allied enterprises are appended to the contract. The contract allocates funds for sociocultural activities (admissions to sanatoria and rest homes, special diets, remedial and extracurricular children's programs, etc.).

Industrial safety is given considerable attention. Safe, healthy working conditions are achieved by improvements in production technology; by mechanization of heavy, labor-consuming operations; and by eliminating causes of accidents and occupational diseases. The workers are protected from harmful effects of chemicals, extreme air temperatures, and excessive humidity by special protective clothing and safety devices (glasses, respirators, and masks), which are issued to workers by the enterprise free of charge. Workers engaged in certain types of production, chemical for example, are given special prophylactic food prepared according to scientific regulations. Employees engaged in production injurious to health have a reduced work day and additional leave.

The administration is obliged to inform the workers of the general rules of behavior expected while in the employ of the enterprise and teach them the operational techniques for the machinery they use during their work time. Every worker must know the technical safety rules; some must take special examinations.

Industrial safety control is provided by both state organs (ministries, departments, the Prosecutor's Office) and the trade unions. Industrial safety commissions are established within the enterprises, and volunteer inspectors to enforce safety and health rules are elected. If the rules are violated, work operations in any production department may be suspended. Persons found guilty of violating labor safety laws are held accountable.

The basic rules of safety and health protection established for agricultural work are also binding on collective farms, which have many different kinds of equipment and machinery and use electricity and various chemicals extensively. Safety and health regulations must also be observed in the care of livestock.

In addition to general rules covering all toilers, labor legislation establishes supplementary rules and standards of industrial safety for *women and adolescents*.

Women are forbidden to do work that is heavy and injurious to health, such as smelting or casting metals. They are barred from a number of enterprises in the chemical, printing, and leather industries. As a general rule, women are not permitted to work underground or in loading and unloading operations. Maternity and infant care are subjects of special legislation. Pregnant women are given 112 days' leave, nearly one-third of a year. Expectant mothers and single women with a child less than one year old may not be dismissed from their jobs.

Adolescents are permitted to work when they reach the age of sixteen, or in exceptional cases fifteen, when a medical checkup is mandatory. Adolescents from sixteen to eighteen years of age work a shorter day but receive the same wages as adult workers or employees on full shift. Adolescents younger than eighteen years are barred from certain kinds of work and training. They are not given night work, overtime, or jobs injurious to health. Workers and employees under eighteen are entitled to a full month's leave, during the summer as a rule.

Possibilities are created for young people to get settled in jobs easily and quickly. Enterprises are assigned quotas for taking on secondary-school graduates. The young workers who combine work with educational training in a school, technical institute, or university are given certain privileges: a reduced work day or week, education leave, and half-price tickets to the location of their examination.

For its scale and rhythm socialist production requires unconditional, strict *labor discipline*.

What does it mean to be a disciplined worker?

Essentially, it means working honestly and conscientiously; reporting for work on time and not leaving ahead of time; using the working hours only for production and performance of official duties; handling tools, machine tools, and other machinery carefully; maintaining cleanliness and neatness in the shop and on the grounds of one's enterprise; leaving one's work station in proper condition for the replacement shift. The conscientious worker tries to turn out only high-quality products, with no rejects.

Socialist labor discipline is inseparable from conscientious and prompt fulfillment of the production manager's orders. Why is it so important that the manager's orders be obeyed without question during the work period? Because he is not merely an official with certain prerogatives but primarily an organizer and production expert.

A high degree of production discipline is also required of the collective farm member. The *Kolkhoz* Statute adopted by the Third All-Union Congress of collective farm members in November 1969 requires all agricultural cooperative members to perform their work honestly and conscientiously, observe the internal rules, and complete job and social assignments made by the *kolkhoz* administration or brigade leader.

Moral obligations imposed by the statutes of the VLKSM [All-Union Leninist Young Communist League] on its members are the same as these legal requirements. According to the statutes, *Komsomol* members are committed to increasing their labor productivity and improving their labor skills, observing labor discipline and public order strictly, and safeguarding socialist property in every possible way.

Socialism consolidates labor discipline by good production organization, the method of persuasion, and a well-thought-out system of rewards to encourage both the individual worker and the entire collective. Enterprise internal-labor regulations include forms of encouragement, such as expression of public appreciation, awarding of Honor Certificates, recording of names in the Honor Book and on the Honor Board, granting of the title Best Worker in the Profession, bonuses, and valuable gifts. The very best workers are given decorations and medals of the Soviet Union and awarded the highest titles, Hero of Socialist Labor or Lenin Prize Laureate and State Prize Laureate.

Violations of labor discipline are punished. Absenteeism without good reason, tardiness, leaving work ahead of time, damage to material and equipment are punished by reprimand, with the culprit being transferred to a lower-paying job or demoted for as long as three months. As an extreme measure, the worker may be dismissed, but only with the concurrence of the trade-union committee.

There may be disagreements between individuals or between groups of workers and employees on one hand and the administration on the other. The *labor-disputes commission* is the first mandatory instance where arguments between administration and workers are reviewed. It is made up of an equal number of permanent representatives of the administration and the trade-union committee. It is obliged to review labor disputes within five days of a request. The labor dispute is considered resolved when both parties—worker and administration—have reached accord. If the worker disagrees with the decision of the labor-disputes commission, he may appeal his case to the *local trade-union committee*. This is the second instance for settlement of labor disputes. Factory, plant, and local committees review requests and complaints concerning labor disputes within seven days of receiving a request. If the worker still disagrees with the decision reached at this level, he may next appeal to the *people's court*, which has jurisdiction over the area of the enterprise's location. The labor-disputes commission is not competent to handle disputes arising from a worker's dismissal approved by the trade-union committee, in which case the worker may appeal directly to the courts. Neither is it competent to handle dismissal or transfer to another job of administrative personnel, shop supervisor, and foremen.

Another category of disputes, which occur very seldom in our country, are those between the administration and the members of the workers' collective regarding such matters as the established output quotas, or application of certain other provisions of the collective contract. These disputes are resolved by agreement between the administration and the trade union. If agreement cannot be reached at this level, the dispute is resolved by higher level trade-union and economic administration organs.

We have said that under socialism the principle of distribution operates according to quantity and quality of labor expended. Let us now see how it operates in practice.

The amount of labor expended by workers is determined by *establishing labor norms*. There are time norms and output norms. It is possible to establish, by the use of *time norms*, the number of hours, minutes, or seconds consumed by the worker to produce an item or part of it. By using *output norms* it is possible to establish the number of items or item parts the worker produces per shift, hour, minute, or second. Norms, therefore, are a type of quota for the worker.

In calculating wages it is not enough to know the amount of labor expended. It is also important to evaluate the product's quality correctly. This is done by means of the *wage rate system*. This system differentiates wages according to the worker's qualifications, skill, and knowledge; the nature, complexity, and danger of the work (the working conditions); and the relative economic importance of the given production branch. It distinguishes between skilled and unskilled workers and between heavy and light work; it also takes into account the complexity and degree of responsibility connected with different kinds of work. Every worker is given a *wage grade* commensurate with his qualifications and specialization. The first grade covers workers engaged in the simplest labor, with the remaining grades reflecting better worker qualifications.

The relationship between wages and various grades is determined by *wage scales*. The higher the grade, the higher the wage. A grade six worker earns 1.62 times more than a grade one worker. Skilled labor brings more benefits to society, creates more and better products per identical unit of time. The worker's qualification (grade) is assessed by the qualification commission and assigned by the enterprise administration and the trade-union committee in a joint decision.

Hourly or daily wages are determined by basic *wage rates*. These represent 70 or 80 percent of salary due. The balance of the wage is in premiums paid on condition of overfulfillment of production norms. Wage scales and rates are the same for all enterprises in a given branch of industry.

Work in any professional field is described in detail in the *rate and skill manuals* compiled for the various branches of the economy. They contain scientifically established requirements for fixing the rates at which the labor performance should be paid, specifying the skills and knowledge for each worker grade.

The piece-rate wage is the best method of establishing the complete, direct relationship between the results of a worker's labor and his earnings. It is applied wherever labor is regulated by norms and wherever calculation of each worker's labor outlay is possible. The time-work wage—for example, in automated assembly-line production—is paid the worker for the exact time he actually spent. All higher administrative, engineering, and technical personnel and office staffs are paid time-work wages.

Labor remuneration may undergo change. In revising the rates upward, the state sees to it that labor productivity increases ahead of wages. Otherwise it would be impossible to expand production and improve the well-being of the people.

Social Organizations of Toilers

The toilers' social organizations occupy an important place in the political system of Soviet society. Under the leadership of the Communist party, acting closely with state organs, they help satisfy the great variety of interests of society's different strata (workers and employees, youth, women, creative workers, etc.); they perform educational functions, helping to form and bring to the fore the Soviet people's collectivist habits and organizational abilities.

Social organizations function as voluntary societies of toilers, having their own statutes. The largest mass social organizations are labor unions, the *Komsomol*, cooperatives, and scientific, technical, sports, and cultural associations. They comprise almost the total adult population in the country.

Labor Unions

The entire working life of workers and government employees is tied in with the labor unions. A labor-union organization exists in every industrial enterprise, at every building site, *sovkhoz*, institution, and school. Labor-union membership totals almost ninety million.

V.I. Lenin saw the labor union as an organization for training and educating the toilers, involving them in the administration of the production process. He saw it as a school for society management, a school of communism. How do the labor unions discharge their task?

The mill, factory, plant, or local labor-union committee enters into a collective contract with the enterprise management. It has the right to participate in drafting the production plan by discussion and suggestions for change at meetings of labor-union members. It also has the right to receive reports from the factory director about his administrative activity, and, should the need arise, the right to present to a higher economic instance any question of replacing an incompetent administrator or punishing him by disciplinary action.

Labor unions enlist the workers and government employees in socialist emulation, within the enterprise itself as well as with other enterprises. They promote the movement for a communist attitude toward work and organize mass public exhibits of inventions. One of their important activities is to extend the application of advanced work methods and facilitate creative mutual assistance among personnel. Labor-union committees see to it that workers, engineers, and other employees improve their professional skills. *Production conferences* organized by labor unions together with the enterprise administration are a method of involving the toilers in production administration.

Also, labor unions are concerned with improving the living conditions of workers and government employees. Mill and factory committees and the enterprise management jointly distribute housing. They have at their disposal a whole network of sanatoria, health resorts, holiday facilities, and tourist centers. Settling children in nurseries and kindergarten and organizing holidays for schoolchildren fall within their competence. They have the right to supervise the state and cooperative trade network, communal meals, and public services.

Labor-union members enjoy a number of advantages over nonmembers. They receive a higher subsidy for temporary disability. Subsidies from the state social-security fund are at the disposal of the labor unions. Members have preference when admission passes to vacation facilities and sanatoria are distributed and when children are admitted to nurseries, kindergartens, and pioneer camps. The unions render material assistance, when necessary, to members, from their own funds.

The labor unions represent a great cultural force; halls of culture, clubs, and libraries are under their supervision.

The Youth League

Our country's youth spends more than ten of the best years of their lives in the ranks of the Leninist *Komsomol*.

The *Komsomol*'s importance in the country's life is due to the fact that it is not simply a youth organization but a *league of communist youth*, closely tied to the Communist party, a militant ally under its direct supervision. The *Komsomol* is an inexhaustible membership source for the CPSU; no other single organization gives so many members to the Party. Millions of the best-trained members of the VLKSM [All-Union Leninist League of Communist Youth] have been accepted into the Communist party. This clearly reflects the succession of generations taking place in Soviet society, and the enthusiastic support of Party policy by Soviet youth.

During the years of the *Komsomol*'s existence more than ninety million persons have undergone training in its ranks for various social activities—a schooling in communism. Two-thirds of the adult population in our country has received its formation from the *Komsomol*.

The League of Communist Youth originated under the direct guidance and initiative of the Communist party and its leader, Vladimir Il'ich Lenin. It was founded at the First All-Russian Congress of Youth Organizations on October 29, 1918, in Moscow, Number 4 Khariton'yevskiy Lane. The basic provisions of the program adopted by the congress read: "The Youth League expresses its solidarity with the Russian Communist Party of the Bolsheviks. Its aim is to spread the ideas of communism and involve worker and peasant youth in active construction of a Soviet Russia." V.I. Lenin was elected honorary chairman of the congress. At its close he received a group of delegates and held a long discussion with them about the situation in their localities and the aims of youth organizations.

In 1924 the Sixth *Komsomol* Congress decided to add the word *Leninist* to the title of the youth league.

The *Komsomol* has given vivid, unforgettable pages to the history of socialism.

The *Civil War period* is the *Komsomol*'s birthdate. The First Congress of the Russian Communist Youth Union [RKSM] solemnly stated: "The world counterrevolution coming to a head in the South will find us solidly opposed to it. We shall dedicate all our revolutionary fervor and youthful strength to fighting it, and we will never retreat. Long live Soviet power." The *Komsomol*'s entire membership went to the front as volunteers. In May 1919, in view of the serious situation on the Eastern Front, the *Komsomol* decreed the first all-Russian mobilization of its members and sent more than three thousand to the front. In 1920 about seventy thousand *Komsomol* members were enlisted in the Red Army, or every sixth member. The Bolsheviks, as S.M. Kirov said, more than once looked with envy on the heroes provided by the *Komsomol* at that time. Nikolay Ostrovskiy's novel *How Steel Was Tempered* conveys that period's heroism.

The Leninist *Komsomol* was awarded the Order of the Red Banner in acknowledgement of the heroism and military success of tens of thousands of members during the Civil War years. The Eighth All-Union Congress of the

VLKSN, in accepting this tribute from the fatherland in the name of the *Komsomol* and all youth, proclaimed: "Our knowledge, our strength, and our life belong to the government of the workers and peasants. We risked them in the years of Civil War fire, and we will offer them again without regret in times of new trials and victories."

Years of Peaceful Socialist Construction. As early as 1920, during the Third *Komsomol* Congress, V.I. Lenin assigned its members the task of economic renewal of the country—reorganization and restoration of agriculture and industry on the basis of contemporary technology. He called on the *Komsomol* to become a shock brigade that would offer help in every type of work with initiative and boldness. In brief, he gave it the task of learning communism.

The *Komsomol* helped the Party restore industry, transportation, and agriculture destroyed by the imperialist Civil War. Its members erected factories and electric-power stations, laid down railroad lines in the taiga and desert sand, built new cities. Dneproges, Magnitogorsk, Kuzbass, Komsomol'sk on the Amur, Donetsk, the Moscow subway—this is hardly a complete list of the *Komsomol*'s industrial construction effort.

In January 1931 the government awarded the Order of the Red Banner of Labor to the Leninist *Komsomol* for its initiative in shock brigade activities and socialist emulation, which ensured the successful fulfillment of the Five-Year Plan for the development of the USSR economy.

Summoned by the Party, *Komsomol* members and other youth fought selflessly for the collectivization of agriculture. The *Komsomol* originated mass marches to help with the harvest and helped train tractor drivers, combine operators, mechanics, truck drivers, and other agricultural machinery operators. It organized schools for peasant children and reading rooms and libraries in the countryside, spread agrotechnical knowledge, and fought superstition and prejudices. The young enthusiasts were not afraid of the bullets from sawed-off shotguns used against them by the *kulaks* [well-to-do peasants]. Nor were they afraid of brutal torture by the Basmachi [members of anticommunist resistance in Central Asia].

At the Party's call *Komsomol* members and other youth strove to conquer the heights of science and culture. They helped the Party solve one of the most important problems of socialist construction, formation of a new intelligentsia with its origins from among the Soviet people. Many Soviet scientists of world fame entered upon their scholarly careers encouraged by their *Komsomol* experience. From its ranks the *Komsomol* produced many talented Party, Soviet, and economic management workers, and members of the military.

The Patriotic War Years. Hundreds of thousands of young persons of both sexes went off to the front as volunteers. "Because I belong to the *Komsomol*, I want to go into battle," wrote the young soldiers in their applications. Of the eleven thousand soldiers awarded the title "Hero of the Soviet Union," seven thousand were *Komsomol* members and *Komsomol*-trained youth; of those designated Hero of the Soviet Union, sixty were *Komsomol*-trained youth. Ivan Kozhedub and Alexander Pokryshkin, awarded the title Hero of the Soviet Union three times, also had *Komsomol* training.

Komsomol members were organizers, along with the communists, of the first partisan detachments in the region temporarily occupied by the fascist armies. Up to 60 percent of the partisan ranks were *Komsomol* members and other young people. Underground *Komsomol* organizations—*rayon*, city, and *oblast* committees of the *Komsomol*—operated in enemy-occupied territory. *Komsomol* newspapers also appeared there.

The names of fearless *Komsomol* sons and daughters have become world famous. The heroic exploits of Victor Talalikhin and Yuriy Smirnov, Alexander Matrosov, Gafur Mamedov, Liza Chaykina and Maria Mel'nikayte, Nicholas Gastello and Feodosiy Smolyachkov, Manshuk Mametova, and Zoya Kosmodem'yanskaya—heroes and heroines of the "Young Guard" and the "Partisan Spark"—are living legends among our people.

"Do your share of work and also that of your comrade who has gone to the front" was the slogan of *Komsomol* members working in industry and agriculture. Hundreds of thousands of youngsters went directly from their school desks into shops and factories and quickly mastered the necessary production techniques. Educational institutions under *Komsomol* sponsorship trained more than two million young workers for industry and transportation. The *Komsomol* organized all-union youth work on Sundays, and the wages earned were turned into a fund for defense and assistance to war orphans.

The Leninist *Komsomol* was awarded the Order of Lenin in June 1945 for outstanding achievement on behalf of the fatherland during the years of the Soviet Union's great Patriotic War against Hitler's Germany, and for excellence in educating Soviet youth in the spirit of absolute devotion to the country. *Komsomol* organizations and newspapers that had especially distinguished themselves were awarded other orders of the Soviet Union.

During the postwar years the *Komsomol* joined the front ranks of peaceful and creative labor. The accomplishments of the young people—builders of gigantic power stations and railroad lines, of new cities; tamers of virgin lands; pioneers in the conquest of the cosmos—have left remarkable pages in the history of the Soviet fatherland. Twice in recent years the Leninist *Komsomol* has been awarded the Order of Lenin for its successful activities and youth education. On its fiftieth anniversary it received the Order of the October Revolution.

Under *Komsomol* leadership Soviet youth takes an active part in the international movement of democratic youth and struggles for peace. Together with democratic youth and student organizations of other countries, the *Komsomol* established the World Federation of Democratic Youth (WFDY) and the International Union of Students (IUS), universally accepted centers of progressive youth and students in all countries. Presently, the All-Union Leninist League of Communist Youth actively cooperates with almost every young people's democratic organization in the world.

The *Komsomol* now has more than twenty-seven million members of both sexes. Its influence extends to the entire Soviet youth. It is in direct charge of the Vladimir Il'ich Lenin Children's Organization of Young Pioneers. The Party has entrusted it with training the rising generation.

Youth represents the people's future, communism's future. Our young people are fully equal to the challenge of the contemporary heroic epoch of the struggle for communism and worthy of their great socialist fatherland. Even though the young sometimes do not have the older generations's knowledge and experience, it has more than enough energy, enthusiasm, and drive to acquire knowledge and experience. By nature young people aspire to work creatively and constructively. Youth knows what labor is. It works on the country's most important construction sites, in electric power stations and plants, in scientific research institutes and laboratories. Construction shock work by the *Komsomol* has been schooling for life for tens of thousands of boys and girls.

In recent years 300,000 young people with *Komsomol* travel passes have gone to *Komsomol* shock work sites of construction to supplement cadres of builders of some of the most important economic projects. They have worked at Noril'sk, Sumgait, Bratsk, and Krasnoyarsk hydroelectric power plants, and at many others. *Komsomol* members and *Komsomol*-trained young people have actively helped develop the productive forces of Siberia, the Soviet North and Far East—the power industry, metallurgy, chemical, petroleum, gas, pulp and paper industries, and transportation installations.

Komsomol members are struggling in the villages for better use of the land, helping to introduce progressive technology into agricultural crop cultivation and mechanization of labor-consuming farm procedures. There is a widespread movement among the village youth to obtain professional knowledge.

The Sixteenth Congress of the VLKSM took place in May 1970. It placed before the young enthusiasts a goal requiring responsibility: to participate in exploiting the natural wealth of Western Siberia and open the world's largest oil and gas deposits there. The Congress called on the young toilers to contribute to greater expansion of the socialist economy and intensification of all its branches, and to make an active effort to introduce scientific and technological achievements into industry and agriculture.

Cooperative Organizations

You know the *kolkhoz* primarily as an *economic* organization. But the *kolkhoz* is, at the same time, a *social* organization of peasants.

A *kolkhoz* is a cooperative; that is, a voluntary association of peasants based on collective production and social self-government. At general meetings *kol-khoz* members personally make such vitally important decisions as electing the *kolkhoz* administrative board, the board chairman, and an auditing commission. They also make decisions about admission and expulsion of *artel* [cooperative] members, priorities for the use of funds, norms for production and compensation, and the mandatory minimum work days; and they establish the size of private plots, among other matters. In the large *kolkhozes* members solve a number of problems at meetings of their authorized representatives and of work brigades. Standing commissions selected by the general membership meeting also function regularly. Thus, all the members have the opportunity to participate in discussions of the problems of *kolkhoz* life.

The *kolkhozes* have been granted broad initiative in planning and organizing agricultural production. They decide independently about improvement and construction in villages and hamlets, and the erection of nurseries and kindergartens, schools, hospitals, clubs, and libraries.

Our country has *consumer cooperatives*, which improve trade in the rural areas, organize the marketing of surplus farm produce, and service the general public. They have more than forty-three million shareholders. Housing construction cooperatives assist the general public in improving housing conditions.

Other Associations

There are many other social organizations in the country, uniting people either by profession or special interest (hunters' associations, for example, societies of anglers, and others). Some of these organize scientific and cultural activities for the masses (the Society for the Propagation of Political and Scientific Knowledge, for instance). There are associations of scientific workers in the fields of education, medicine, and others; numerous scientific technical associations; associations of efficiency experts and inventors; unions of writers, newspapermen, composers, artists; actors and workers in the motion-picture industry; architects; and other groups of creative intelligentsia.

Other associations organize physical culture activities and promote defense skills and information. There are sports associations and organizations, the Voluntary Society for Cooperation with the Army, Navy, and Air Force, the Red Cross, the Red Crescent Society, and the Society for the Protection of Nature and Plants.

A number of volunteer groups organize Soviet citizens for peace campaigns and promote friendship with peoples of other countries. These are called Soviet Societies for Friendship and Cultural Ties with Foreign Countries, the Soviet Committee for Defense of Peace, the Committee of Soviet Women, and the Committee of Youth Organizations of the USSR.

All these and numerous other voluntary associations operate on the principle of social self-help. Their influence extends to many millions of persons.

Whatever their specific aim, in the final analysis all these social organizations pursue one common purpose, to develop the toilers' initiative and active participation and to help the Party and the state solve the tasks of communist construction.

The Communist party binds together all these social organizations and unions and coordinates their activities. The Party does not issue orders to them but directs their activity mostly through their active communist members. In their activities the social organizations strive to be consistent in carrying out the policy of the Party, the most authoritative sociopolitical organization of socialist society, and its acknowledged leader.

Gradual Transformation of Socialism into Communism

Complete and Final Victory

In summing up the study of the economic and sociopolitical structure of Soviet society, we conclude with good reason that *socialism has won complete and final victory in the USSR*.

Social ownership of the means of production and the socialist system of management based on it have full dominion over our country's *economy*. In *social* relations exploitation of man by man and national oppression have been eliminated. Union and collaboration of all classes and strata of the population and friendship among peoples of our multinational fatherland have been firmly established: the sociopolitical unity of the entire Soviet people has been created. In the *political* sphere the Soviet state, as an instrument of the toilers' power, has proven itself by the test of time. Socialist democracy has been steadily developing. The Marxist-Leninist ideology has been victorious in the *ideological* sphere. It has unified the workers, *kolkhoz* peasantry, and the people's intelligentsia by giving them a single purpose, rallying them around the Communist party.

Thus, socialism has gained victory in all spheres of society's life and activity: it has prevailed *completely*.

World reactionary forces and imperialism have never reconciled themselves to socialism's victory in the USSR. World imperialism nurtured German fascism, using it in an attempt to annihilate the first socialist state of workers and peasants in the world. Even under contemporary conditions imperialism is not abandoning hope of liquidating socialism and reestablishing the capitalist system in our country.

However, attempts of this kind are now hopeless. Why? Because the Soviet Union has become a great industrial power, a leader in many critical branches of science and technology, and because it has at its disposal powerful modern armed forces. The community of socialist countries has become a reality. (The notion of "capitalist encirclement" is therefore obsolete and without meaning.)

There is no force in the world today that could reinstate capitalism in our country and crush the socialist camp. Since the danger of the restoration of capitalism is excluded, socialism has gained final victory in our country.

The question may arise as to whether it is correct to talk about socialism's complete victory if there are still difficulties in our country with housing, if there is an irregular supply of consumer goods, if vestiges of the past remain in the people's consciousness and lives—in short, if many complex questions and unsolved problems still exist.

There are two different problems. On the one hand there is the question of the success of socialism as a progressive social system. On the other, there is the question of degree of economic maturity, of the stage of development of socialism. Socialism's final victory does not mean that the new society has already achieved the apex of economic and cultural development. Upon socialism's complete victory, all its inherent tremendous possibilities for the development of production and culture and for improvement in the standard of living for the toilers become apparent. The more fully these possibilities are realized, the more perfect will be the condition attained by socialist society. And the process of perfecting socialism is at the same time the process of its transformation into communism. This is the dialectic of the new society's development.

Characteristics of the Transition to the Higher Phase, Communism

When he was developing plans for socialist construction, Vladimir Il'ich Lenin wrote: "Even while we strive for socialism, we are convinced that it will turn into communism."

Socialism is communism's first phase, and there is no stone wall between the two phases of the same formation. Communism develops gradually from socialism. Therefore, there is no need to break up everything and build anew: it is necessary to develop, perfect, and—where needed—transform the production base and social relations existing under socialism.

As it is transformed directly from socialism, communism is at the same time superior to it in all respects. *Qualitative* changes take place in economics and social relations, as well as in the people's consciousness and psychology. However, this qualitative "revolution" occurs gradually, by way of developing and perfecting the socialist economy and social relations and by increased communist consciousness on the part of the masses.

Because it is gradual this in no way means the process is slow. On the contrary, the more deeply we enter communism, the faster will we move forward: the rate of communist construction will be increasing all the time.

The conversion of socialism into communism is an *objective, law-governed process*. Therefore, the strictest consistency is necessary in constructing a communist society: there should be no racing ahead or lagging behind in making various urgent transformations. Lenin taught us realism in politics. Even though capable of looking into the future, we must keep our feet on the ground and always consider actual, real-life circumstances.

Let us take as an example the problem of private plots held by *kolkhoz* peasants. The future of these plots is perfectly clear: they must disappear. And the reasons are equally clear. In the first place, they preclude application of powerful agricultural technology and require large expenditure of labor for small output. Briefly, labor in a private plot is not truly productive, and it would be absurd to retain it under communism. Second, and this is the main point, the private plot cannot be made compatible by any means with the tenet that in communist society all people will work only in social production, only for society, and have their needs satisfied only from social resources.

However, as of now, the *kolkhoz* peasants cannot give up the private plots, since they contribute to fuller satisfaction of their personal needs and to improvement of their living standard. Under those conditions it would be a mistake to raise the question of liquidating private plots. They must become economically obsolete. Any attempt to speed up this process artifically, to race ahead of events, could only damage the cause.

The gradual character and continuity of socialism's conversion into communism do not mean that it is spontaneous. The construction of communism requires active, creative solution of the tasks facing society. Communism is being built by conscientious, purposeful activity of the toilers of our country under the leadership of the Communist party.

Contradictions and Problems of Growth

Clearly, constructing a new society is an exceptionally intricate task: the emergence of anything new is always accompanied by contradictions to be resolved and by the breakup of old, established, habitual forms of life that once played a positive role but then began to hamper progress.

Socialism's contradictions differ from those of capitalism, arising from the rapid advance of socialist economy, from the people's increasing material and cultural needs. They are contradictions between the old and the new, between backwardness and progress.

In capitalist society contradiction between productive forces and production relations unavoidably evolves into a conflict that cannot be resolved within the framework of capitalism, and therefore leads to its downfall. Under socialism social ownership predominates, and this excludes any conflict between productive forces and production relations. Social ownership favors the growth of productive forces. What, then, is the nature of the contradictions in the socialist mode of production? With development of productive forces certain sectors of production relations fall behind. Substitution of some sectors by others does not change the nature of socialist relations; it only develops and enriches them. These specific contradictions are being successfully solved by society, which is thus lifted up to a new level of development.

Contradictions are by no means overcome automatically but only through struggle against conservatism, inertia, and backwardness.

Other kinds of difficulties confront our society.

We are obliged to allot considerable resources, for example, to strengthen our country's defenses. This imposes a certain burden on the national budget. But we are compelled to make expenditures to equip the army with modern weapons. As long as the danger of military attack by the imperialist powers exists, we must keep our powder dry.

There are difficulties of a temporary nature, often from objective causes; for example, drought or earthquake leading to considerable losses. The severe natural environment of the Far East and Siberia obviously hamper opening the country's richest regions. Complex problems that can be solved only by continuous effort emerge in the area of labor distribution, training, and retraining. For example, exhaustion of mineral deposits at individual mining sites may lead to local labor surplus. Understandably, organizing the resettlement of people and re-employing them according to their skills in the same locality are by no means simple. Scientific and technical progress leads to extinction of a number of professions. It is thus necessary to provide new jobs without curtailing wages. A multitude of such problems arise in the life of society. While some are predictable, many spring up quite unexpectedly.

Problems may come from subjective causes as well. It has already been stated that shortcomings in planning and inaccurate decisions about distribution of resources and labor are apt to lead to disproportions in the economy, adversely affecting the rate of development.

Obviously, in a task as complex as constructing a new society, it is impossible to guarantee fully the absence of errors. One cannot proceed without endless search, experimentation, suggestion, and testing of new forms of economic and social development never attempted in practice. The problem is to reduce miscalculations and errors to a minimum, and one of the chief concerns of the Communist party is ensuring the optimum solutions of all social problems.

In the process of constructing communism, the Soviet people are successfully overcoming these contradictions and growth problems. Where do we concentrate our efforts?

A Threefold Task

The basis of society is production of material goods. The most important task of communist construction, therefore, is creation of the *material and technical base of communism*. This is the chief task, but not the only one. Clearly inculcating *communist social relations* is essential for the victory of communism. This is the second objective in building the communist society. Inasmuch as the final aim of total communist transformation is all-around development of the human personality, the third task is *to train the new man*.

The close interdependence of the chief tasks of communist construction is clear at a glance. By building new plants and factories and by increasing the social wealth, we are preparing the conditions for transition to the communist principle of labor and distribution; we are perfecting social relations. Development of social relations requires reorienting the people's consciousness, inculcating new moral qualities. Formation of communist social relations and education of the new man will, in turn, powerfully influence the growth of productive forces.

The powerful productive forces of communism are not created by fairy-tale "wishing." They will appear as a result of the strenuous toil of millions of Soviet people led by the Communist party. The success of the cause therefore depends to the greatest degree on how conscientiously each of us works in his own sector and on how well the builders of communism are imbued with the communist attitude towards labor.

The interdependence and unity of these three fundamental tasks of constructing communism are so great that they are called the *threefold task*.

Review Questions

1. What is society's class composition under socialism? What is the explanation for the leading role of the workers in constructing communism?
2. What is the source of the strength of the friendship among peoples, and of the strength of proletarian internationalism? Why are communists irreconcilable enemies of bourgeois nationalism?
3. What are the main directions of Soviet state activity?
4. What basic obligations do society and the state impose on the Soviet people and especially on the youth?
5. What is the role of mass organizations in the life of our society?

Points to Consider and Discuss

1. Using your knowledge of history, try to compare the social composition of the population of Czarist Russia with that of the socialist Soviet Union.

2. Recount how the Soviets ensure the development of mass initiative and creativity. To understand better the mechanism of the Soviets' activities, become familiar with the work of a local administrative organ. Arrange for a talk at your school by an employee of the local Soviet Executive Committee.
3. Why is it necessary not merely to claim one's rights but, first and most important, to be honest and conscientious in fulfilling one's duties as imposed by society and the state? Why is it so important to respect Soviet laws?
4. Arrange a discussion on the following subject: the role of the *Komsomol* in the life of Soviet youth and measures necessary to improve the work of the *Komsomol* organization in your school. The value of this discussion will be judged, naturally, not only by interesting speeches but practical results.
5. Recall the first topics in this textbook and exchange opinions on the following subject: how are the laws of dialectic demonstrated in the process of socialism's development into communism?

6

Creation of the Material-Technical Base of Communism and Formation of Communist Social Relations

Foundations of Communism

Most Important Factor for Victory of the New Social Order

To construct communism is, first and foremost, to create its material-technical base. If the base—the foundation—is lacking, even thinking about constructing communism is impossible, just as it is unthinkable to erect a structure without a foundation.

By the *material-technical base* of a society we mean the developmental level of production on which a specific social system is established and evolves in a comprehensive way. Clearly, the material-technical base of communism, which is expected to produce abundance of material and cultural goods, must surpass anything hitherto known.

But how will such gigantic growth of production in all branches of industry and agriculture be achieved? The simplest means would seem to be an expansion of production: to obtain many various kinds of products, build as many plants, factories and mines as possible; increase the areas under tillage, the size of herds, and so forth.

However, if we were to take this road and develop production only in breadth, it would take us a very long time to establish communism. Just doubling the number of industrial enterprises would require decades, even at our present high construction rate. And a doubled output would still not bring us abundance.

Time is not the only problem. The no-less-complicated question arises as to where to find the tens of millions of workers to service this multitude of enterprises. A simple increase in the number of plants and factories, therefore, is not sufficient to construct the material-technical base of communism.

Is there any other road to abundance? Yes, there is.

Let us recall what enabled capitalism to become established as a social formation more progressive than feudalism. History and political economy give the answer: the main reason was that capitalism achieved higher productivity of social labor.

Socialism and, even more so, communism open up unprecedented possibilities of growth in labor productivity by efficient utilization of all the material and labor resources available to society. Whereas the numerical increase of the labor force has its limits (depending directly upon the overall strength of the

177

population capable of working), under socialism the rise of labor productivity has no limits. The rise of labor productivity is the fundamental source of social production development. We must never forget V.I. Lenin's words: "Labor productivity is in the final analysis the important element for the triumph of the new social order." Labor productivity growth is the main criterion of success in creating the material-technical base of communism.

How can labor productivity be raised? One of the most important means is the fullest possible use of the achievements of the *scientific and technical revolution* that has spread throughout the modern world, embracing all areas of science and technology. It applies to power engineering, industrial materials, and production techniques, and to the nature of the work process itself (automation).

Power Engineering

Power! Obtained in various ways, under man's control it races through long-distance power lines to every destination; it performs countless labor operations, every kind of work, where crude power is needed and where the most delicate operations are performed.

In technology under the communist system the enormous advantages of electric power will be fully utilized: it is easily converted into other types of energy (mechanical, thermal, chemical; it may be infinitely split (permitting its use in the most diversified mechanisms and finest precision instruments); and it may be transmitted over great distances (promoting better geographical distribution of industry). This is what makes electric power the foundation of modern technical progress.

The growing demand for electric power as a result of the vigorous development of the economy and growth of labor productivity can be satisfied only by the country's total electrification.

Increased generation of electric energy does not mean merely an increase in the numbers of our mechanical aids. Electric power is an exceptionally flexible production *tool*, with extensive use in the economy. New chemical production processes, especially smelting of light metals such as aluminum, magnesium, titanium, and pure nickel; production of synthetic fibers and fertilizers—these branches of technology have an especially high rate of power consumption.

There is expanded and improved use of electric power not only in the many branches of the economy. The demand for personal everyday needs will be increasingly satisfied (electric household machines and appliances, radio and television sets). Use of electric power for cooking and for heating and air-conditioning of residential buildings has begun.

Large electric-power plants are linked together into "rings," in order to provide mutual back-up in the event of unexpected breakdowns, and also to take care of the uneven load at various times of the year and even of the day. The plants linked together operate as a "common boiler," a common electrical network feeding a great number of power-users. A power system is thus formed. This is not merely a group of electric-power plants but a single combine for generation and transmission (transport and distribution) of energy.

The country's total electrification will require further development of power systems: the linking up not only of individual power plants but of whole systems for parallel operation. Merging of the power systems will be accomplished by creation of a *unified power system of the USSR*. Under this title a unified complex of absolutely fantastic scope and intricacy will go into operation, making the USSR power economy thrifty and giving it maximum maneuverability.

Rapid development of electrification does not mean that the need for fuel and other energy sources will disappear. Many electric-power plants run on coal, oil, and gas, after all. The biggest users of solid and liquid fuel have been and will continue to be many branches of heavy and light industry, transport, and agriculture.

In addition to being first-class fuels, oil and natural gas are also raw materials for various synthetic products, such as artificial fibers, plastics, synthetic rubber, synthetic leather, soap, alcohol, dyes, cosmetics, medicines. At present, several thousand substances are made of oil, and their number is steadily increasing.

Science and technology are opening up prospects for large-scale use of many new sources of electric power.

The use of atomic energy is becoming widespread. The first electric-power plant in the world to run on nuclear fuel has been operating in the USSR since 1954. Beloyarsk and Voronezh and other atomic electric-power plants are now in operation.

What remains is to harness the extremely rich source of energy, the sun. Great possibilities are in prospect; solar electric-power plants with silicon semiconductors, for example. Every square meter of the surface of the semiconductor battery yields one hundred watts of power during almost the entire period of sunshine. Similar batteries are in operation on Soviet artificial earth satellites and spaceships. Mighty solar electric-power plants are being designed.

Soviet power engineering is on the threshold of wide-scale use of the earth's interior heat. The earth's natural heat is being employed in the form of steam or boiling water in Kamchatka, the Kurile Islands, the Caucasus, and Central Asia. So-called geothermal electric-power plants are already being constructed. Other power plants to convert into electricity the energy of sea tides—a gigantic wave caused by moon and sun—are also under design. This wave travels twice around the globe every twenty-four hours and in some places reaches ten, fifteen, and even twenty meters. It will be harnessed by special dams equipped with hydraulic turbines. The first tidal wave station in the USSR will be built on the Kola Peninsula, in the bay of the Barents Sea, where the tides are expectionally high.

Materials

If power constitutes the first prerequisite for modern industry, the second is materials, from which machines are manufactured, buildings constructed, and numerous consumer goods made.

In creating materials, nature was indifferent as to whether they would be convenient or even usable for human needs. In their natural state materials cannot always satisfy the requirements of modern technology. Not so long ago designers developing new machinery and architects designing apartment houses or industrial buildings were restricted in their selection to those basic materials available in the technology of recent decades. Having learned how to explain and anticipate the properties of various complex molecules, physics and chemistry have now acquired the ability to "design" new substances with properties currently required. The designer is gradually being liberated from restrictions imposed by the specialist on industrial materials. He is now free to choose materials which fully meet his technical intentions and, no less important, facilitate processing the manufactured item. If the necessary materials cannot be found in nature, the designer has only to specify what properties he requires, and they will be made available. Such materials as heat-resistant steels and semiconductors, unbreakable glass, noninflammable fibers, acid-resistant utensils, spark-free gears, bolts requiring no insulation from electric current, and resins for bridge construction have been introduced into technology.

No new modern technological advances would have been possible—a spaceship flight, total automation of any production process, or the creation of a "thinking" computer—without the production of new materials with certain specified, widely varying properties. Certain devices require exceptional hardness maintainable at extreme temperatures; others, adaptability to rapid changes in an electromagnetic field; still others, resistance to the most corrosive chemical media.

Fundamental change in the interrelationship between available materials and possible achievements in technology will allow even more rapid technical advance by supplying designers with materials actually needed instead of what is on hand. When this challenge is met, a new period will follow, perhaps called "the era of unlimited choice."

Enormous iron-ore resources that permit increased production of inexpensive metal and potential improvement of its structural qualities will maintain iron's importance in machine building, production of instruments and various devices, and other articles in all the economy's branches.

At the same time, metals are being replaced at an increasing rate by more economical materials, reinforced concrete and plastics, primarily.

The time is rapidly approaching when iron in its technically pure state (nonenriched or, as technicians say, unalloyed) will be used only in rare, exceptional cases. All industrial metal will be alloyed in varying degrees, and its strength considerably increased. Consequently, a half ton of alloyed steel will suffice where a ton of ordinary rolled metal was once required.

Twentieth-century technology has already made colossal strides owing to the discovery of the properties of certain rare metals. Even greater advantages may be expected from the metals just beginning to come into industrial use.

Here are some examples. Copper-berrylium bronze (alloy of copper with 3-4 percent berrylium) is hard and resilient; it is irreplaceable for components subject to frequent load change. In the very near future, not a single branch of technology will be able to operate without photocells, just as now the normal operation of industry is inconceivable without the use of electrical instruments. As a result, such rare elements as germanium, cesium, thallium, and others will be introduced into daily use. They will function in countless automatic control devices. The valuable physico-mechanical properties and high corrosion resistance of titanium in combination with enormous supplies of minerals containing titanium has awakened interest in this new metal. (A large aircraft can be made several tons lighter simply by using titanium in its construction. A diesel locomotive manufactured with titanium is only half as heavy as one of steel.)

New types of materials manufactured on the basis of macromolecular compounds occupy an ever greater place in modern technology and household use. Because of the character of their structure, giant molecules of polymers and other macromolecular substances have unique properties. In various combinations with fillers and structural support (glass, for instance), and also by themselves, they can be used as very durable structural materials, fibers, and rubber substitutes.

Polymer-base plastics are highly favored in technology and can easily be converted into finished products. This is due to the property reflected in their designation of "high plasticity." They reach plasticity under comparatively low heat, making it possible to mold them into desired shapes that are hardened by cooling. Plastics can be made into finished articles by pressing and also by advanced methods such as vacuum molding, pressure casting, use of centrifugal force for large articles, continuous pipe casting, and stretching into shape.

Plastics applied in numerous ways are complete substitutes for metals and often even surpass them. In this sense they are correctly called "irreplaceable replacements."

Furniture and building materials, machine-tool cases and gears, and automobile bodies can all be manufactured from plastics. In the future almost all metal parts of machine tools, machinery, and aircraft will be replaced with light, durable macromolecular compounds.

The polymer family is constantly growing. Since there is an infinite multiplicity of polymer "internal structures," this family's growth potential is infinite.

Chemistry makes it possible to create new indispensable materials. The chemical industry output will double during the current five-year plan period.

And this is not a chance development. Expansion of chemical production in all branches of the economy promises great benefits.

First of all, products created by chemical processes require less expenditure than exploitation of natural raw materials does. Also, the quality of products made from chemical and synthetic materials is incomparably higher, which makes a substantial savings in socially indispensable labor.

Second, new chemical materials allow increased production of variety of consumer goods in popular demand. Thus, chemistry brings us closer to the promised shores of communist abundance.

Third, more widespread, economical and efficient use of our raw material resources is tremendously important.

For example, in the course of logging operations by means of mechanical equipment, nearly two-thirds of lumber material (branches, sawdust, shavings, slabs, etc.) goes to waste. Chemistry, however, makes it possible to use nearly all this waste material to make wood alcohol, pulp, paper, and other products.

Mechanization and Automation

Mechanization and automation are tremendous factors in creating the material-technical base of communism. They are the most important means of increasing labor productivity and making work easier. When we speak of easier work, this' by no means implies that under communism one will be permitted to work at half his capacity, taking his time. Work is work, and it will always require a definite expenditure of physical and intellectual forces and concern and effort on man's part. By making work easier we mean constant expansion in technical labor equipment. Development of heavy industry (particularly machine building), mechanization of industrial productive processes, of transportation and agriculture lead to steady curtailment of heavy manual labor and disappearance of occupations that are health hazards and shorten the life span.

The unskilled laborer using a shovel has yielded place to an excavator manned by a driver and mechanic. Heavy labor by woodcutters and loggers in the timber industry has been lightened by electric saws and logging tractors. In machine building, metalworking, and construction work the labor of carriers and loaders has been replaced by crane and lift operations. In crude oil production there are no more bailers and similar laborers. Drilling crews operating complex mechanical devices do their work instead.

Similar changes have taken place in agriculture, where a mechanic working as a tractor or combine operator has become the key person in the production process.

Heavy manual labor still goes on in many production branches, because certain work operations are not easily adapted to mechanization. Obstacles of this kind, however, can be overcome, and in the future heavy manual labor will be eliminated due to technical progress.

Socialist production mechanization and automation call for improving the workers' qualifications, imparting an increasingly creative character to labor. Handling a shovel and operating a powerful crane are two vastly different things. Using a shovel hardly requires a great deal of knowledge. Neither does it provide opportunities for creative work; no particular intelligence is asked for. A crane operator must not only have the required minimum scientific and technical knowledge; effective use of his machine depends on his skill and creative inventiveness: he looks for the most rational approaches and methods in his work. Many operators even strive to improve their machines. These new work conditions have brought to life that mass form of the people's creativity known as streamlining and inventiveness.

Labor's character and conditions have been altered even more by automation. There are many examples of various automated production processes, and no doubt you all read about them and have personally observed them during school excursions. We shall consider at some length a few general principles of automation applicable not merely to individual machines but to entire shops, plants, and even complete economic branches.

The productivity of machines can be increased not only be speeding up the basic operation of material processing, metal cutting for instance, but also by curtailing the time needed for those auxiliary operations—done manually. But increasing the speed of manually performed auxiliary operations quickly reaches a physical limit, and they are also being automated.

Machinery automation is considerably increased by introduction of new mechanisms for automatic adjustment of working parts during the production process, for automatic quality and quantity control of produce, automatic feeding of the material to be processed, and removal of waste materials.

If the automatic work cycle is interrupted at any stage and requires the operator's intervention, we have a semiautomatic machine. Most of these lack the mechanism for "feeding" in the work piece as well as devices for removing the finished product, both of which operations remain the worker's duty.

An automatic machine not only speeds up particular operations but also makes it possible to *combine* them. For instance, one cutter at an automatic lathe is completing the external surface of a work piece; the second is cutting the butt-end; while the third has already begun to work on the conical surface. All these operations are performed simultaneously.

If one could conceive of a nonautomatic machine combining different operations as successfully as an automatic one, the worker in charge of this imaginary machine would have to possess one hundred pairs of hands and eyes, all strictly coordinated. The automatic machine, instead, is controlled by mechanical "hands" and electronic "eyes."

Where idling operations have been completely integrated with working operations, we have a continuous-action machine.

A typical example of a continuous-action machine is a rotary printing press: the object in process, the paper, is in constant motion and the printing process also continues without interruption. These machines are now quickly replacing the flat printing presses, which operate with interruptions, because the rotary presses have incomparably higher rate of productivity.

Continuous-action machines can function in all branches of industry. In metalworking there is use of automatic machines with the operative parts located inside their perimeter. An item is completely processed as the machine itself rotates without stop. When every section of the rotary machine arrives at the one feed mechanism, it takes over the item to be processed and upon completion of processing (in one rotation of the machine) ejects it at the unloading place. Rotary automatic lines, so-called, operate on this principle.

By concentrating a number of automatically executed operations, a multistation automatic machine can be constructed, a so-called combine or automatic transfer line, with the material in process kept in constant motion during the entire action.

The highest level of automation is achieved in the fully automated plant, where an automatic system of machines operates in perfect coordination.

Processes in continuous action at enormous speeds are impossible to control without modern automatic devices and computer technology and without creating systems of programmed regulation, self-adjustment, and self-tuning that select optimum modes of operation—all opening new vistas.

A machine can be designed that will not only sustain an assigned mode of operation but also select the best one. It ensures the most economical operation of a steam boiler by maintaining its fuel supply; selects the most favorable conditions as a chemical process progresses; or establishes an efficient method of oil-well drilling.

Conditions are especially favorable for wide application of *automation in the chemical industry* due to continuity in most technological processes involved in making chemical products. Impressive successes have been achieved in automating the production of synthetic alcohol, rubber, nitrogen fertilizers, calcinated soda, and sulphuric acid.

A decisive stage has been reached in the introduction of *automation into the field of power engineering.* The automatic unit control in all large and medium electric-power plants operating in the USSR has been achieved. All new hydroelectric power plants are equipped from the beginning with automatic control and, in cases where operating conditions require, with remote control. In large hydroelectric power plants service personnel per shift now consists of four to six persons; and in medium-size plants, two to three. Many hydroelectric power stations with the rate capacity of up to twenty thousand kilowatts function without any full-time personnel.

Transportation throughout the country will be converted to operate eventually like a single conveyer.

Coordinated and efficient operation of all types of transport depends not only on improving the chief means of transportation (conversion of railroads to electric traction, increased speed and capacity of trucks and ships). It also depends on improved operation of auxiliary functions; here it is especially important to mechanize completely all types of loading and unloading.

Likewise, *construction* is increasingly becoming a mechanized process of assembling and erecting buildings and installations out of prefabricated sections and parts manufactured at plants. Construction sites are beginning to look like plant assembly shops. Factory buildings and residential structures are assembled on the spot from parts, like machines.

Capitalist and Socialist Automation

You know from the newspapers that many automatic installations and transfer lines are in use in the developed capitalist countries also. What are the results and consequences of introducing automation under the different conditions of the two opposite social systems?

Modern automatic equipment economizes on human labor, its chief merit but not its only one. As we have seen, the introduction of self-regulating control systems in the production process makes possible the best use of all the other production elements: raw material, auxiliary material, and equipment. This is an even more important factor, because material expenditures predominate in the overall production costs in many industrial branches. This is the circumstance that most often attracts the capitalist businessman. But in a socialist society, automation's economic advantages do not have the same impact as in capitalist society. Its *social consequences are directly the opposite*.

Full employment is the most important among the problems caused by development of automation in a capitalist society: under its economy automation inevitably swells the army of unemployed.

In bourgeois countries there is also a *market problem* created by introduction of automation. Many companies are afraid to automate their plants, thus sharply increasing production, because it is impossible to find buyers for their products. An automated radio-receiver factory in England, for example, was unable to operate at its projected output capacity for twelve years because of marketing difficulties.

To be sure, the problem of unemployment, like the market problem, is nothing new for capitalism, nor is it the result of automation alone. But automation complicates and aggravates both problems drastically.

Automation is frequently called the "demonic force" in the West. George Thompson, an English physicist, in his book *The Foreseeable Future* has even estimated that within one generation remote-control automatic machinery will permanently deprive millions of persons of employment.

But is automation really responsible for all the misfourtunes suffered by the working class in capitalist countries? Of course not. Automation becomes an evil in capitalist countries chiefly because of *private ownership, the cause of production anarchy due to lack of planning.*

Precisely because automation represents the highest level of society's productive forces, at this stage it urgently requires establishment of production relations capable of opening new avenues for productive forces to develop immediately and in the future.

Under socialism and communism automation provides society with enormous, heretofore unheard-of opportunities for growth of productive forces and improvement of the people's living standard. The CPSU Program states: "As distinguished from capitalism, the socialist system of planned economy combines accelerated technical progress with full employment of every person in the population capable of working. Automation and complex mechanization are the material basis for gradual transformation of socialist labor into communist labor."

Naturally, in Soviet plants too the introduction of highly productive automatic equipment curtails the need for human labor. At times, significant groups of workers are released from employment in particular production sectors, shops, and even plants, in connection with the introduction of new automatic lines. However, the workers released as a result of replacing obsolete equipment are not threatened by unemployment, nor is there danger of glutting the market with additional products obtained from steady expansion of social production.

Of course, it is not a simple matter to find new jobs for these workers. Various solutions are possible. In some instances, when the plant is automated and expanded simultaneously, the released workers can be employed at the same plant. In other cases, it will be necessary to transfer the workers and employees to other enterprises in the same city or district, or from one economic region to other regions and other cities.

Concentration and Specialization of Production

The rapid progress of science and technology makes great demands on production organization. What tendencies does one observe in this area?

One of the main trends is further consolidation and *concentration of production.* Small enterprises cannot ensure high labor productivity nor cope with mass production of manufactured articles and goods. This is precisely where large enterprises offer broad opportunity. Their use of complex machines and, especially, of comprehensive mechanization and automation is more profitable. All the advantages of modern equipment can be put to full use in large enterprises.

There are more large enterprises in the USSR than in any other country. But the possibilities for further concentration of production are far from exhausted. As we move closer to communism, the few small, backward factories that still exist will be gradually phased out, yielding to large, technically advanced industrial production.

Specialization is the second important organizational principle of present-day production. Essentially, it is the strict division of labor, where enterprises or their particular shops, engaged in making a variety of products switch over to uniform production. This permits better utilization of machinery and raw materials, introduction of highly productive equipment (especially automated machines), improvement of production technology, improvement of product quality, and considerable reduction of production cost.

Automobile and tractor plants producing a single finished product serve as examples of specialized enterprises. Plants are also being developed to manufacture individual machine components: automobile and aircraft engines, ball bearings, tires, and so forth. Also, specialization is being introduced by separating specific production operations—in foundries, for example, or forge and press plants.

A major part (about two-thirds) of standard metal hardware (nuts, bolts, etc.) is manufactured in our country by specialized enterprises in profitable conditions of automated mass production. However, in 1963, to produce the remaining one-third of this type of hardware, nonspecialized small shops at other metalworking plants spent considerably more funds than the specialized plants did for their two-thirds share of this total production. In terms of the entire output of machine-building, this meant an overexpenditure of tens of millions of rubles per year, millions that "leaked out" through the many barely noticeable "streamlets."

Specialization is also being introduced into agriculture. For example, regions of the country's northwest, the Baltic republics, many areas in Belorussia and the Ukrainian Poles'ye specialize mainly in producing milk, bacon, and industrial crops.

The Transcaucasian republics and those in Central Asia have the most favorable environment for growing fruits, grapes, citrus fruits, tea, and cotton. These crops will be developed there on an even broader scale.

In the central Black Earth Belt region and the Ukraine and northern Caucasus, grain-growing and livestock-raising will be developed at more rapid rates.

Vegetable farms and dairy farms are being expanded around Moscow, Leningrad, Kiyev, Gor'kiy, Sverdlovsk, and other large industrial centers.

The interdependence of various economic branches with individual enterprises increases with growing specialization, especially in industry. Operation of a machine-tool plant, for instance, depends to a great extent on deliveries from the foundries that make half-finished parts, from the motor works, and instrument-making enterprises. A tractor plant cannot operate without electrical equipment supplied by a specialized factory. Close production relations are being established between various factories and economic branches in order to ensure industry's normal operation. Establishing these ties is known as *production cooperation*.

Combination of production will be increasingly important in the future. Its enormous advantages are due to many factors. There is the elimination of unproductive intermediate steps in the technological process, a more complete use of raw materials, more rational employment of equipment, and cuts in transportation costs.

Combination, it goes without saying, throughout the particular economic branches is effected in various forms and directions. In the lumber industry, for example, the various methods of processing timber are combined, the primary with the secondary. It is more sensible and efficient to haul planks than logs by rail over long distances. It is more profitable to undertake chemical processing of lumber waste on the spot, extracting acetic acid, turpentine, and other valuable products, and pressing fiberboard out of the sawdust. It is profitable to combine metallurgy with chemical production. When a mixture of oxygen and natural gas is blown into a blast furnace, the composition of the blast-furnace gas changes: it becomes a valuable chemical raw material. About three hundred kilograms of inexpensive synthetic ammonia can be obtained from blast-furnace gas per ton of pig iron.

Adoption of combined technology leads in a number of cases to complete restructuring of entire branches of industry: many specialized branches are gradually disappearing, and their production is being transferred to another branch, and thus is much more profitable. For example, future plans call for about two-thirds of soda and nearly one-half of sulphuric acid production in the country to be concentrated in nonferrous metallurgy, i.e., to be obtained as by-products of extraction of precious metals. Such combined methods have another advantage of no small importance: in most cases they eliminate pollution of the atmosphere and water reservoirs. The so-called industrial waste of one branch represents very valuable raw material for another. Large amounts of waste are a sure sign of a scientifically defective technological process.

Conditions are especially favorable for creating combined enterprises in the food-processing industry and in agriculture. This is understandable: agricultural raw material is complex in composition; it is available at various seasons, and in every season the same type of equipment can be used in a combined enterprise to process it. This will strengthen production ties between *kolkhozes* and *sovkhozes* on the one hand, and the local industrial enterprises on the other. As the CPSU Program points out, agricultural-industrial combines will gradually emerge.

Scientific Organization of Agriculture

Creation of the material-technical basis of communism presupposes vigorous development of both industry and agriculture.

Increased output of farm produce can be obtained in two ways: by expanding the areas under cultivation without changing the agrotechnical basis (extensive development) or by obtaining an ever increasing amount of farm produce per unit of area under cultivation (intensive development). "The chief means of advancing agriculture and satisfying the country's increasing need in farm produce," says the CPSU Program, "is overall mechanization and consistent *intensification*."

The soil is the chief means of production in agriculture. Degree of farming intensity is therefore primarily decided by how this natural basic factor is used. Any machine wears out, but the soil does not. If it is well cultivated and fertilized, and if the various crops are sown in reasonable sequence or, as the agronomists say, if crop rotation is practiced correctly, the soil's fertility will constantly increase.

What are the chief features of farming intensification?

Intensive farming means, first of all, obtaining higher yield from each hectare of land, and second, increasing labor productivity and lowering production costs by *mechanization and use of chemicals*.

Within the next few years the *kolkhozes* and *sovkhozes* will receive new machine systems of high technical-economic performance, geared to conditions in each agricultural zone. Of course, intensive farming requires not only increased numbers of farm implements per unit of area under cultivation, but also highly productive operation and careful storage of farm equipment.

All-inclusive *electrification* of agriculture is fundamental for efficient intensification of agricultural production.

Experience of many years in the use of fertilizers and chemicals to protect plants and animals, as well as evaluation of these procedures' economic effects, have demonstrated that use of chemicals is one of the most powerful means of agriculture intensification. Academician D.N. Pryanishnikov, the eminent Soviet agrochemist, has written that chemistry is creating "new continents" by providing quantities of additional farm produce comparable to the agricultural output of entire large countries.

In recent years chemists, physiologists, and biochemists have had considerable success in making and applying new chemicals to regulate plant growth and fertility. Among them are chemical preparations that act as growth stimulants when used in small quantities, whereas in large doses they suppress plant development and even kill plants. The following preparations will be used with increasing frequency in agriculture: herbicides, for selective destruction of weeds among useful plant crops; growth stimulants, for fruits and vegetables; chemical compounds, to inhibit budding and blossoming of trees during a cold spring; and preparations that prevent stored potatoes from sprouting, and eliminate runaway shoots on fruit trees, cotton bushes, and other crops (chemical chopping).

Mechanized harvesting of cotton and a number of garden crops is made easier by defoliants, which remove leaves, and dessicants, compounds that promote drying of stalks, leaves, and tops of potatoes, tomatoes, soy beans, and other plants. Use of defoliants makes possible cotton-picking by machine. This will relieve an enormous number of people of seasonal overwork because of heavy physical labor in the central Asian republics and other southern regions.

Agriculture up to this time has been greatly dependent on the weather. Can agriculture be made independent of the weather's caprice? Man has not yet mastered weather control.

In dry regions irrigation of the fields is a dependable way of obtaining stable harvests, making possible utilization of the rich soils of the south, where sunshine is plentiful, but not moisture. Because of irrigation, millions of hectares will be brought under cultivation in Central Asia, the southern regions of the Russian Federation, the Ukraine, and the republics of Transcaucasia. Because of irrigation there is certainty of always obtaining required amounts of such valuable agricultural products as wheat, cotton, rice, and corn, and of increasing production of meat, milk, butter, and wool. Irrigated fields promise an additional one to one and a half billion poods [one pood equals thirty-six pounds] of grain. In the European part of the USSR, outside the Black Earth Belt, drainage and eventual cultivation of swampland covering approximately twenty million hectares are in planning.

The Special Plenum of the CPSU Central Committee of May 1966 was devoted to improvement and irrigation problems of low-productivity soils. The Plenum decided on a broad program of irrigation and amelioration to be carried out over several five-year-plan periods.

Great tasks faced us in livestock breeding, where guaranteed milk and increased meat yields are needed. And the most dependable way to attain these goals is by introducing progressive work methods, new and more advanced equipment, and the latest scientific achievements.

Chemistry plays an important role in livestock-raising, also. Chemicals enter this branch of farm economy chiefly in three ways: chemically prepared fodder, preservative chemicals, and compounds regulating life processes.

The economic effectiveness of chemical stimulants is considerable. For example, feeding urea (carbamide) to ruminants increases the milk yield and weight of the stock; in the case of sheep, it also results in higher yield of wool.

Many animal diseases are caused by bites of blood-sucking insects (gadflies, horseflies, mosquitoes, flies, etc.) and are transmitted by infected water and fodder. Chemicals play an important role in prevention and treatment of these ailments.

The system of animal-feeding is also being changed. The use of chemicals to preserve fodder has considerably reduced storage losses of crops with high moisture content (clover, timothy, and other grasses). As a result, actual fodder harvest is almost doubled. Chemistry also has created the possibility of enriching fodders with mineral substances, especially phosphates and other microelements.

The struggle for improvement of livestock-raising is identical with the struggle for more rapid development of all branches of agricultural economy, and for speedy creation of abundance of farm products. Livestock-raising is directly connected with grain-farming. Not only abundant production of meat and milk but also more use of valuable natural fertilizers to enlarge the crop yield of grain cereals, and, thus, the overall grain harvest, are tied in with expansion of livestock-raising.

Science, the Great Productive Force

In the beginning, science entered production as complex mechanical equipment. The laws of mechanics helped design machinery; physics and chemistry made possible improvement of the technology developed experimentally.

Now the situation has radically changed. From explanation of natural phenomena science has moved to artificial reproduction of the natural processes and of chemical reactions. Actually, in many ways, science has gone farther than nature. For example, concentrating light energy into fine pencils—lasers—is unknown in nature; we do not encounter in nature many of the substances created by synthetic means.

Science is providing its own powerful production base. Think of such modern sicentific "instruments" as the gigantic elementary-particle accelerators with magnets measuring several hundred meters in diameter and service crews of nearly a thousand people; the huge wind tunnels; electron microscopes; and computers. From the engineering viewpoint they are all highly complex installations.

Production based on the latest scientific achievements more and more frequently represents a hugely magnified process of laboratory research. Every contemporary large technical transformation begins with the stage of scientific research. Inventiveness in industrial production now inevitably includes scientific research.

In other words, science is gradually being converted into a direct productive force. But this prospect is only possible in a society advancing toward communism. Why is this so?

The expansion of the sphere of technological application of science, however important, is not the decisive requirement of its conversion into a direct productive force. Only when there is harmonious development of social production can science become fully productive; its technological application ensures the progress of the means of production and promotes the individual person's development, the basic productive force in society.

And this merging of science with the main productive force of society—man himself as creator, bearer, and champion of science—is only possible in a society where development does not occur spontaneously. Communism possesses all the necessary preconditions for this merger for the first time in history. And the closer our society draws to communism, the more manifest is dominion by man, armed with scientific knowledge, over the means of production.

We have traced the main courses of development of the material, tangible base upon which new, communist human relations will grow. The material-technical base of future communist society will surpass the level of productive forces created by capitalism considerably; it will absorb the highest achievements of scientific and technical progress and equip our country with the most modern and powerful technology.

All this—the oceanlike wave of energy, the untold wealth of materials, the army of intelligent machines—is not going to appear unaided. Every one of us must make his contribution.

Toward a Classless Society

As a result of the construction of socialism, the main evil of a class society, the oppression of man by man, has been wiped out forever. Everyone labors in a social economy, is paid according to his labor, and has an equal right to take part in state affairs.

However, class and other related social distinctions (between town and country, between manual labor and intellectual) have not been completely eradicated. As long as they persist, there cannot be full equality of working and living conditions for the people. That is why overcoming these distinctions and creating a classless society is an all-important objective of communist construction.

Communist Ownership, Basis of Classless Society

The fundamental reason for the class distinctions that still exist is that the labor of workers is tied in with the all-people property, while that of the peasants is tied in with the *kolkhoz* (cooperation) property. These distinctions will disappear when a *single communist ownership of the means of production* replaces the two forms of socialist ownership.

How will this be accomplished?

The *all-people property develops* in the course of the construction of the material-technical base of communism. Its volume widens: every year thousands of new plants and factories, schools and apartment houses, cinemas and clubs, polyclinics and stadiums are made ready for use; equipment of industrial enterprises is modernized and their production potential increases. At the same time, as has been stated, there is concentration of production, specialization and cooperation of enterprises, improved distribution of productive forces and improved economic management.

Socialist all-people ownership develops directly into communist ownership.

Matters are more complex with *kolkhoz* ownership: it must be brought into alignment with all-people ownership and merge with it. How can this objective be achieved?

The simplest solution would appear to be: "Let us convert all the *kolkhozes* into *sovkshozes*, and the task will be done," But such transformation will not solve the problem, nor will it ensure an automatic rise in the entire agricultural production. We need bread, meat, milk, and other products in ever-increasing quantities. To obtain them it is necessary to introduce new equipment, apply scientific advances in agriculture and livestock-raising broadly, and improve labor organization; that is, bring about a sharp rise in agriculture's productive forces. This is the key to the solution, because rise in *kolkhoz* production brings development of *kolkhoz* ownership, to merge directly with all-people ownership.

Is the *kolkhoz* form of ownership capable of ensuring this development, this upswing of productive forces? Certainly it is, as proven by the fact that, alongside existing backward *kolkhozes*, there are many *kolkhozes* whose performance is no worse, and sometimes even better, than that of *sovkhozes*. Obviously, the *kolkhoz* form of production has not exhausted its potential and possesses enormous hidden reserves that must be fully utilized. Therefore, in agriculture we should develop both the *sovkhoz* and *kolkhoz* forms of production.

Convergence of the Two Forms
of Socialist Ownership

Let us see how the upsurge in *kolkhoz* production and the conversion of *kolkhozes* into actual factories of agricultural products lead to a higher level of socialization of cooperative ownership, causing it to draw closer to all-people ownership.

With growth of *kolkhoz* production the *amount of unshared funds belonging to the communal property is growing*, as compared with shares belonging to individual members (which account for less than 3 percent of *kolkhoz* funds and are on the decrease). The larger the proportion of unshared funds, the closer *kolkhoz* property draws to all-people ownership, as far as concerns its economic nature.

The labor of the entire Soviet people—the *kolkhoz* peasantry, the workers, and the intelligentsia—is embodied in the powerful tractors and combines, in all the diversified, advanced mechanized equipment of modern agriculture.

Internal kolkhoz production relations are improving with the development of communal economy in the *kolkhozes*. They increasingly satisfy the needs of their members, not only in grain but other farm products, and on this basis gradual elimination of the family plots will be achieved. Paid vacations and other payments, similar to those in state enterprises, are being introduced.

Recent years have seen successful *development of interkolkhoz production ties,* various forms of cooperation among *kolkhozes.* One *kolkhoz* by itself is often not in a position to build even a small electric-power plant, a factory for initial processing of agricultural raw materials, or other production installations; a rest home for its members, and other facilities. Several neighboring *kolkhozes,* therefore, combine their resources and build jointly. Often *kolkhozes* undertake construction jointly with state enterprises. Clearly, these joint ventures and installations can no longer be considered purely cooperative property; they hardly differ from objects of all-people property. *Direct consolidation of kolkhoz means of production with state resources* is thus taking place.

One of the chief advantages of socialist ownership, as we know, is the possibility of planning production. In this respect, too, the present difference between the two forms of socialist ownership is being overcome: *advanced ways and methods of planning* developed in industry are being successfully applied in the *kolkhozes* (with due consideration to their peculiar features as cooperative enterprises).

Growth of unshared funds, development of cooperation among *kolkhozes* and between the *kolkhozes* and the state, and improvement of other aspects of production relations indicate that *kolkhoz* ownership is converging with all-people ownership. But does this mean that the two forms of socialist ownership are developing separately, the one leading the way and the other catching up? Clearly, it does not. *Kolkhoz* production (and, therefore, the socialization level of *kolkhoz* property) is increasing mainly because of electrification, introduction of chemicals, complex mechanization and automation of farm labor. This is being effected by industry, which supplies the countryside with powerful equipment and fertilizers, thus reorganizing agricultural production.

The development of the two forms of ownership is most closely interconnected, and the leading role belongs to all-people ownership. The result will be the merger of the two forms. When this process is completed, the chief distinction between the classes will vanish. How will this be manifested?

All production workers will labor in industrial and agricultural enterprises owned by the entire people.

All will toil under approximately the same working conditions.[a]

All will be paid for their work out of public funds and have equal access to the benefits distributed from public funds.

Town and Country

Ways the Countryside Develops

The process of *elimination of the social distinctions between town and countryside* is connected with the formation of communist ownership. This process is of utmost importance for the creation of a classless society.

---

[a]The use of the word "approximately" is not by chance. The point is that for an indefinite period distinction between working conditions connected with the specifics of agricultural production will persist. But this distinction no longer has a social character.

But, one must remember, social distinctions between town and countryside cannot be completely identified with class distinctions. This would be a mistake, since not only *kolkhoz* members but also *sovkhoz* workers and a large segment of rural intelligentsia live and work in our rural areas. Moreover, the reason for persistant distinctions lies not only in the original antagonism of the classes but also in the historical circumstances of society's development. As locations of industrial concentration, the cities have long enjoyed a higher level of working and living conditions, whereas the exploiter classes attempted to perpetuate the comparative backwardness of the villages.

The victory of socialist relations in all branches of social production led to the disappearance of this contradiction. The villages ceased to be primitive raw-material sources to the city. They were converted into one of the equal components in the social system of socialism.

The town offers various kinds of assistance to the countryside. In the most crucial moments in the history of village life the workers sent tens of thousands of their best sons to help the toiling peasantry organize the *kolkhozes* and put an end to want and backwardness. The town has given the countryside first-class equipment, thus ensuring a rapid rise in productivity of agricultural labor.

A great deal has been done for the countryside in recent years. The state has allocated tens of billions of rubles for capital investment in agriculture and granted credits for construction of communal buildings, housing, and cultural and service facilities in the rural areas.

Along with economic development, a cultural revolution has changed the face of the countryside. Hundreds of thousands of qualified specialists with higher and secondary-school education—agronomists, veterinarians, physicians, engineers, educators—are now working in the rural areas. Millions of inhabitants in the countryside have acquired various mechanical skills. It is difficult to imagine the present-day village without a school, hospital, cultural center, library, motion-picture house, radio receivers, amateur art groups, and sports organizations.

But substantial distinctions between town and countryside still persist. The village is seriously lagging behind the town in housing conditions, household conveniences and comforts, and cultural development. In this we see the remnants of the original social inequality, which will decidedly vanish in the process of constructing communism.

The Communist party has outlined a whole system of measures to overcome the cultural and day-to-day backwardness of the countryside. Rural settlements will receive all the modern facilities needed to satisfy demands for everyday repairs and other services. At the same time, the system of public education and network of cultural institutions will be expanded.

The rural population will be able to enjoy all material and cultural benefits on a par with city-dwellers.

Imagine a person living in a rural area and having all kinds of conveniences and services. Would he feel any less favored than the city-dweller? Certainly he would not. Rather, it would be the reverse; other things being equal, rural life has a number of advantages over urban life: clean air, absence of noise, and the aesthetic enjoyment that comes from continuous contact with living nature.

Indeed, the problem is how to make the cities healthier places in which to live, which will also be solved under communism. Even now there are great projects in our country to establish green areas in our cities. Around Moscow and other large industrial centers the first satellite towns are being created, combining the best features of town and country life. In other words, as the rural areas are upgraded to the town level in regard to everyday living conditions and culture, the urban areas will be upgraded to the level of the health conditions in the countryside and to its closeness to nature.

All this will lead to disappearance of the very notion of village, in the present sense of the word. Efficiently planned cities, freed from overpopulation, purified from soot and smoke, will merge with endless rows of well-built settlements with all conveniences.

In addition, the excellent means of communication will leave no reason for any feeling of isolation in a remote spot. The TU-104 now brings Leningraders to Moscow in fifty minutes, the exact time it takes for a Muscovite residing on the city outskirts to get to its center. These airplanes will be replaced soon by supersonic passenger aircraft and, later, by rocket planes. In brief, trips between various centers on official or personal business will become no more difficult than it is now to visit with relatives in a neighboring village.

Far more powerful radio and telecommunication equipment than is now available, current newspapers, telephone service that will do away with preordering calls and tiresome waiting—all of this will enable people, no matter where they live, to get the latest news immediately and thus be well informed about all current events.

Conversion of Agricultural Labor into One Variety of Industrial Labor

Finally (and this is of the greatest importance), due to mechanization and, later, automation of agricultural production and to the introduction of science into soil cultivation and livestock raising, *agricultural labor will become another variety of industrial labor*.

Only in this way can the gap between countryside and town be closed. If agricultural labor with its special characteristics were not adaptable to mechanization and automation, all effort to eliminate the social distinctions between town and countryside would necessarily be doomed to failure. Judge for yourselves. Could there be any serious discussion about equal cultural development of persons in the town and countryside if manual labor were to have ascendancy in agriculture? Certainly there could not. All milkmaids may be given a higher education, but this would be an artificial situation if they were not able to find a place to apply their acquired knowledge and further it in creative labor.

An entirely different situation arises when agricultural labor is reorganized on the basis of modern technology. This requires personnel with much greater specialized knowledge and general culture. It is unthinkable to employ scientific methods to increase livestock productivity without some knowledge of biology, veterinary science, and other skills. Limitless opportunities are being created to search out the most efficient methods of managing farms, to experiment and innovate.

The *kolkhozes* and *sovkhozes* will be converted into real factories of grain, meat, milk, and other products. And what is factory work but industrial labor that requires not only a higher degree of culture but also a higher level of collectivistic outlook on the part of the toilers?

One must bear in mind that difficulties will be encountered: the task of automating agricultural labor is more complex because of its specific nature. Production processes in soil cultivation and livestock-raising are heterogeneous; not only men and equipment take part, but nature as well. Nature fixes the time for ripening of crops and growth of livestock. This, however, does not at all preclude automation of several labor processes even now. (For example, there is an automatic tractor invented by F. Loginov, a farm mechanization specialist.) The more distant future will see the successful automation of most farm-labor operations.

The conversion of agricultural labor into one variety of industrial labor will create the circumstances for the workers in agriculture to combine intellectual and physical labor in their operations, just as industrial workers do.

Labor: Intellectual and Manual

From Opposites to Unity

The utopian socialists dreamed of the day when it would be possible to put an end to one of the greatest injustices of class society: the division of persons into intellectual and manual workers.

Socialism has done away with the original antithesis. Under socialism intellectual work has ceased to be an inherited privilege; knowledge has been made available to everyone. The Soviet intelligentsia is kith and kin with the workers and the *kolkhoz* peasantry, sharing the same interests and the same destiny with the basic classes of society. The cultural revolution has brought science, technology, and art within reach of the broad masses of the people now. The more than two million inventors and efficiency experts, the hundreds of thousands of amateur art group members, the millions of workers and peasants who occupy their leisure time with study and creative efforts are intelligent, in the highest sense of the word.

However, all this does not change the fact that the division of people into intellectual and manual workers has been retained in society. Can it be abolished once and for all? And how can this be done? One solution, already suggested by the utopian socialists, is to alternate intellectual and manual labor.

This alternation already takes place in many persons' activity. A manual worker, for example, his assignment completed, sits down to study or work on some technical improvement; a mathematician who has been working through the day at theoretical computations tends a garden in his free time. In these cases, as we see, the alternation of occupations occurs during the nonworking time; the man's basic profession remains the same, and either manual or intellectual work, as before, predominates.

Work alternation will be even more developed with the shortening of work time. This will be useful both for the individual and society. However, modern production and science demand that people specialize. Regardless of the job, whether repairman, agronomist, teacher, there is always need for certain skills, experience, and qualifications. To become really skilled, a person must dedicate himself mainly to one field; he can hardly be expected to achieve serious results in production, science, or art otherwise. All indications are for the need of far-reaching specialization: persons must have complete mastery in their chosen profession.

Where, then, can this problem's solution be found?

The answer, apparently, is to change the nature of manual labor, bringing it nearer to intellectual labor. It is essential, in other words, that production work itself require of the toilers a high degree of intellectual culture and offer them the possibility of creative activity.

This is exactly the goal to which the construction of the material-technical base of communism is leading. First of all, heavy manual labor is disappearing forever. Everywhere machinery is coming to man's aid; in the last two or three decades alone several hundred occupations requiring unreasonable expenditure of human energy, causing great injury to health, and shortening workers' lives have become obsolete.

The more complex machinery becomes, the higher the demands on the worker-operator, who must know fundamental principles of various sciences and thoroughly understand production technology. It is no longer possible for him to limit himself to mechanical repetitive actions he once learned; he must therefore rely upon his knowledge, combining it directly with his labor. Conditions are being created for *organic unification of intellectual and manual labor in men's productive activity*.

These objective conditions will be supplemented by such organization of public education as to assure the all-round development of each of society's members. Every person will make a thorough study of his chosen specialty, will be familiar with the fundamentals of contemporary science, and will acquire the habit of participating directly in productive labor.

Automation and Labor

Whereas elimination of heavy manual labor is a matter for the near future, the organic unification of intellectual and manual labor, a far more complex task, can be completely achieved only under the conditions of automated communist production.

A legend of a pushbutton paradise was born at the dawn of automation. There were those who thought that the "blessed time" was coming for the worker when "simply by pressing a button" he would activate powerful machinery and make obedient robots execute any order.

First of all, "simply pressing a button" is by no means as easy as it appears at first glance. Pushbutton control has facilitated the worker's labor; operators of automated rolling mills and crane-hoists, engineers in control of electric power plants, use it. But actually the only thing that is simplified is the transmission of command. The decision preceding that command, the most important thing, demands great knowledge and experience, as well as instantaneous orientation— strenuous concentration of all the faculties, in other words.

But even this concentration serves only temporarily. The speed of modern machinery's production processes has greatly increased, and man is not in a position to cope with it. If the normal sequence of this process is interrupted, a man cannot respond with speed sufficient to correct a deficiency or prevent breakdown. Man, the great inventor of all these magnificent machines and devices, with all his buttons that have "only to be pressed," thus becomes himself a hindrance to the productive process of the equipment he has created.

Electronic computers come to man's assistance. They are capable of executing thousands of operations in a second. In addition to their operating speed, these machines have another important feature: they "remember" individual stages of the process, compare their results, and make the best selection from among them. The machine can be ordered to determine the best operating schedule, and maintain it, by "commands." These electrical commands are instantly "obeyed" and carried out by electronic operating devices. To put it even more briefly, high-speed computers can "run" a production process without human intervention.

The important question arises as to what is left for a man to do in automated production?

We can answer with confidence: the most important and most interesting task.

To man belongs not only the design and manufacture of the automatic equipment (in itself an exceptionally fascinating function) but also the programing of the automatic devices. Even the most "clever" machine can "think" only within strictly defined limits after it has been "set" with the aid of a suitable, frequently extremely complex program, which must be fed to it by none other than man himself.

As you see, production work in the future will be neither excessively burdensome nor monotonous. Man will hand over to machines monotonous operations to be performed automatically, and he will take over their control and regulation. This has already become a profession in the engineering technology field.

Once communism is established, therefore, the old division of labor, which doomed a considerable majority of persons to heavy, uninspiring work, will vanish. Whatever the occupation, it will have a creative character and require a combination of high-caliber specialization with broad mastery of scientific and technical knowledge. Harmoniously combined "brainwork" and "handwork" will convert any labor into a source of enjoyment and delight. Obviously, this does not mean that work will become a delightful pastime. Work will always demand of man the strenuous concentration of his intellectual and physical forces and great expenditure of energy.

To be more exact, in the future men will cease altogether to question what should be uppermost in their labor activity, the intellectual or the manual, just as a surgeon, let us say, does not even think of this question, since he works simultaneously with his brain and hands.

At the same time it would be an oversimplification to imagine that the "dosage" of intellectual and manual labor will be identical for all men. Different professions will always require varying correlations of intellectual and manual effort. For example, take a geologist: his muscular exertion is heavier than that of some manual workers.

With the passage of time, therefore, men will cease to be divided into manual and intellectual workers, and the intelligentsia as a social stratum will disappear.

Formation of a single communist ownership of the means of production, elimination of the social distinction between town and countryside, the organic unification of manual and intellectual labor in the productive activity of persons—all these are objective social processes leading to the ultimate eradication of class distinctions.

Toward Communist Labor and Distribution

Two Prerequisites for Transition to
Communism's Fundamental Principle

The principle of compensation according to labor performed embodies one of the greatest achievements of socialism; it negates the monstrous inequality in distribution of material and cultural goods that exists under capitalism.

But compensation according to labor still does not signify full equality of living conditions. Persons employed in jobs requiring higher qualifications earn more and live better, naturally, than those whose work calls for lower qualifications. Families differ in size, which also leads to difference in living standard. These vestiges of social inequality will vanish when society is able to implement fully the communist principle of labor and distribution: "From each according to his ability; to each according to his need." What are the indispensable conditions for this?

Simple common sense suggests that, first of all, an *abundance of material and cultural goods* must be ensured and such development of productive forces and high level of productivity of social labor achieved as will enable society to satisfy generously the needs of all its members.

Also, people's needs are constantly growing; therefore, the social wealth must grow even faster.

The situation is comparatively simple in regard to most vital needs: food, clothing, footwear, housing. Scientists have calculated the amount of calories required for the human organism to carry on its life processes; the amount of proteins, fats, carbohydrates, and vitamins in food; the amount of shoes, dresses, suits, and other clothing in an individual person's wardrobe; the amount of housing space for healthy and civilized living. These indices are called *rational norms*. With knowledge of population figures at present and their anticipated increase, it is possible to figure out when full satisfaction of one need or another will come about.

Of course, human needs do not remain static: people's aesthetic tastes develop, and fashion gives rise to new models in clothing, footwear, and furniture. But these changes are not extremely significant, and a smoothly running industry can serve various requirements and satisfy the most exacting tastes, once it has ensured satisfaction of the basic needs in conformity with the rational norms.

Growing production, science, and technology at the same time create entirely new needs, which become no less vital to us than, let us say, the need to be well dressed. A few centuries ago people got along without books, but for you and us spiritual nourishment is no less essential than physical nourishment. Thirty years ago a TV set was not a need, but now everyone finds a small screen at home essential, and our radio-TV industry is assigned to satisfying this need within the next few years. Videophone is just beginning to come into use, but undoubtedly everyone will want to avail himself of this useful and convenient device within one or two decades. And at this time we cannot even imagine what new needs will be generated by the vigorous development of science and technology under communism.

Abundance of material and cultural goods is the first but not the only prerequisite for transition to the communist principle: the whole point is that this is a principle not of distribution alone but of labor as well. And what is to be the source of this abundance? Who can satisfy men's growing needs except men themselves, with selfless labor for society's good? This is why the second paramount condition for the introduction of the communist principle is readiness on the part of all members of society to labor to the full measure of their abilities, to give generously of their knowledge and skill, talent and energy, to society. In the course of the construction of communism, labor itself is being transformed into the *first, vital need* of the human organism, as natural and indispensable as the need to breathe. V.I. Lenin wrote:

Communist labor is unremunerated labor for the good of society—labor performed not to fulfill some official duty, acquire the right to obtain certain products, in conformity with prescribed and legalized norms—but voluntary labor beyond norms, given without counting on renumeration and independently of it, performed as a habit of working for the common good . . . labor as a need of a healthy organism.

You see that both parts of the communist principle of labor and distribution are inseparable and interconnected: without labor according to ability there can be no distribution according to need. Two problems, therefore, need solution at the same time: creating an abundance of vital goods and inculcating the communist attitude toward labor into society's members. The key to the eventual solution of both lies in the consistent, practical application of the principle of material incentive, in order to make each working person interested in the result of his labor.

Without material incentive there can be no steady increase in labor productivity nor any continued growth of the social wealth. Without it millions of persons will not be led to communism, neither can the circumstances be created where work according to ability becomes habitual, a vital need of all persons. Therefore, the construction of communism must rely on the principle of material incentive. Compensation according to labor performed remains the basic source from which the material needs of the toilers are satisfied.

It is definitely a good thing if a man works conscientiously in order to acquire certain necessary products and to spend his earnings for his own satisfaction and his own good. But it sometimes happens that the more a man earns, the more insatiable becomes his thirst for acquisition. The pursuit of the almighty ruble becomes his life goal, and he begins to work not so much for himself as for his strongbox. When he yields to his thirst for profit, he not infrequently falls into dishonest practices and ends by becoming a criminal.

We are not ascetics; any denial of the legitimate desire to live better, more affluently, is alien to us. But we must not allow ourselves or our comrades to fall under the power of the "golden calf." Therefore, material stimuli to labor must always be combined with moral stimuli. In our society moral stimuli to labor—above all, people's awareness that they are working not for exploiters but for themselves and society as a whole—have acquired enormous importance. The Party fosters in Soviet citizens profound understanding of their labor's social significance and conscientiousness toward labor on their part. We are working not for profit but for the triumph of the great cause of communism. And our labor is being repaid a hundredfold by ensuring an uninterrupted growth of social wealth.

Distribution by Means of Social Funds

The wealth created by socialist society is distributed also by means of social funds. During the first years of the Soviet regime, when the first boarding schools, nurseries, and other similar institutions were emerging, Lenin called them sprouts of communism. He urged us to protect and strengthen them. We now possess an entire system of these institutions. Public education and medical care, maintenace of hospitals and Pioneer Camps, old age and disability pensions—all are being financed by the state from social funds.

Why do we see in the distribution by means of social funds the communist way of satisfying needs? Because it is chiefly done irrespective of the quantity and quality of the labor of the different persons involved.

Clearly, we would have been incorrect to identify distribution by means of social funds with the communist principle of distribution according to need and assert that therefore the principle has already been partially introduced. First of all, social funds are still not large enough for complete satisfaction of all the needs for which they are intended. Second, in certain cases the results of the existing distribution according to labor are taken into account in the distribution of these funds.

The amount of pensions depends upon wages, for example. Justice demands an identical pension for everyone: after all, those who work long and honestly at their occupations, important or modest, deserve the same attention and support from society. It is not possible to introduce this procedure now, but we are aiming at this objective. In recent years there has been an increase in pensions for the low-paid categories of workers. Preference is being given to the less-well-off and their children in distribution of labor-union travel passes to vacation facilities, assignments to boarding schools, scholarship grants in the institutions of higher education. This helps narrow the gap in living standards of toilers with higher and lower skills.

Distribution by means of social funds promotes extension of *communal forms of satisfying the people's needs*. And this involves a gigantic savings of social labor and brings great benefit both to society as a whole and to individual persons.

Take communal meals as an example. Increasing numbers of people prefer to eat in public dining halls. After all, this saves a great deal of time! The chief gainers are women, who now have the thankless burden of housework. Also, mechanized preparation of food emerges as a general possibility, even necessity.

As soon as the basic principle of communism was formulated, the opponents of communist teaching stated that it was impossible to carry it out. Bourgeois ideologists continue to assert this. "Laziness," they claim, "is deeply rooted in human nature, and man will work only if forced by hunger or roused by thirst for profit. As soon as society takes over the task of satisfying everyone according to his needs, no one will lift a finger to do a thing."

What lack of faith in man these slanderous accusations express! By his very nature man is not an idle contemplative; he is a doer. To paraphrase a well-known saying: Man is born to work, as the bird is born to fly.

Balzac, a man of genius, experienced extreme need for money throughout his life. But who would ever try to prove that we owe *The Human Comedy* to selfish greed for profit? The author was inspired by his creative passion, the loftiest manifestation of the human intellect. This passion inspires many persons of the most varied professions, whether a gardener who spares no effort to grow a beautiful flower or an engineer who devotes all his time to work out details in a new design.

In our country at present a large part of the population already works to the full measure of its ability and can do no more. Millions participating in the movement for communist labor are the best refutation of our critics.

But what is to be done about idlers. Quite simply, there will be none. Laziness, after all, is caused by inactivity and bad upbringing. In the new society the individual is trained from childhood to work, and he learns to view constructive labor as the highest aim and meaning in life. Under these conditions, even if some are negligent and work only halfheartedly, society can be an influence on them. Even now we are conducting a successful campaign against persons who prefer idling to honest work. Why should we assume that in the future, when labor according to ability will be a vital need for all or almost all, one idler will be able to corrupt, let us say, ten thousand toilers? On the contrary, thousands of toilers will be able to compel the do-nothing to work conscientiously.

Another argument of bourgeois ideologists goes: As soon as society begins to satisfy everyone according to his needs, people will be overwhelmed by an "instinct" for self-enrichment and every man will try to get as much for himself as he can, with the result that the social wealth will be pillaged. Other bourgeois ideologists maintain that the communist society will try to regulate and control a person's needs, giving every one an equal ration of identical products, dressing every one in standard clothing, and so forth. Having painted this gloomy picture, the slanderers weep over the fate of the "unfortunate communist people" who must abandon all of life's joys and turn into standardized dummies.

Here again we have an example of how the bourgeoisie tries to judge the communist man by its own image and likeness. If people brought up in the spirit of bourgeois morality were suddenly to land in the middle of communist society, they would, in fact, shout: "Grab what you can!" But the whole point is that such money-grabbers never will land there. As has been explained, the communist principle of distribution will be fully introduced only after communist morality has triumphed in society and a sufficiently high level of communist conviction on the part of all persons has been attained. Furthermore, one of the most significant characteristics of persons with communist convictions is that they will not have extravagant wants; their needs will always be reasonable.

A conscientious member of communist society will never express such a wild demand as, say, a hundred-room private home when a three-room apartment would be quite sufficient for his needs. Or cover his apartment walls with magnificent canvasses, whose proper place is in a museum or other public building for everyone to admire. Or cram his trunks with clothing and his cellar with food supplies, when he can quite easily get all he really needs from stores and public food reserves.

Within the limits of reasonably understood needs, everyone will be able to satisfy his own personal tastes and inclinations: to furnish his apartment, select and order his clothes, regulate his own life as he pleases. Lovers of exquisite food, if they do not mind spending time on it, will find it possible to satisfy their gastronomic cravings at home. (After all, no one is forced to eat in public dining halls.) And the fashion plates and dandies[b] will be able to busy themselves with the beauty of their personal attire.

For some time the voices of those who take a petty-bourgeois socialist position have been added to communism's bourgeois critics. The principle of material incentives has nearly always been the most important target of their attacks. If one were to believe them, higher pay for greater output and better quality labor turns people into profit-seekers and money-grabbers; and improved living standards for the Soviet people and their acquisition of TV sets and refrigerators supposedly deprives them of their revolutionary spirit, leading to the "degeneration" of Soviet society, to the "restoration of capitalism" in the USSR.

Such arguments most strikingly reflect typical petty-bourgeois conceptions about socialism as the realm of all-around egalitarianism, and about the revolutionary spirit as exclusively the character of half-starving people. If it really were as these ultrarevolutionaries say, communism would be altogether

---

[b]These two words are now used mostly in a pejorative sense: we apply them to women and men who have nothing more in their heads than the latest fashions and try to stand out by the exaggerated originality and pretentiousness of their attire. But the wish to be well dressed is perfectly justified in itself, especially in the younger years. The whole point is that it must not cut off a person from the real world, making him or her the slave of showy clothes. With this reservation it is not reprehensible but, on the contrary, commendable to have a desire to be elegantly dressed. The culture of dress, and culture in general, will undoubtedly develop further within a society of abundance.

mpossible, inasmuch as any socialist society would be in danger of unavoidably degenerating into capitalism as its prosperity grows. That is the kind of absurdity to which the views of the petty-bourgeois revolutionaries lead!

No, dear friends, we tell them, one cannot build communism with such views. People rise in revolutions in order to struggle for socialism and win a free, happy life for themselves and their children. They are achieving this by their heroic labor, thus giving an example to their brothers in capitalist countries. Our revolutionary character and our greatest international duty toward the toilers of the entire world today consist in our building communism successfully.

Development of Statehood into
Communist Social Self-government

The State During the Period of
Communist Construction

The role of the socialist state has been steadily gaining importance in the process of the construction of communism. The state is necessary for the management of our multibranch economy according to a single plan, for ensuring labor discipline and public order, for control of labor norms and consumption. We must wage a battle against idlers, loafers, swindlers, hooligans, and other violators of community rules, using the power of law and the pressure of public influence.

The state also needs to organize the country's defense and protect its interests in the international arena. Also, it must fulfill a number of important tasks resulting from our international duty to the proletarians of the whole world.

At the same time, in a society that has completed the building of socialism, class suppression is no longer a necessity. This fundamentally changes the character of state activities and the organizational forms of power. The dictatorship of the proletariat ceases to be necessary, and the state begins to turn into a political organization of the people as a whole, the all-people state.

This by no means implies that the working class is no longer the directing force of social development. As long as classes continue to exist, the workers, as the most progressive and conscious class, remain the shock detachment of communist construction, its main driving force.

The all-people state is not a rigid political organization, but rather a new, important stage on the road of development of socialist statehood into communist social self-government. The most important feature of this stage is the thorough practice and perfection of *socialist democracy*.

There are two means by which the toilers may be attracted to taking part in state affairs: *representative democracy and direct democracy*.

Participation in the administration is either direct or through representatives.

All citizens, therefore, elect to the Soviets individuals who have the most authority and general respect because of their personal labor, organizational ability, and sensitivity. The deputies, as representatives of the people, decide on behalf of the people state affairs of all importance, large or small.

Moreover, millions of citizens take direct part in matters of state; for example, at the general meetings of collectives in industrial enterprises, *kolkhozes*, and other institutions, where the most significant production problems are discussed and decisions are taken in common.

Direct and representative types of democracy are indissolubly combined within social organizations. These organizations are directed by Party bureaus, labor-union and *Komsomol* committees, and other elective organs. Nevertheless, the most important questions are discussed by general meetings, where decisions are adopted by voice vote.

Precisely the same situation occurs in people's participation organs: tenant committees attached to housing boards, parents' committees at schools, comrade courts, many versions of people's councils and commissions, of which there are hundreds of thousands in our country. They all operate in close contact with representative governmental organs and with the Soviets, under the leadership of Party organizations.

From the State to Communist Social Self-government

One of the most important predictions of the Marxist-Leninist scientific theory is that under communism the state will wither away, yielding place to social self-goverment. The state emerged by necessity under definite historical conditions. With the same inevitability it must disappear in the future from the arena of social life.

The withering away of the state is not an instantaneous act or a sudden explosion, but rather a protracted and gradual process. "For the total withering away of the state," V.I. Lenin pointed out, "total communism is necessary."

The conditions, the prerequisites, for the withering away of the state are being created during the construction of communism. These are, first of all, economic prerequisites. Among them is attainment of a level of development of productive forces that will satisfy fully and without fail the people's growing material and spiritual needs, with the result that control of labor and distribution norms will become unnecessary.

Indispensable social prerequisites for the state's withering away also exist. What is important in this area is elimination of all traces of class division and class distinction, elimination of distinctions between town and countryside and between intellectual and manual labor. Only then will human relations within society lose their political character.

Finally, there are ideological prerequisites: a high level of consciousness and of culture on the part of society's members, the overcoming in men's minds and everyday life of capitalism's vestiges, the complete victory of communist morality.

These are the chief internal prerequisites for the state's withering away. However, without specific external conditions, the state cannot wither away. These are the total and final victory of socialism in the international arena and the elimination of any danger of armed attack on the part of imperialism.

The withering away of the state and emergence of communist social self-government should not be considered two separate and independent processes. In fact, it would be most unreasonable to ignore the great experience accumulated by the socialist state, those forms and methods of managing society's affairs that have proven themselves with time and may be successfully used under communism. The problem is not merely one of common sense. Objectively, one cannot imagine a course of events in which the state first withers away and then, on the "cleared" space, construction of a system of social self-government begins. This is an indivisible process, the *process of development of socialist statehood into communist social self-government.*

Will there be authority of any kind in communist society?

The kind of public power personified by a special stratum of persons employed exclusively in administration will not exist under communism. But whatever the form of social organization, it will always require some authority and, as a result, some subordination. Without reasonable centralization and leadership, a complex and perfect economic organism such as the communist production system simply cannot operate. Therefore, authority will exist under communism, but it will be devoid of political character and based on self-discipline at work and in everyday community life.

The withering away of the state as a "coercive apparatus" and disappearance of law as the sum total of rules of conduct enforced by state power by no means signify that rules of conduct will not exist under communist society. Organized human society calls for norms and rules for everyday community life, mandatory for all its members. Observance of generally accepted standards will become a need and habit for people living in communist society.

Of course, even under communism individual excesses like present-day violations of law may occur. One cannot rule out cases of serious misbehavior, cases of delinquency caused by lack of concern in daily life. The speedy reaction of neighbors, however, confident that their actions will be immediately supported by the entire collective, will be sufficient to suppress excesses by individuals.

Administrative functions now discharged by state organs—management of economy and culture, bringing up and educating the young generation, organization of labor and consumption—will not disappear under communism but will be transformed in conformity with society's development. Society's affairs will be administered by a specific social mechanism, without the state apparatus—a system of social self-government. And although this mechanism will be devoid of political character, it will prove stronger than that of any state by virtue of its enormous moral authority.

The withering away of the state is a complex social process. It is perfectly clear that when it is installed, the system of communist self-government will not immediately reach the necessary organizational perfection. There are, therefore, good grounds for affirming that the Communist party will last for some time, even after the withering away of the state. When the Party will have ensured reliable, well-coordinated functioning of all the links of social self-government, its historic mission will be fulfilled and it will merge with the whole of society.

Review Questions

1. What is the significance for the construction of communism of increased labor productivity?
2. What are the chief trends of development in the scientific and technical revolution? What is this revolution's influence on creating the material-technical base of communism?
3. What are the chief means of creating the single communist ownership of the means of production?
4. What are the signs of the new interrelation between the socialist town and the socialist countryside?
5. How does society achieve the organic integration of intellectual and manual labor?
6. How is the process of development of socialist statehood into communist social self-government manifested?

Points to Consider and Discuss

1. What do you understand by "communist labor"? What will your personal contribution to the construction of communism be?
2. Show what social consumption funds provide by taking as an example your family and people you know.
3. Bourgeois sociologists are trying to prove that class distinctions within Soviet society are not fading away but that, on the contrary, stratification into isolated, unequal social groups is taking place, with new classes emerging. Petty-bourgeois ultrarevolutionaries, in their turn, consider imposters, thieves, speculators—criminal elements of every shade—a class. Give them your answer.
4. There is an argument between two persons. One maintains that professional art should be discontinued under communism, that abundant leisure will

provide everyone with the possibility of creating art masterpieces without abandoning his work in the production process; the second man's objection is that without concentration of all the spiritual powers on a single subject, nothing worthwhile can be created; that repudiation of professional art would lead to art's ruin. The debaters come to you and ask that you arbitrate.

5. Read and evaluate these books: *Utopia* by Thomas More and *The City of the Sun* by Tommaso Campanella. Which predictions of the utopians have proved correct? And where did the science and practice of communism set them straight?

7

Education of the New Man

Communist Man Is Being Born Today

Dispute About Man

Communism brings men abundance of material and spiritual goods and creates the conditions for happiness. Nevertheless, it also makes serious demands of men. We must earn these vital goods by our own labor. Equality will not be firmly established until man begins treating his fellow man as friend and brother. The man who is subject to religious prejudices cannot become truly free. No one who is spiritually poor, a stranger to the joy of knowledge, deaf and blind to the beauty of art, can become happy.

In other words, along with constructing communism, society must make ready for it: it must instill lofty qualities in its members and help them rid themselves of everything that tarnishes human dignity. And these matters are much more complicated than presented in certain utopian novels, which do not make clear where all the "ready-made" communists come from, nor where all those who do not meet communism's demands vanish. Of necessity, we must construct communism with the "human material" produced by history, and this material is not homogeneous. There is much in it that is good, but not a little is bad.

To shape the new men means refashioning their psychology, their attitude toward labor, society, family; means effecting a *revolution* (in the fullest sense) *in their consciousness and behavior.*

Is this objective at all possible?

The bourgeois sociologists and moralists say no. Man, they say, is by his very nature a vile creature. For two thousand years he has been taught: Do not kill, do not steal, do not deceive. And, as before, blood is still being shed in the world, pillage abounds, and brother betrays brother. To some degree, of course, men can adjust themselves to community living; they can be made to observe external decency. But one will never succeed in exterminating the beast in man and save him from his vices.

The Marxists say: Yes, man can be reeducated.

The bourgeois sociologists and moralists are wrong. Human vices will inevitably die out with the eradication of the social conditions that generate them. Private ownership and exploitation of man by man are the chief ones.

211

Private ownership divides society into a handful of the rich, who make extravagant use of all the good things in life, and the multimillion mass of toilers, who are robbed materially and spiritually, and deprived of the opportunity to develop and apply their own creative capacities. In the world of private business bourgeois individualism inevitably prevails, setting men against each other and asserting the laws of wolfish bourgeois morality: "Every man for himself"; "Rob others before they rob you"; "To the rich and powerful all things are permitted"; *"homo homini lupus."*

It is not only the objective conditions of social life in the capitalist world which produce the relationship of "war of all against all others" (as the English philosopher Hobbes characterized the exploiter society). Another contributing element is the whole bourgeois ideology glorifying the cult of the "strong individual" who know how to trample on the neck of his competitors and conquer power and wealth by brutality and deceit. This was expressed most openly and cynically in the fascist theories, which reflected the views of the reactionary imperialistic bourgeoisie. The ideological precursor of fascism, the German philosopher Nietzsche, proclaimed the advent of the era of the "superman" and the "blond beast" who would drown the world in blood and subject the entire human race to slavery.

The corrupt bourgeois morality is opposed by the revolutionary morality of the proletariat, which carefully preserves all the best ethical qualities cultivated by humanity on its historical path. And not only preserves them but defends them against the bourgeois ideology. This circumstance alone convincingly exposes the slander against human nature by the bourgeois ideologists. No, it is not nature that is responsible for human vices, but rather the system of capitalism that deforms actual human nature.

Of course, a revolution in consciousness is the most complex of all revolutions. But it will inevitably be a success in a society where the very conditions of life objectively promote an alteration in human psychology and the triumph of the new communist morality.

The dispute about man and his destiny has long ago progressed from theory to practice.

In the other part of the world, which was split in two in 1917, it is being persistently insinuated to the working man that he is a pygmy. In eager rivalry, church preachers, radio and TV commentators, and authors of philosophical treatises attempt to convince him that all life on earth is like a spore of mold on a cheese rind, and he himself just a dust particle holding out against the elements and a subservient executor of the will of "higher beings."

In contrast, at our socialist pole of the universe, the higher, communist concept of human nature is proclaimed. Man is not the slave of the elements; rather, he is the creator of his own happiness, and nature's ruler—not a grain of sand in the maelstrom of social storms but history's maker. He is capable of ridding himself of everything within himself that denies human dignity, and he does it independently, building the new world with his own hands.

Communist Education

Objective factors at the base of the complex process of creating the new man are: social ownership of the means of production, socialist democracy, and the sociopolitical unity of the entire people established under socialism.

The whole structure of our life is a training school for the new man. As children the Soviet people enter a world where everything is subordinate to the laws of comradeship, where there are no exploiters and exploited, where every person capable of work is obliged to work. The great power of collective labor leaves its imprint on our way of thinking and brings out the best moral qualities.

The fact that the economic and political system of socialism facilitates formation of a well-developed person does not at all mean that the revolution in consciousness is accomplished spontaneously. Society cannot entirely depend on objective factors, simply waiting for them to take effect. It strives to speed up the process of remolding consciousness by every ideological means. The school, literature, and art; the press, radio, TV, and other means of influencing men's minds and hearts tirelessly popularize the heroism of labor, the ideas of collectivism and humanism, instilling the traits befitting the communist man.

The combination of objective factors with ideological influence is a reliable guarantee that society will manage to solve the immense task of educating the new man. However, the length of time required depends to a considerable extent on a person's attitude. You must agree that it is not easy to teach reading to someone who does not want to be literate. It is difficult to instill good qualities into the person who refuses to admit his shortcomings. In brief, nothing speeds up and facilitates the training process more than a responsive, honest desire on the part of men to become purer and better, to *educate themselves.*

Therefore, communist education is our common affair.

But how are we to develop? Whom should be emulate? Should we, perhaps, look for the ideal communist man in the science-fiction novels of our writers? These novels are populated by persons who are fantastic, in the full sense of the word. But, in fact, it is not necessary to imitate mere literary heroes when there are living ones. The communist traits of consciousness are reflected in the thought and actions of the progressive-minded Soviet people, in their attitude towards labor, their capacity for wholehearted devotion to our great cause, their loyalty to principles, their honesty and other great moral qualities. They are the very best models to imitate.

What are the traits that can be called communist? What ought to be the essence of the new communist consciousness? First, and most important, the *scientific view of the world.*

The Scientific World-View

The Path to Spiritual Freedom

Imagine a person who has no world-view. How can he understand reality around him and find his place in life? Someone like this will have no ideals, clear aims, or convictions. Like a sea, life will toss him here and there, and he will not be able to understand events as they occur. He is a slave of circumstance.

It is clear, therefore, how absurd are the views of bourgeois philosophers who consider that the individual's spiritual freedom presupposes freedom from any ideology and any world-view.

Deeper insight into man's spiritual world gives us the conviction that actually there is no one who does not have some world outlook. Every person has views of the world and life's meaning, but these are by no means always scientific. And then man is a prisoner of false ideas, of religious or narrow-minded notions, for example.

The scientific world-view is the door to the world of spiritual freedom, inasmuch as it provides man with genuinely free choice of action. In everyone's life there are complex situations when it is necessary to make independent decisions. Without ideological training, without having learned how to judge events correctly, one may easily make a mistake, take a wrong—possibly irreversible—step. Communist consciousness helps one make correct decisions.

All of us have often observed and taken part in heated debates about human actions and views, and about events in domestic and international life. Various viewpoints are expressed. How is one to decide which are right and which wrong? How can one convince the others that they are mistaken, and prove his case? One should not forget that often he encounters backward views and attitudes reflecting an alien, bourgeois ideology. He must know how to identify hostile ideas and dispel them. This is a sign of a person's ideological maturity, which is inconceivable unless he has the scientific world outlook. This outlook makes us understand the course and development of world progress, helps us grasp the events inside our country and in the international arena, and permits us to build our lives consciously in the communist style.

What does mastery of the scientific world-view require? First, factual knowledge, which provides the material from which the scientific world-view is constructed. However, bits and pieces of knowledge are worth little if they are helter-skelter like single bricks. They must be thought through and organized into a system. The study of Marxism-Leninism and Party documents is helpful, but most important is the verification of theoretical knowledge by life experience, the application of this knowledge in practical action. Only in this way will knowledge be transformed into solid communist convictions.

In the prerevolutionary school classroom, learning by repetition was a favorite instruction method. We approach it differently: practical application is the mother of learning. To think, to "turn over in one's mind," to try to apply—in classroom assignments, thoughts, dreams, and later in practice—what we are working at, what we are studying, that is the goal for which to strive.

In his speech to the Third Congress of the *Komsomol*, Lenin pointed out that without effort, without struggle, the knowledge of communism acquired from pamphlets and articles is worth nothing. Only by working together with the workers and peasants can we become real communists. That is why the Communist party insists that in the conduct of each person communist ideas must be organically joined to communist deeds.

Social Duty: Socialist Patriotism and
Internationalism

The communist world-view and devotion to its tenets lie at the basis of a man's understanding of his duty to society and at the basis of patriotic and internationalist awareness.

Social duty is one's moral responsibility to his own society and people, his readiness to do everything for their good. "Duty," said F.E. Dzerzhinskiy, fearless knight of the revolution, "is not obligation but necessity, need, profound conviction, the meaning of life."

Social duty does not always coincide with personal plans and intentions; sometimes conflicts arise. And it is then that the extent of a man's communist awareness, his world outlook and fidelity to principles are revealed. The ability to subordinate what he desires to what he should do is the indication of a person's political and moral maturity. Thousands of Soviet people behaved this way when they abandoned a comfortable life in the cities and accepted a difficult existence, full of privations, in order to provide the country with grain from the virgin lands or make accessible to the people the wealth in the harsh northern regions.

The ideological qualities of *socialist patriotism and internationalism* are part and parcel with a clear understanding of social duty.

Patriotism is profound social sentiment, reinforced by centuries and millenia of the existence of separate native lands. By it we express our love for the country in which we were born and grew up, its history and people, of whom we feel ourselves to be inseparably part. Socialist patriotism is linked with selfless devotion to the progressive social order, to the communist cause; with a feeling of great pride in the Soviet people, who are forging a radiant future for the entire human race.

Patriotism is one of the finest features of human nature, urging men on to active deeds in the name of their own people. Poets and writers have often described how in the face of death a man returns in his thoughts to his native land, his own home with its weeping willow or birch tree. For Soviet citizens their fatherland is personified not only in cherished memories of nature in their native country. We find it also in recollections of Pioneer meetings, of our youth spent in the *Komsomol*, and in the unique atmosphere of comradeship characterizing the life of every Soviet collective. Native land and the socialist system blend together in the mind of the Soviet citizen.

Socialist patriotism is not blind sentiment. Utterly alien to communists is the "my country right or wrong" type of patriotism, the unbridled exaltation of everything in our country. That type of "patriot" is ready to boast even about his country's defects. He takes a scornful attitude toward everything "foreign."

Real love of one's country is love with eyes wide open.

We rightly pride ourselves on our marvelous achievements, but we boldly reveal our shortcomings and make every effort to eliminate them. We consider it no shame to take over the best of the accomplishments of other peoples and even, in certain matters, to learn from capitalists.

The distinctive feature of socialist patriotism is its intrinsic bond with internationalism, respect for other peoples and their national cultures and traditions. National egotism and chauvinism are alien to Soviet citizens. In their struggle for the victory of communism they are fulfilling their internationalist duty to the working class and the toilers of all countries. The internationalism of the Soviet people is expressed in the material, political, and moral support they lend to all peoples struggling for freedom and national independence. The member of socialist society is always ready to stretch out a hand of fraternal help to the representative of any nation.

The unity of socialist patriotism and internationalism is clearly seen now that socialism has become a world system. Fostered by the October Revolution, socialist patriotism has transcended the boundaries of a single fatherland; in our times it means loyalty not only to one's native land but to the entire community of socialist countries.

In communist society of the future, all the world's peoples will be a single friendly family. Patriotism and internationalism will then completely merge into one great sentiment: love for all mankind and for mankind's cradle, the planet Earth.

Marxist Atheism

To have a complete understanding of the communist world-view it is necessary to talk about Marxist atheism. "Atheism," literally, means godlessness. Atheism is the negation of god, of religion. To be an atheist does not mean simply to be an agnostic but, rather, someone who passionately and uncompromisingly struggles against all forms of religion, someone who does not swerve from the position of the scientific, materialist explanation of nature and society. Communism saves people from the drug of religion.

We have already discussed religion's roots, essence, and reactionary role in society's life. Now we must look into the problem of its withering away and how to overcome its vestiges. Unlike the men of the seventeenth- and eighteenth-century Enlightenment, who merely linked that problem with the propagation of knowledge, Marxism-Leninism has carried the struggle against religion onto the social ground, specifically, combining it with liquidation of the exploiter regime and change of the entire system of social relations.

The chief means of overcoming religious beliefs and consolidating the scientific world-view is the new socialist way of life, the creative effort of millions of toilers. One can keep repeating to a believer that there is no god, but it will hardly influence his religious conviction. Precisely by the practical activity of constructing communism is religious dogma revealed as completely groundless and man's ability to regulate his life without god's help, without any intervention by "divine providence," made clear.

By eliminating class antagonisms, socialism has undercut the principal social roots of religion's existence in our country. Socialism has guaranteed the toilers freedom of conscience, the right to practice any religion or to be an atheist and conduct atheistic propaganda. The decree of January 23, 1918 separated the church from the state, and the school from the church. This act brought an end to the church's privileges and to all violence against the consciences of citizens. His relationship with religion is the private domain of each citizen, the domain of his own conscience. All the same, no one in the Soviet Union has the right to avoid his obligations as citizen by pleading religious conviction. All Soviet citizens are equal before the law.

Socialism and contemporary science are driving religion out of every pore of social and cultural life. Today every schoolboy knows how the earth originated, how life emerged, and the brain functions. Man has boldly invaded the universe's space; his artificial satellites, space vehicles, and interplanetary stations are solving one after another of the "world's enigmas." Every new achievement by science demonstrates how powerful the human mind is. A proverb says, not without reason, "The friend of science does not need god."

Understandably, religion and the church do not surrender their position without resistance. In the past the ministers of the church conducted aggressive anti-Soviet activity, which placed them in direct opposition to the masses of believers who had wholeheartedly accepted the Soviet system. The church has been compelled to change its attitude toward the Soviet power and become more loyal. However, it would be incorrect to think that religion and the church have since become harmless. They are poisoning people's consciousness, endangering their spiritual and moral growth, interfering with their social activities. Under socialism religion represents a stronghold of ignorance and hampers the spiritual maturity of society.

Certain sects[a] are characterized by crude fanaticism. They practice rites that not infrequently result in psychiatric disorders or premature death.

Religion implants the ideology of slavish submissiveness, corrupting the will and consciousness of believers. Communism asserts the joy of life on earth. It steels the will.

During the many centuries of its existence, the church accumulated great experience in luring people into its nets. Furthermore, members of churches and religious sects show particular interest in lonely persons, those who suffer some misfortune in life or experience a great loss. These persons are in need of compassion, and if they do not find it within their collective or society, they not infrequently are attracted by the church. One should always remember this.

Religion is attempting to adjust to the new phenomena of contemporary social life. The church eagerly makes advances towards communism, saying that all that is "wholesome" and "just" in communist principles supposedly has its origin in religion. But in fact, communism and religion are irreconcilably antagonistic. The communist society of the future shall succeed in vanquishing religious prejudice and shall place religion and the church in storage in museums for antiques. When they visit these museums, people will marvel at how fantastically deformed were the minds of believers in their understanding of natural phenomena and social relations.

Communism, Not god, Upholds Moral Ideas

In constructing communism we are carrying on a stubborn struggle to uphold the moral ideals of the new—the communist—society, of justice and humanism. And what does religion teach? What kind of morality does it preach?

Religion is quite willing to ascribe to itself all the sound rules of community life, traditions, and habits. In fact, however, this is not so. For example, let us take the best-known religious moral commandments: "Thou shall not kill"; "Thou shall not steal"; "Honor thy father and mother"; and the like. Are they of divine origin? Not at all. These norms have been borrowed by the church from the practical life of society and elevated to the dignity of the divine. These commandments, moreover, are not the essence of religious morality.

If the verbal shell is thrown away, the essence of religious sermons becomes clear: man ought to be concerned exclusively with preparation for the eternal life beyond the grave; he must ignore earthly interests and goods.

Religious consciousness and morality perpetuate lack of culture, ignorance,

[a]A sect is a religious group that split from the original church (Orthodox, Catholic, Protestant) and the Moslem and other faiths. Recently, various sects of Western origin—Baptists, Adventists, Pentecostals, and others—have become active. Activities of religious groups whose teaching and ritual infringe upon citizens' rights or jeopardize their health are incompatible with Soviet laws concerning religious denominations.

hypocrisy, and bigotry. Long ago Calvin expressed the church's motto in these words: "Believer's ignorance is better than philosopher's insolence."

Let us turn to the religious holidays. As is well known, they are connected not only with mystical rites but also with drinking, fights, and infringements of work discipline. And what about religion's attitude toward labor? Because it considers labor to be a punishment from god, religion denigrates man's work, depriving it of joy and beauty. It is no accident, therefore, that the ranks of the clergy are often replenished from parasitic elements, spongers, and morally unscrupulous persons.

Let Us Declare Decisive War on the Vestiges of Religion

Religious superstitions, as we can see, are gradually being overcome. However, we must not wait until they vanish spontaneously from our lives. A decisive struggle against them must be carried on, not by administrative measures, but instead by scientific and atheistic education. Why do we emphasize education? Because the chief reasons for the existence of religion in our country are no longer social in character but predominantly ideological, moral, and psychological. Therefore, the struggle against religion is a struggle against religious ideology and morality, but in no case is it directed against believers themselves, whom we should assist in formulating the scientific world-view, the communist mode of action and morality.

As for communists and *Komsomol* members, religion is not their private affair. The Party and the *Komsomol* demand that their members struggle against religious consciousness and morality. Every communist and *Komsomol* member has the *duty* to expose stupefaction caused by religion and to propagate scientific atheism.

There are different forms and means of atheistic propaganda: evening discussions, lectures, concerts on the theme of atheism, new nonreligious holidays, as well as conversion work with individual believers. Schoolboys and schoolgirls can actively participate, since the knowledge of biology and physics, mathematics and astronomy, history and social science acquired in school can be put to good use here. It is also helpful to organize clubs of atheists, to talk or read books with believers and expose religious "miracles."

Religious rantings most often take place in the family circle, where society's cleansing power does not reach. It is precisely from there, the family and daily life, that religious superstitions must be driven out.

The actions of a young Leningrad worker and *Komsomol* member, Robert Malozemov, are instructive. His mother and father belong to a religious sect. They were forcing Robert and his brothers and sisters to practice religious rites and depriving them of going to motion pictures and theaters. Workers and communists in the Soviet army helped Robert to break with religion. He could have simply left his parents, but his brothers and sisters would have been abandoned. Therefore, Robert managed to obtain the guardianship of his six brothers and sisters, and he was assisted in this by his factory collective, *Komsomol*, and labor-union organizations. He was also supported by the "*Komsomol'skaya Pravda.*" The children were snatched from the grip of the religious sectarians.

The decisive struggle against religion is the struggle for man's soul and sentiments, for his communist education.

The New Man Is Being Tempered by Labor

The School of Labor

The poetry of work! What an extraordinary surge of energy, what joy you experience when you have worked well and accomplished something useful! As if the sun were shining more brightly and the world around you were smiling! As if your heart were expanding from an abundance of good and wholesome feelings!

The poet V. Ya. Bryusov wrote:

> *A great joy is in your work*
> *In the fields, at the lathe, at your desk.*
> *Toil 'til you're dripping with sweat,*
> *And without clock-watching.*
> *All earthly happiness is in labor.*

Work is the source of courage and spiritual elation for man. Such qualities as independence, initiative, keenness, efficiency, and strength of character are instilled in him by labor.

K.D. Ushinskiy, a Russian educator, speaking about the importance of labor for man, said:

Without personal labor a man cannot advance or even hold his own; he must retreat. Man's body, heart, and mind require work; and this requirement is so insistent that if for any reason at all a man does not work for a livelihood, he misses the right path. Two other paths are open to him, both equally fatal: either constant dissatisfaction with life, gloomy apathy, and bottomless boredom; or the path of deliberate, slow self-destruction, leading to infantile vices or brutish pleasures. Both result in the death of a person while he is still alive, because work—personal, free work— is life itself.

Exploitation kills joy in work. In the inhuman system of a capitalist enterprise man turns into an appendage of the machine. The fruits of his labor are appropriated by the capitalist, with labor becoming a heavy burden for the worker, which he must carry on his back in order to earn a livelihood. But even this work is by no means available to all. Millions of sound, physically strong persons are deprived of the elementary human right to work. And despite all this, working people are noted even under capitalism for their high moral standards. Concerning the workers' moral traits, Karl Marx wrote, "Human nobility radiates upon us from their toilworn faces."

Socialism liberates labor from the shackles of exploitation. Before our eyes free labor turns into creative labor. Technological progress facilitates this enormously. Take the job a steelmaker has in a metallurgical plant: modern equipment requires a great deal of knowledge on his part. And the work of the automatic lathe operator? It used to be said of a master worker that he had "golden hands." Nowadays this is not enough—he needs a "golden head" as well.

The wise power of a builder is hidden in every person, and . . . it must be allowed to develop and mature in order to enrich the earth with even greater miracles.

M. Gorky

But this does not mean that we must wait until technology has changed labor's character everywhere, converting it entirely into creativity. After all, any work can be made interesting and creative if one has a conscientious attitude towards it. This means that the worker must pour all his skill into the job and perform his work as best he can. Also, he can always use his intelligence to devise some sort of improvement, thus increasing labor productivity. With this approach, the most "ordinary" occupation can become absorbing.

The strong desire to put a living idea into what one is doing stimulates the toiler's innate ability and talent, raising them to a higher level, as it were. A conscientious attitude toward labor and fascination with a task make it possible for workers in the most commonplace occupations to show and develop their personal gifts.

Creativity brings happiness and delight to work and gives man deep satisfaction with his personal activity, enriching his interior world. Ultimately, this work becomes life's primary need.

New relations between men are formed in collective labor: friendship, mutual assistance, and comradely collaboration are strengthened; conforming one's own actions to the requirements and opinions of the collective becomes a habit. The conviction that others need his work aids the person in overcoming difficulties, and gives him increased strength. Take a look at creative persons. Their lives, permeated with their quest for the new, are always interesting; every day broad horizons open to them. These are truly happy people; they already live for tomorrow.

For Soviet citizens work is a matter of honor, the chief content of their lives, which is why the progressive Soviet people angrily condemn those who do not care about their work or even shirk it altogether.

The spiritual world of a slacker or a parasite is narrow and worthless; his interests and desires, petty. Such a person is a moral cripple, deprived of the chief joy in life. He robs not only society but, first of all, himself.

A Generation's Heroic Exploits

We are proud of the achievements of the generation of Vasiliy Chapayev and Sergey Lazo, Nicholas Ostrovskiy and Arkadiy Gardan, Oleg Koshevoy and Zoya Kosmodem'yanskaya. Some young men and women envy them but feel that the days of heroic struggle are a thing of the past. But there is always room for heroic deeds in life. All it requires is the correct understanding of the tasks of one's times and the boldness to tackle their solution.

Our daily life abounds with heroic exploits: a young geologist sacrificing his life to save the map of an ore deposit just discovered; an army engineer risking his own safety to deactivate a German underground ammunition depot threatening the security of an entire town; the locomotive driver who uncouples burning cars from his train despite danger to his own existence. . . .

Our brave falcons who blazed the trail into cosmic space for mankind brilliantly embodied the traits of heroism and Soviet patriotism. The pioneers who opened outer space and approached the stars have become the incarnation of the bravery, beauty, moral power, and spiritual wealth of the Soviet man.

Yuriy Gagarin, one of the most famous heroes of our time, will always be a shining example for humanity. Son of the Land of the Soviets and of the Party of the Communists, he had the honor of being the first to throw open to man the gates to cosmic space. This happened on April 12, 1961.

Yuriy Alekeseyevich Gagarin's life was like that of thousands upon thousands of Soviet men. He was born into the family of a Smolensk *kolkhoz* member on March 9, 1934; he graduated with honors from a trade school in the town of Lyubertsy, Moscow Province; and he studied at the Saratov technical-industrial school. Love for aviation led him to join an amateur pilot club and then to the Chkalov Air Force Pilot School.

As a talented and fearless fighter-pilot, Yu. A. Gagarin was one of the first to be included in the astronaut group. Here his outstanding qualities were most clearly shown. With persistence and energy he would solve complicated problems connected with space and space engineering; he spent much of his time and energy teaching and training astronaut crews. He was warmly loved as a person of great charm and modesty. Millions will remember Gagarin's kind smile. On March 27, 1968, his short and famous life came to an abrupt end when he perished during a training flight.

Socialism has greatly expanded the possibilities for heroism, and its doors are wide open in the main area of human life, work. "There is no heroism in the world more majestic than the heroism of labor, of creativity," said A.M. Gorky.

Once you have grasped the deeper meaning of your work, understood its social significance, and come to feel yourself to be a true fighting man, the inner readiness for heroic deeds will emerge. Then you will sense the heroic in the most ordinary profession or occupation. Then you will have enough courage to struggle for justice and truth always and everywhere, to measure your personal life not in terms of petty satisfaction but in terms of joy from the good you have done for your motherland, without even counting on being lifted up to the status of a hero. The communist attitude toward work reflects ideological maturity and conviction, great honesty, and citizenlike understanding of one's duty toward the motherland.

Thousands of heroes have matured in the front line of the struggle for communism: the fitter-mechanic Victor Yermilov, the miner Nicholas Mamay, the tractor operator Alexander Gitalov, the cutter Constantine Masliy, the turning-lathe operator Clara Kucherova, the mechanization specialist Tursunoy Akhunova, the woman *kolkhoz* member Stepanida Vishtak, and others.

A little over a quarter of a century has passed since the creation of a distinctive honorary title for the highest achievements in the fields of economic and cultural construction, the title of Hero of Socialist Labor. There are now over thirteen thousand Heroes of Socialist Labor in the USSR. Among them are workers in industry, agriculture, transportation, communications; builders, scientists, physicians, and teachers.

For exceptional service to the motherland, more than sixty-five Heroes of Socialist Labor have been awarded the golden medal of Sickle and Hammer for the second and third time. They include: M.V. Keldysh, President of the USSR Academy of Sciences; I.I. Brid'ko, a miner; S.P. Korolev, designer of spaceships; A.N. Tupolev, aircraft designer; A.A. Ulesov, builder; Basti Masymkyzy Bagirova, a woman *kolkhoz* member; and others.

The stronger an individual's drive to selfless labor, the richer and more beautiful he becomes. Those who have taught themselves a conscientious attitude toward labor are called pioneers of the future. In the process of performing their heroic deeds, they acquire through their labor the invaluable moral qualities of the new man. That is why forming a conscientious attitude toward work is *paramount in communist education.*

Collectivism and Humanism

All for One and One for All

Our world is a world of collectivism. From our youth we live in a collective, gratefully accept its assistance, and give it in return our own knowledge and experience. A man feels much more secure if he is a full-fledged, respected member of a collective. People take deeply to heart any disagreement with their collective.

A sociable man is often called a collectivist. And this is true, if under sociability one understands not simply politeness or benevolence toward comrades but a deep-seated interest in the collective's affairs and a feeling of personal responsibility for its success and failure. Learning to live in a collective means becoming part of it and remaining always, in every way, loyal to collectivism's basic rule: *all for one and one for all.* By observing this rule it is possible to harmonize personal and community interests.

A Soviet man's personal interests differ radically from the private property ambitions promoted by capitalism. Under socialism, material and cultural needs of an individual toiler are considered his personal interests. They develop under the influence of socialist society and are satisfied according to the degree of the success of production. Thus, the chief personal interests coincide with that of the community, i.e., construction of a new society.

Contradictions do occasionally arise between personal and social interests. For example, the need to express criticism of another person clashes with doubts as to whether that person would not feel insulted. Is it necessary to state that we must at all times, in all matters, give preference to the interests of the collective?

Strong will does not mean only to desire something and succeed in getting it, but also to be able forcibly to deny oneself something needed. Will is not simply a desire and its satisfaction, but also a desire and its rejection and renunciation.

A.S. Makarenko

Essentially, this is a simple requirement of discipline.

But a higher form of discipline exists: the individual's creative activity, his drive to do everything to enable the collective to solve successfully the tasks facing it. This creative activity is an adornment of the collective and its members, expressing not simply the subordination of personal to social interests, but their natural blending.

A shining example of deep understanding of personal responsibility for the affairs of the collective is the noble action of Valentina Gaganova. In transferring to a lagging work brigade, she gave up a guaranteed high wage and the companionship of those with whom, in her own words, "working was like singing a song." Her new associates, having lost confidence in their ability, received her with mistrust, but Gaganova, being an experienced spinner, helped them onto their feet so that they advanced to the rank of a leading work brigade. Without suspecting it, Valentina Gaganova thus began a new page in the history of our collectivism.

The collective has much to offer its individual member, and it also has the right to demand much of him. Whoever violates the principles of collectivism, whoever embarrasses or dishonors his comrades, deserves severe condemnation. "Don't whitewash mistakes, don't tolerate defects, but conscientiously bring them into the open": this is an important rule, without which no healthy collective can exist.

Criticism, even if just, is not easy to take. But there is nothing more disgusting than a person who is stubborn in his error. And anyone who desires to be respected by others must possess the highly valuable, necessary qualities of being able to listen attentively to his comrades' comments, suppress his false pride, and attempt to correct his mistakes. Self-criticism bespeaks not only a man's honesty but his *modesty* as well. I.P. Pavlov wrote, in addressing the young:

Never think you already know everything. And no matter how highly you are praised, always have the courage to say, I am ignorant. Don't let conceit get hold of you. It will make you stubbornly resist when you ought to agree. It will make you refuse useful advice and friendly help and lose the necessary degree of objectivity.

Collective labor has become a powerful means of educating the new man. It is no accident that Soviet citizens are progressing towards communist labor, as a rule, in collectives: teams, brigades, sections, shops, and enterprises. Life experience has refuted the assertion of bourgeois ideologists that collectivism standardizes the person and leads to loss of personality. The more ties with the collective the individual has, the richer and more beautiful is his spiritual world, and the more fully and clearly is his individuality revealed.

Man – the Friend, Comrade, and Brother of Man

Being a collectivist also means loving people, wishing them well. As moral qualities, collectivism and humanism are twins. "A man should love people," said M.I. Kalinin, "and if he does, then he will live better and more happily, for nothing is as miserable as the life of a misanthrope."

The profound humanity of Soviet citizens is evident. Someone gives up his place on the waiting list for an apartment and lets his comrade have it; a young girl, a *Komsomol* member, risks her life to snatch a child from under the wheels of a train; a volunteer policeman takes a blow meant for another from a hooligan.

Humane actions are important not merely from the point of view of their concrete results. The person who experiences attention and concern has his faith in people strengthened and his belief in the justice of our collectivist system reinforced. He, in turn, will try to help others. Humane behavior thus produces a "chain reaction" of a kind.

No rules can be established as criteria of tactfulness and concern for human beings. It is necessary simply to bear in mind that a person's dignity must always be respected. This is the essential requirement of humanism.

History shows many examples of great nobility and humanity in personal relations. But humanism was practically excluded from relations between the individual person and official society.

Under socialism the principle of "man the friend, comrade, and brother of man" is becoming a moral principle for the whole of society. Socialist humanism is vividly reflected in the state's care for the well-being of every individual person and for his all-around development, and in the individual's concern for the prosperity of the motherland as well as for his comrades.

Our humanism demands that every individual be a knight, in the highest sense: courteous and sensitive, considerate and obliging to others. If you see a weak person being abused, you are obliged to defend him; it is your duty to surround your parents with love and attention, to respect your elders for the good things of life, the knowledge and experience received from them; it is your duty to help the young grow up into strong, honest adults. All these are elementary requirements of our communal living. But they may acquire profound significance if you discharge your duty not merely as an obligation but lovingly and cordially.

To love people means also to expect much of them and to help them rid themselves of their personal shortcomings, of everything debasing. Is real friendship conceivable without frankness? No. Falsehood and hypocrisy are inevitable in a relationship based on mutual "forgiveness of sins" and on "reticence."

Our socialist humanism has nothing in common with the universal "love in Christ" hypocritically preached by bourgeois ethics. Love for human beings by its very nature compels us to hate with our soul's strength those who condemn the toilers to cruel exploitation, oppress peoples, and threaten mankind with the horrors of war. We reject the good-for-nothing theory of "nonresistance to evil" and are ready to fight evil with the one and only weapon it recognizes—force.

War on the Vestiges of the Past!

Our society enjoys good health, and the maladies inherent in capitalism are alien to it. In the USSR no social grounds exist for the nurturing of individualism, money-grubbing, parasitism, and other symptoms of bourgeois morality. However, traces of these diseases still do exist in the form of vestiges of the past, and they are doing considerable harm to the cause of communist construction.

The Most Malicious Vestiges of All

About three-quarters of the population in the USSR were born and brought up under the Soviet regime. How, then, can vestiges of the past affect the middle-aged and youth who never lived under capitalism?

We know that the development of man's consciousness lags somewhat behind social existence. Hence, the vestiges of the past are preserved for a long time after the disappearance of economic conditions that caused them. Such "birth-marks" of the past, having acquired the force of habit and tradition, hold fast, as it were, in the new life. They are passed from person to person, securing a strong hold on the new society. Nor should one forget that the old notions, ideas, and customs are supported by bourgeois influence from abroad.

Also, antisocial phenomena are tied in with scarcities that we still experience in day-to-day life.

Take, for example, the type of parasitism that black-marketeering is. It can occur only as long as we do not have sufficient supplies of certain commodities. The closer we approach abundance, the less chance there is for profiteering. This does not mean, of course, that we ought, meanwhile, to tolerate the black-market parasites who are living off other people's labor.

Another most repulsive product of the former world is Philistinism. Its essence is total lack of any ideology, indifference to everything but one's own ego.

The interests of a collective and of society are of no concern to the Philistine. He is interested only in obtaining worldly goods from his labor. He will permit any squandering, provided he cannot be made directly responsible for it. The Philistine will not sacrifice even one hair of his head in order to prevent injustice or render unselfish assistance to anyone.

Our society has put an end to many manifestations of Philistinism. But a stubborn struggle with the greedy, resourceful, and narrow-minded Philistine hiding behind many faces still lies ahead.

The Public Opinion Institute of the *Komsomol'skaya Pravda* made a survey of our country's young men and women on the topic, "What do you think about your own generation?" Among other questions there was one about purpose in life. Thousands of letters described personal fascination with work, a restless but happy life. "My whole life is a constant striving towards one objective: to become a good person. I wish that my own life would bring more warmth, light, and well-being into the lives of the largest possible number of individuals. I would like to become, if I may say so, a little sun for other people," wrote Natasha, a proofreader from Lyubertsy.

And here are dreams of another kind—Philistine dreams—of a young girl from the Primorskiy Kray. She sees her purpose in life as "getting married, living in security and having fun, not in working. After all, even horses die from work." It is hard to find words to express one's revulsion at such vile thoughts.

When Philistinism, which in the final analysis is the private-ownership instinct, appears in this overt form, it is easier to fight. Unfortunately, Philistine traits sometimes penetrate into the minds of otherwise decent persons. Can every one of you say, sincerely, that his conscience is clear, that he has never forsaken justice to satisfy his own ease and comfort? You see something wrong where you work, and you keep quiet about it: that is Philistinism. You see a hooligan insulting a woman, and you walk past: that is Philistinism. You notice that the machinery in a *kolkhoz* is rusting outdoors, and you ignore it: that is Philistinism. Philistine indifference is responsible to an enormous extent for the tenacity of such vestiges of the old world as red tape, venality, careerism, and groveling. These can only survive where they are tolerated instead of opposed.

A hooligan is the Philistine's relative, too. M. Gorky called a hooligan a creature deprived of any social sentiment. That is why, he said, a hooligan does not admit that anything of value exists around him and even loses awareness of his own life's value.

Drunkenness does tremendous harm to society. The abuse of alcohol is one of the main causes of hooliganism and thievery. Statistics show that most criminal acts are perpetrated by persons in a state of intoxication. Also, natural consequences of alcoholism are serious and protracted illness, loss of professional skills, and censure by society. By his conduct a drunkard sows dissension in his family and disturbs peaceful labor and the tranquility of others.

Overcoming the Vestiges of the Past

Communism is incompatible with the vestiges of the past. But these "birth-marks" from the former life can be removed only by the combined efforts of the entire people. Vladimir Il'ich Lenin wrote:

Only the voluntary and conscientious collaboration of the *masses* of workers and peasants imbued with revolutionary enthusiasm can expose and control *cheaters, parasites, and hooligans,* and thus conquer these vestiges of the accursed capitalist society, these dregs of mankind, these hopelessly rotten and dead limbs, this infection, plague, and ulcer inherited by socialism from capitalism.

The essential conditions for the eradication of these vestiges of the past are being created by the achievements of communist construction. But, at the same time, a persistent educational effort to reach every individual is needed: it is the collective's business to help those burdened with the vestiges of the past to rid themselves of the burden. In certain cases friendly advice is necessary or even a warning or sharp comradely criticism. As for vicious parasites, criminals, hooligans, members of fanatic religious sects, and other elements dangerous to society—they will be severely punished.

Social organizations have a leading role in the struggle against the vestiges of capitalism. At their disposal are such powerful weapons as public opinion and persuasion in order to prevent amoral acts and reform certain persons.

A good example of personal and social life is the best means of persuasion. If a man lives and works according to communist moral principles, he will not ignore amoral actions; he will come out against those who have lost their honor and conscience, resist the hooligan, call to account the person living beyond his means, and expose the lawlessness and willfulness of the bureaucrat and the careerist.

The amoral man is most often a coward. He fears publicity and exposure, since he functions on the principle of Molière's Tartuffe: "He who sins quietly does not sin at all." When honest men act boldly and persistently in accordance with principle, falsehood always retreats.

For practical training, some ninth-grade girls were assigned to a store where instances of shortweight occurred. The schoolgirls began blaming the saleswomen. But apparently cheating the customers had become a habit there. To protect the personnel against the just charges, the manager of the store accused the girls of unwillingness to work. At first, neither the girls' school nor the local Department of Public Education helped them. But the girls did not give in, and an inspection commission was sent to the store. The irregularities were discovered and the culprits punished.

In brief, the time required to eradicate the vestiges of the past depends directly upon the degree of our impatience with evil.

Communist Morality and Way of Life

Way of Life Is Not a Private Affair

The area of moral relations is very broad: it covers the individual person's working and social life as well as his everyday family and personal life. Everyday life is the social environment in which an individual exists when he is not working or involved in social activites, when he is, so to speak, on his own. The question arises as to whether a person's everyday life is not his private affair. No, it is not. It is bound up closely with his social life, is part of it, as it were. Everyone realizes that it is in a man's everyday life that many of his character features are formed, and that his disposition and his working ability depend on his day-to-day comforts. All this considerably affects his moral outlook, his attitude to labor and to the collective.

Everyday life is determined by the nature of the social system. Socialism has destroyed the bases of the old ways: taverns and slums, tapers for illumination and churches, card games and ignorance have been replaced by clubs, theaters, universities for culture, comfortable apartments, books, electricity, and television. The expansion of the nursery and kindergarten network, increased communal meal facilities, improved repair and other services—including public health—all these taken together are definitely changing everyday life for the Soviet people.

But it is a mistake to think that the communist way of life will establish itself automatically, in correspondence with the creation of appropriate material conditions. Its victory depends on the persons themselves, the growth of their cultural level, and their adoption of communist moral principles.

It is hardly enough to erect beautiful new buildings for housing and beautiful city blocks; one must learn how to live a new, fine life in them. And to do this we must show affectionate interest in improving and planting greenery in every street and courtyard; we must see to it that the dining halls, stores, and shops for everyday services really satisfy the needs of the population; we must voluntarily observe the rules of socialist communal living.

As we organize our daily lives, we learn to make appropriate use of leisure time, which is constantly increasing. A considerable amount of it now goes to reading and supplementing our skills and knowledge; to communal activities, art, and sports. But many persons are no longer satisfied with the role of spectator, reader, or listener; they themselves are learning how to handle an artist's brush, trying their hand at literature, taking part in theatricals and competitive sport.

All this proves that the new, the communist, element is penetrating our way of life more and more powerfully.

The Family and Marriage

The family, a social unit based on kinship relations, plays an enormous role in man's life. The family is intimately connected with the economic and social order. In miniature, it reproduces the basic characteristics of the existing order.

Socialism removes the fetters of private ownership relations from the family. Money considerations yield place to natural human feelings. Marriage based on financial calculations is considered monstrous in our society, an immoral phenomenon. The socialist revolution has liberated woman and given her equal rights with man.

Shoulder to shoulder with men, women actively take part in communist construction. The world of social affairs is open wide to them. As a result, the basis for any economic or intellectual dependence of wives upon their husbands has disappeared. As a consequence, the moral and ideological foundations of the family—love, friendship, mutual respect and frankness between the partners, community of views and interests, love of work, care of the children—have acquired all the greater importance. The Soviet citizen seeks in the family not profit but rather satisfaction of the moral need for love of and friendship with persons close to him.

Love occupies a great place in man's life. It is both a great joy and deep emotional experience, as well as a moral obligation. V.I. Lenin severely condemned the bourgeois concept of "free love," which justifies sexual promiscuity. Love is a great, radiant sentiment, demanding the whole man. Beware of turning it into small change.

The writer Lydia Obukohova has commented on this subject well:

When Lermontov says that he "loved with the full intensity of all spiritual powers," we should seriously reflect on the poet's words. The passing excitement or youthful yearning for now one, now another cannot be considered love yet, even though many ardent and pure experiences may be involved. "Absolute intensity of all spiritual powers," the moral and physical impossibility of living without the other person, is exactly what love is. And this sentiment does not come all at once; at first it needs testing. Do not be afraid that it will be smothered by excessive severity: the dearer the other person becomes (in the sense of the efforts we make for the sake of that person), the more inextricably entwined with our own being will that person become. But do not believe either that passion justifies all kinds of thoughtless actions: these come from inner lack of balance or even from sham.

No one can give a ready-made prescription for loving. It is a sentiment that is profoundly individual, always new and fresh, always uniquely expressed. Only one wish may be made: always retain integrity of feeling and human dignity under all circumstances, both the bitterest and the happiest. And avoid debasing yourself with petty, vulgar behavior. These are stains hard to wash off later.

It may be said, "It takes two to love. What is society's interest here?" Certainly, it would be vulgar and downright indecent to intrude into all the aspects of two lovers' intimacy, to check on their every step. No one requires that. But love is not a "personal matter" only. V.I. Lenin said, "It takes two to love, and a third life results. Here is where society's interest begins, and where the duty to the collective arises." The logical continuation of love, its development and deepening, is the family and the upbringing of children.

Contracting marriage is a very serious matter, requiring maturity and imposing various obligations to society. Sometimes young people marry too early, before they have fully realized what these obligations are or before they are able to fulfill them. Certain resources and conditions are necessary in order to support a family. Living with the financial support of parents is a kind of parasitism unworthy of a Soviet citizen. The family also places responsibilities on the marriage partners: food purchasing, meal preparation, dishwashing. And all of it takes up much time. When young people marry without taking all this into account, without having learned a trade and completed their studies, either they will seek a divorce, because the strain has been unbearable, or they must make unjustifiable sacrifices, such as giving up their studies and accepting jobs of no interest to them, and the like. That is the reason it is not advisable to rush into marriage, even if your partner is a real friend and your own feelings have been tested. It is better to wait until you are firmly on your feet and can say with certainty: "Yes, I will be able to fulfill all the duties married life brings with it."

There is an idea that under communism society will take entirely upon itself the upbringing of children, freeing the family of this obligation. It is true, of course, that communal upbringing of children is acquiring ever-increasing importance among us and in the future will be the main form of training and education. However, this does not mean that the family will no longer have any part in this important task. Everyone knows what a real role maternal affection has in a small child's life. It would be simply absurd to forego the powerful moral influence of parents on the formation of the child's mind and moral qualities.

Man Must Strive for Excellence in Every Way

The *all-around, harmonious development of a human being* presupposes the combination of spiritual wealth, moral integrity, and physical perfection.

Spiritual Wealth

In communist society the foundation of a man's spiritual wealth is the scientific world-view and a solid belief in ideology. Our ideological convictions are not blind faith, demanded by religion, nor are they the kind of fanaticism that requires unquestioning execution. The new man relies on a clear understanding of the laws of development of nature and society, uses them in his practical activity, and by his knowledge of these laws is convinced of the total victory of communism.

Another feature of our spiritual wealth is diversified knowledge. One should not imagine, of course, that every member of society will be able to master the whole range of knowledge and all the recent achievements of science, technology, and art. That is not the point. Polytechnical education will give the new man thorough knowledge of the fundamentals of science and production, helping him find his vocation quickly and become an outstanding specialist in any field.

Spiritual wealth is inconceivable without, also, knowledge of literature and art, without the ability to find and understand beauty, and to create it. This constitutes the essence of *aesthetic education.*

Unfortunately, one still encounters the opinion that only work in science and technology represents considerable importance, while literature and art are simply lyric. This is a mistaken notion. We know that the road to the stars for our space heroes led not only through complex mechanisms, laboratories, and mathematical calculations, but through favorite poetry, novels, and motion pictures, too. As they flew at incredible speed and hitherto unheard of altitude in their spaceships, Soviet men were admiring the earth's beauty and recalling lines of favorite poems and songs.

But why is it that magnificent works of art do not affect all persons to the same degree? Some are deeply moved when they look at an artist's painting; others pass by with scarcely an indifferent glance. The reason is not only that each person comes to an understanding of the beautiful in his own way. It also takes work to grasp beauty: to enjoy art one must be artistically educated and know at least the most important works of literature and art, and develop his personal sensitivity and imagination.

Aesthetic training not only enriches our spiritual world, it ennobles it. The deeper one penetrates into the world of beauty, the more strongly does he feel its effect; the purer and better he himself becomes.

Moral Integrity

The moral features of the new man are clearly defined in the CPSU Program's *moral code for the builders of communism:*

— devotion to the cause of communism, love of the socialist motherland and of socialist countries;
— conscientious labor for the good of society: he who does not work does not eat;
— concern on everyone's part for the preservation and growth of social wealth;
— high degree of awareness of social duty, intolerance of violations of society's interest;
— collectivism and comradely mutual assistance: one for all and all for one;
— kind relations and mutual respect among people: man is the friend, comrade, and brother of man;
— honesty and truthfulness, moral integrity, simplicity, and modesty in social and personal life;
— mutual respect in the family, concern in the upbringing of children;
— intolerance of injustice, parasitism, dishonesty, careerism, money-grubbing;
— friendship and brotherhood of all the peoples of the USSR, intolerance of national and racial enmity;
— implacability towards the enemies of communism, of the cause of peace and freedom of peoples;
— fraternal solidarity with the workers of all countries, with all peoples.

These moral principles embody not only the requirements of the revolutionary proletarian ethics and the best features of the progressive people of our society, but also the moral rules common to all mankind, worked out by the popular masses in the millenia of struggle against social oppression and moral vice.

And understandably, the moral code, as we see it, is not a sum total of principles that will have their impact in some undetermined future, but instead a kind of moral compass by which the Soviet people now measures its actions and deeds. It gives a correct answer to the question: What kind of person should one be? Its strength lies precisely in the fact that its norms are not pious hopes for the future but indispensable today for every builder of communism and living in all progressive persons and heroes of our times. The moral code helps the collective and each individual to decide whether various acts are upright and whether his own conduct as well as that of others is correct.

Physical Perfection

Man's spiritual and moral perfection is inextricably bound up with his harmonious physical development. Vladimir Il'ich Lenin was always reminding us of the necessity of combining study and research with various kinds of sports; of complementing one's various intellectual interests with the relaxation of calisthenics, swimming, excursions, and physical exercise.

We would like the external appearance of the person to correspond with the rich inner content of his mind and with his generous actions. This does not mean, obviously, that under communism everyone will be fabulously handsome. But everyone will be healthy, tough, and brave. Moreover, no matter how intellectually rich and morally pure a man's life may be, he is deprived of many joys unless he is well developed physically.

An important means of preserving and strengthening one's health is physical labor as well as physical training.

When one neglects physical exercise and does not lead a regular life and maintain a regular diet in his youth and middle age, the result will usually be premature infirmity. By about forty years of age, he will look flabby and complain of shortness of breath, tiredness, headaches. On the contrary, those who systematically take part in sports and observe an appropriate life regime excel by their great work capacity, energy, and joy of living.

Physical training exercises strengthen the health, prepare us for successful labor activity, and make us combat-ready in the event of the need to defend our country. The physically well-developed person is quicker at mastering his profession. The quality and productivity of his work will be higher than those of the person who shuns physical training and sports.

Irrespective of his specific responsibility within the system of automated production, in the final analysis a person must always deal with motor power. And irrespective of automation's progress, the personnel operating the automatic equipment must possess high-level physical and labor skills, requiring, first of all, broad understanding of information, endurance, and ability to solve control problems correctly, swiftly, calmly, without fuss. At the same time, the operator of automated equipment must be able to maintain his alertness during lulls, when he receives only a few signals, and monotonous ones at that. He must always be prepared for swift operational intervention. As we can see, it is not merely a matter of knowledge. Physical training and sports have no insignificant part in developing the skills required of workers operating complex automated devices.

Scientists-cyberneticists assert that pure physical labor never made such extensive and complex demands upon man's physical development as does contemporary, essentially intellectual work in an intricate, highly automated control system.

Sports not only help one acquire many qualities essential in life: courage, endurance, decisiveness, perseverance, and inventiveness. It also develops aesthetic taste, enabling the participant to acquire good bearing, grace, agility, dexterity, and precision of movements. Ski trips and hiking expeditions bring a deeper grasp of the sentiment of comradeship and stress the collective's importance. After a good rest in the fresh air, work and life are easier. Sensibly combined with other activities, sports are an important source of both physical and spiritual development for man.

For centuries communism was a far-off dream of the oppressed and disenfranchised. Now it is becoming reality. And people no longer need to look for Man, as old Diogenes did, lantern in hand in broad daylight. The new man is born, maturing, and reaching adulthood.

Review Questions

1. Why does the Party assign top priority to inculcating the scientific world-view into all members of our society?
2. What is self-education's part in forming the qualities of the new man?
3. Who do we call heroes of our time, and why?
4. Why are vestiges of the past harmful, and what are the ways to banish them from the life of our society?

Points to Consider and Discuss

1. Obtain information about persons who chose their vocations in their youth and followed them throughout their life span. Tell about them.
2. Organize a discussion on each of the following themes: What kind of person should a real friend be? How do you visualize the man of communist society? What is the meaning of our life?

8 The Party, Our Helmsman

The party of the Communists is the militant, experienced vanguard of the Soviet people, uniting the progressive, most aware members of the working class, the *kolkhoz* peasantry, and the intelligentsia on a voluntary basis.

The Communist Party of the Soviet Union was created by Vladimir Il'ich Lenin, who was present at the merger of Marxist groups into a single revolutionary organization, and formulated its structural principles, norms of internal life, and operational methods. Lenin, its recognized leader for a quarter of a century, formulated the Party's strategy and tactics in the critical stages of the struggle for socialism. He left the Party an invaluable treasure of ideas, which even today serves as its most effective weapon.

The Communist Party of the Soviet Union is rightly called the Party of Lenin. Mayakovskiy has a vivid and precise description for this: "The Party and Lenin are twin brothers."

The Party's Role in Soviet Society

Vanguard of the Soviet People

The character, organizational principles, and operational methods of political parties are determined by the interests of the classes and population strata they personify. The Communist Party of the Soviet Union originated on the threshold between the nineteenth and twentieth centuries, representing the interests of the Russian proletariat as its vanguard.

The history of the workers' movement includes many political trends and organizations acting in the name of the proletariat and pretending to express its interests. Some took revolutionary positions but could not succeed because they lacked a clear program of struggle. Others, applying anarchistic methods or means, degenerated into conspiratorial sects that lost touch with the working class. A third trend was under the influence of reformists and adopted the course of compromising with the bourgeoisie, limiting its goal to achieving petty reforms within the framework of the capitalist system.

The Communist party created by V.I. Lenin was successful in leading the Russian proletariat and in achieving the revolution precisely because, from the beginning, it expressed the *fundamental interests* of the working class and was guided in all its activity by the *scientific program of struggle* for the liberation of the toilers, i.e., Marxism-Leninism.

237

Like the proletariat, the toiling peasantry of Russia was vitally interested in liquidating capitalist conditions and in the socialist transformation of society. Objective identity of basic interests of both the proletariat and the peasantry was the precondition for the decisive influence of the Communist party in the countryside and the active support it obtained from the poor and middle peasants. By class origin and aims a party of workers, the CPSU led all the exploited classes of the country in an assault against capitalism.

Having received a mandate from the overwhelming majority of the population, the Party became the leading force in the system of the dictatorship of the proletariat after the October Revolution. The Party Program, with its plan for the construction of socialism prepared by V.I. Lenin, became the basis of the socialist state's entire policy. Party congresses reviewed development in the economy and culture and established future objectives, which acquired the force of directives for governmental and administrative organs, labor unions, the *Komsomol*, and other toilers' social organizations.

Practical application of the Program, however excellent it may be in theory, is the test of the activity of a political party. The half-century journey just completed by the Land of the Soviets under the Communist party leadership represents the great triumph of its Leninist general policy and ideas.

Our Party's history is rich in heroism and important events, and it is characterized not only by the joy of victories but the bitterness of defeat, by wise political decisions as well as serious miscalculations and errors. Nevertheless, this cannot minimize the importance of what has been achieved. A backward Russia in rope-soled shoes has given place to a powerful socialist country second in the world in volume of industrial output, pioneer of the trail into the cosmos, and stronghold of peace and beacon of progress for all humanity. This is the outcome of the struggle and labor of the entire Soviet people and, equally, of the Party's activity—the intelligence, energy, willpower, and self-sacrifice of millions of communists.

Every great revolution produces its heroes, spokesmen for the people, military leaders, and organizers like Spartacus, Muenzer, Marat, and Robespierre. The era of the October Revolution produced its outstanding figures, too, among whom were Lenin's companions in arms and disciples who became organizers and leaders in the first socialist state, men endowed with the most various gifts: remarkable organizers of the masses like Sverdlov and Kirov, talented military leaders like Frunze and Blyukher, brilliant writers like Lunarcharskiy and Ol'minskiy. All had certain characteristics in common: great devotion to the Party aims and ideology, unbending resolve, personal courage, and high principles that caused them to demand much of themselves. All possessed the qualities Dzerzhinskiy (The Knight of the Revolution) required of his Chekists [Employees of the notorious *Cheka* (Extraordinary Commission for Combating Counterrevolution and Sabotage), the first Soviet Secret Police, whose function is now assumed by the Committee for State Security (KGB)], which may generally be considered the indispensable characteristics of every genuine communist: "clean hands, cool intellect, and burning heart."

Not only did these qualities belong to outstanding Party members but they became the norm of morality for tens and hundreds of thousands of communists of all generations. During the period of the Civil War and foreign military intervention, in the time of struggle with hunger and chaos, in the harsh years of the Patriotic War [World War II], the communists always filled the most difficult places. Their slogan was "Communists, forward."

This is the biography of a communist. There are very many like him.

Kiril Orlovskiy entered the Party when he was twenty-three years old. His whole life is a model of service to the Party and the people. In 1918 he routed the German occupation forces at the head of a partisan group near Bobruysk. In the 1920s he fought the White Poles [anticommunist Poles]. In 1936 he fought in Spain. The year 1941 found him in the forests of Byelorussia. Years of struggle with fascist armies passed, including dozens of daring raids and battles. One of these ended tragically with heavy injury, amputation of an arm, complicated surgery on the other, and almost total loss of hearing.

"My physical defects do not allow me to continue military service," wrote Lt. Col. Orlovskiy to his Party organization. "However, I was educated by the Communist party and I know no greater happiness in life—or any other purpose—than to work for the good of my beloved motherland. I am now faced with a question of whether I have done all I could for the motherland and the Party." In 1945 he moved from Moscow to a Byelorussian village, Myshkovichi, which had been devastated by the fascists, and for more than twenty years he has headed the *kolkhoz* "Rassvet" [Dawn], one of the best *kolkhozes* in the country.

Hero of the Soviet Union and of Socialist Labor, K.P. Orlovskiy will always remain in popular memory as an efficient organizer of *kolkhoz* farming and as one always concerned about the rural workers' welfare.

To complete the construction of socialism has been the chief goal of the Party as leader and organizer, for which it has gained the solid confidence and support of the Soviet people. They have long regarded the Party as the political organization not only of the working class but also of the *kolkhoz* peasantry and of the working intelligentsia—of all strata of our society.

With the construction of socialism completed, neither classes nor social strata whose interests would be antagonistic to the workers' interests, as a result, remained in the country, and thus *the sociopolitical unity of the people* was established. Even in a society composed solely of laboring classes and social groups, multiple variations of interests connected with the specific production and life conditions of various groups of the toilers naturally continue to exist. However, these shades of different interests, these specific needs of different population strata, do not represent irreconcilable contradictions. On the contrary, they can best be accommodated and concerted within the framework of a single Party policy expressing the common interest of all the toilers.

Socialist society has thus made possible a phenomenon hitherto unknown in history: a political party as spokesman not of a single class but of an entire people.

But this is only one aspect of the problem. Conceivably, certain strata of the population are satisfied with the Party leadership as long as its policy protects their interest, but do not accept its whole program. Sooner or later, in this case, conflict is inevitable. Because the building of socialism has been completed, however, the *ideological unity of the Soviet people*, as well as its sociopolitical unity, has been established. The Party's ideology has thus become the ideology of the entire people: the communist goals and ideals of the working class, scientifically formulated in the Marxist-Leninist theory, have been embraced by the other social strata, by the whole of society, as their own aims and ideals.

There are fourteen million members and candidate-members in the Communist party ranks, more than half of whom are workers and *kolkhoz* peasants. Among communist professional workers the overwhelming majority is engineering and technical personnel, agricultural specialists, teachers, doctors, and others engaged in intellectual work. More than 70 percent of communists are employed in branches of industrial production. They work in plants, factories, on construction sites, in transportation, in *kolkhozes* and *sovkhozes*. One hundred thirty-one nationalities and ethnic groups are represented in the Party ranks. At present more than half of CPSU members and candidate-members are below the age of forty. Lenin, always proud that the youth was joining our Party, regarded it as proof of generation succession, of the Party's revolutionary spirit and fighting tradition.

Methods and Forms of Party Control

The CPSU is a ruling party, and it is confirmed in this role by the constitution of the Soviet state. How is the Party control realized? What are the forms and methods?

Among methods, the first is the *formulation of the basic principles of the socialist state's domestic and foreign policy*. Along with the Party's programmatic documents, which supply general directives for the policy of an entire historical period, Party congresses and Central Committee Plenums handle specific political tasks, setting the time and manner for their solution.

The Party's economic policy is part of the most important and significant area—since it is the largest in extent—of the Party's political activity: elaboration of directives on the country's economic development; determination of the most universal principles and methods of economy management, which must guarantee Soviet society's steady progress; and creation of the material-technical base of communism. The economic activity, V.I. Lenin said, represents the policy of the most interest for us. Accordingly, following Lenin's advice, problems of economic development are given the main attention of Party congresses, and most Central Committee Plenum sessions are taken up with them.

The second important area of Party control is its direct *organizational activity*, reflected in the mobilization of the toilers by Party organizations in order to put into effect the policy of the Party and the Soviet state. As a ruling party, the CPSU devotes great attention to selection and education of cadres. In recommending workers for responsible positions, Party organizations take into consideration the opinions of the toilers' collectives, labor unions, and other social organizations. A person's fitness for a job, his political qualifications, specialized knowledge, general culture, organizational ability, honesty and devotion to principles are weighed in the recommendation.

Verifying execution is an important part of the Party's organizational activity. It is accomplished through the agency of Party, state, and social control. The people's control organs function under the leadership of the Party and government, helping to broaden involvement of the toilers in the administration of state affairs even more.

The control organs systematically verify execution of Party and government directives by means of the Soviets and economic and other organizations. They see to it that Party and state discipline and socialist legality are observed. They not only investigate and call to account those who violate Soviet laws, they also try to prevent abuses and educate the people.

The persons taking part in the control form a vast army of fighters, including rank-and-file toilers, workers, village correspondents, and young members of "The Komsomol Searchlight" posts—in brief, all those who have an irreconcilable attitude towards shortcomings and consider it their duty to strive for a high labor productivity rate, for coordinated effort in all segments of the Soviet state apparatus.

The CPSU directs communist construction through *state and social organizations*. The Party does not give orders to, substitute for, or tolerate petty surveillance of state organs, economic administrative organs, and mass organizations. While it acts according to its own organizational and ideological-educational methods, the Party strives at the same time to ensure that all state and social organizations develop full initiative within the framework of their prerogatives and functions. The Party line is obligatory for all its members working in these organizations. However, in no way does this diminish their independence, full competence, and responsibility. The Leninist *Komsomol*, as active Party helper and source of membership, also works under CPSU leadership.

Close connection exists between the Party's political-organizational activity and its *ideological activity*—propagation of the Marxist-Leninist world-view; clarification of Party policy and mobilization of the toilers to carry it out; uncompromising struggle with bourgeois ideology and with the vestiges of the past lingering in the minds of the people; concern about education and the general advancement of culture; development in the sciences, literature, art, and all areas of creativity, by professionals and the masses alike. Results of ideological activity are also seen in our economic successes: the fulfillment of production goals, increased labor productivity, and strengthened labor discipline.

The Party's political, organizationl, and ideological activity has a *scientific character*: it is based on in-depth investigation of the laws of social development and of the actual processes taking place in society. Any retreat from this rule, any subjective or arbitrary approach in solving important problems results in serious and costly errors and may do great damage to the cause.

During the many years of its control over society, the CPSU has accumulated a complete arsenal of various operational forms and methods. However, life poses ever new tasks. Therefore, forms and methods of control over society are being continuously developed and enriched: means of involving the masses in formulation of policy are being improved, new requirements for the selection of cadres are being established, improved methods of verifying policy execution are being sought, and forms of ideological work are being refined.

The Party's Policy

The Communist party's policy serves as a reliable point of reference for its great variety of activity as it leads Soviet society and directs the functions of all state, economic, and social organizations. This policy demonstrates the ways to solve the economic, sociopolitical, ideological, and foreign-policy tasks confronting the country.

The present policy originates from resolutions passed by the October (1964) Plenum of the Central Committee, the CPSU Twenty-third Congress, and subsequent Central Committee Plenums. The October (1964) Plenum expressed the Party's firm resolve to assert the Leninist style in all its activities, to avoid subjectivism and arbitrariness when dealing with complex economic and political problems. The Twenty-third Congress of the CPSU, which took place in March and April 1966, creatively expanded the resolutions of the October Central Committee Plenum, adopted directives for the Five-Year Plan for the Developmen of the USSR Economy for 1966-70, worked out measures to improve further the Party's organizational activity, increase its ideological work throughout the country, and strengthen the Soviet state and raise the standard of the population's welfare. The Congress's resolutions were inspired by concern for consolidating the unity of the world socialist system, defending the peace and security of peoples, and resisting imperialism.

As in the past, the Party considers the economy—the creation of an appropriate material-technical base—the chief battleground in the struggle for communism. Clearly, the rate of our progress and the outcome of the confrontation of the two worlds, socialism and capitalism, as well as our contribution to the unfolding of the whole contemporary international revolutionary process, depend on the degree of success we achieve in developing our economy. The Party's policy is therefore directed toward the scientific formulation of economic decisions, toward the highest possible rise in the country's productive forces. At the same time, the CPSU policy proceeds from the assumption that all the aspects of communist construction are interdependent. In order to build communism, the Party's goal is to use with maximum effectiveness new social gains as well as modern scientific and technological achievements, the rising cultural and educational level of the people, and the ideological-educational effort of the Party.

Fundamental Law of Party Life

In order to complete successfully the complex and multiform tasks of control over society, the Party itself must be an exemplary, democratic, and disciplined organization. The fundamentals of the CPSU structure were formulated by V.I. Lenin and are set down in the Party Rules, which, in the full meaning of the word, represent the fundamental law of its existence.

Understandably, the tasks facing the Party in each new historical stage and in specific operational conditions require constant improvement of its structure. When the Party was an organization of professional revolutionaries, comparatively few in number and operating underground, this presented a specific type of problem. A completely different situation emerged when the Party assumed power, became a party of the masses, and roused the people to build socialism. Finally, it is another matter for the fourteen-million-member Communist party, today, to be in charge of building communism. Everything new and valuable suggested by life itself is incorporated in specific form into the Party Rules.

Taking into account changing circumstances and new historical tasks, the Party has courageously reformulated the forms and methods of its activity and leadership, as reflected in the Party Rules adopted by the CPSU Twenty-second Congress and amended by the Twenty-third Congress.

Party Structure

The Party is organized according to the *production-territory principle*. The basic unit of the Party (formerly called the Party cell) is represented by the *primary Party organization*, which is established wherever there are no fewer than three Party members, i.e., wherever a communist collective exists.

Communists join primary Party organizations at their job locations: industrial enterprises, construction sites, *sovkhozes* and *kolkhozes*, government offices, institutes, Soviet Army units, educational institutions, etc. Only those communists who are not employed in social production for various reasons (pensioners and housewives) join Party organizations in their places of residence. The *production principle* thus is applied within the Party structure.

Large primary Party organizations can be subdivided into smaller organizations in shops, sections of construction sites, farms, work brigades, and various departments. There are about three hundred and fifty thousand primary organizations in the CPSU, composing the basis of the Party. For all practical purposes, there is not a single collective or sector of any importance where no Party organization exists.

The most important organ of the primary organization is the Party meeting. It discusses problems of Party policy and those of its organization and the entire collective; it makes decisions on questions related to admission and expulsion from the Party. Non-Party people are invited to attend open Party meetings. At an annual meeting held to hear reports and elect officials, the communists elect a *bureau or committee*, which is headed by a *secretary* and conducts current Party business. All important current affairs are decided by the secretary, not unilaterally but together with other bureau members, in other words, *jointly*.

What is most important in a primary organization's activity?

Dealing with people—their political and moral education; rendering all possible help in forming their habits in administrating state and social affairs, and in organizing work and daily life. The *personal example* of a communist and his exemplary fulfillment of *Party assignments* are an important part in this.

Let us consider the work of the bureau members, the secretary, and the rank-and-file communists. They are asked for advice and help with the most varied problems. Communists are concerned about everything: reorganization of the shop, conditions in the plant, the kindergarten, labor-improvement suggestions, a family dispute, procedure at a meeting, any case of injustice, the housing problem, and organization of leisure activities. And they are not merely interested. If the Party bureau or the entire primary organization proposes, the management, labor-union committee, or *Komsomol* committee will be called in on various important questions. The appropriate decision is made and its implementation is checked upon by the Party bureau.

Primary Party organizations located on the territory of a *rayon*, [district], city, *okrug* [region], *oblast* [province], *kray* [territory], and republic are part of their respective territorial Party organizations. This arrangement expresses the *territorial* principle of the CPSU structure.

Of what advantage to the Party is the combination of production and territory principles? Briefly, it guarantees independent activity to each communist collective, at the same time uniting them into one large organization equipped with a single resolve, ready for action.

The basic problems in the life of a society are decided in the production process. The struggle to fulfill the plans of communist construction, increase labor productivity, and advance the people's well-being and culture take place here. Understandably, the communist collectives in enterprises or offices can have a direct influence on the course of events, since they function in the midst of the popular masses.

On the other hand, consolidation of Party organizations into district, city, and other organizations makes it possible to guarantee combined Party leadership of all state power organs and the economy and culture in all their different parts.

Higher Party Organs

The highest CPSU organ is the Party congress. Each Party congress represents an important landmark in the Party's life and that of the people. The congress reviews and assesses all that was accomplished during the interim period and charts new future tasks. It receives and approves reports from the Central Committee, the Central Auditing Commission, and other central organizations. It approves, reviews, and when necessary alters the CPSU Program and Rules; it defines the Party line on questions of domestic and foreign policy; it discusses and decides the most important problems of communist construction; it elects the Central Committee and the Central Auditing Commission.

Congresses are regularly held no less than once every four years. No later than one and one half months before each meeting, all communists and Party organizations must be informed of the congress's convocation and agenda topics, thus permitting the Party to be more fully prepared for the convocation of its highest organ. In the event of urgent need to decide very important problems prior to the regular session, CPSU Rules provide for convocation of an extraordinary congress.

In intervals between congresses, the entire activity of the CPSU is directed by the CPSU Central Committee (CC of the CPSU). Depending on the circumstances, the Central Committee can hold All-Union Party conferences.

The CC of the CPSU is a kind of heart and brain for the Communist party. It formulates policy of the Party and state; decides about development in the economy and culture; provides for the toilers' education in the spirit of communism, works to strengthen the country's defenses, and helps promote cooperation and communication without friction with fraternal parties and socialist countries. The *CPSU Central Committee is the collective leader of the Party and the Soviet people, the general staff of the ideological, political, and organizational control over communist construction.*

The Party elects to the Central Committee communists who have the most experience and are familiar with building the Party and the economy, with industry, agriculture, culture, science, military affairs, and foreign policy.

Central Committee decisions are binding on all Party organizations and on every individual member.

The Central Committee meets in plenary sessions (plenums) no less than once every six months. It elects the CPSU Central Committee Politburo, which directs its work between plenums, and a secretariat to conduct current business mainly in the selection of cadres and organizing policy execution. In addition, it elects the Secretary General of the CC of the CPSU.

Democratic Centralism

The Party structure and operations are based on the principle of democratic centralism.

This principle stipulates, first of all, that *all controlling Party organs from bottom to top must be elective*. The communists conduct Party affairs themselves, either directly or through their representatives, in whom they place full confidence. All communists enjoy equal rights without exception. All Party institutions are elective, answerable, and subject to removal—individual Party officials as well as collective organs of control. The principles of systematic renewal of their composition and of continuity of leadership are observed in elections of all Party organs, from the bureau of the primary Party organization up to the Central Committee.

The highest controlling organ of a Party organization is the general meeting (in the case of a primary Party organization), the conference (for district, city, region, province, and territory Party organizations), or the congress (for Communist parties of union republics and for the Communist Party of the Soviet Union). Bureaus and committees elected by the meetings, conferences, or congresses are executive organs and conduct their organizations' current business.

The principle of democratic centralism requires, furthermore, that *Party organs periodically be answerable to their Party organizations and to higher Party organs*. The fact that Party organs are elective, answerable, and subject to removal guarantees active participation by all communists in the formation of controlling collective organs as well as in discussion and solution of all important problems of Party life and practical operation.

In finding solutions to the problems of Party life, communists apply Party criticism and self-criticism based on principles and facts. Thus they are able to fight sluggishness and routine, overcome backwardness and the bureaucratic attitude, introduce new and progressive methods, and improve the operations of Party, state, and social organizations. The Party cannot acquiesce in conceit and complacency, and its attention is always concentrated on the tasks to be solved.

Democratic centralism also signifies *strict Party discipline and subordination of the minority to the majority. Decisions of higher organs are binding on lower ones.*

The fact that the Party is so well organized multiplies its power, enabling it to solve the most complex tasks. Intra-Party democracy is inconceivable without freedom of opinion and free, matter-of-fact discussion of all political problems, something natural and necessary. Communists have different degrees of theoretical preparation, and their political and life experience also vary. Everyone has his own approach to solving problems. Free exchange of opinion permits finding the best solution. Once a solution has been worked out, however, unity of action and strict discipline are necessary. The ideological firmness and political maturity of a communist are shown in his strict observance of party discipline.

Whoever violates Party discipline takes the path of factionalism and has no place in the Party. Trotskyites and other opportunistic groups were expelled from the Party ranks precisely for this reason.

Concern for the purity of the Party ranks, ensuring that every communist carry with dignity and justification the proud name of CPSU member, is a law of life for our Party and all its organizations.

Communist, a Proud Name

Persons are brought into the ranks of the CPSU by ideological motives, their grasp of the just cause for which the Party struggles, and the wish to serve selflessly communism's ideals. Who, then, is worthy of the proud name, communist?

Any citizen of the Soviet Union may become a Communist party member. To this end he, first of all, must *accept the CPSU Program and Rules.* Why is this so important? Because the Communist party is a party of people with identical ideas, and it is precisely its Program and Rules that express the common ideological platform on which all communists are united.

But that's not all. It is possible to accept the guidance of Party directives and not be a communist. A communist is one who *struggles* to carry out the Program and Rules requirements of the Party and its policy.

The qualities of a communist become fully apparent in a collective. CPSU Rules require that a person be considered a communist only if he participates in one of the many Party organizations, carries out Party decisions, and pays membership dues.

A communist should serve as a model in fulfilling party assignments where he works, by his personal example inspire others to work selflessly, and show concern about the interests of the people and the country. V.I. Lenin once remarked: "Party members must be ahead of all others in labor discipline and energy." Aware and conscientious, a communist cannot tolerate any interference with our progress or any contradiction to the ideals of communism.

Of course, unworthy persons do get into the Party. As the saying goes, one cannot look into a man's soul. Therefore, errors are being made in admission of new members to the Party. Also, one may see the following situation: an individual was a model communist, honestly fulfilling his Party duties, but then he did not last. He became contaminated by greed or showed an immoral lack of scruples and political maturity, or he turned into a petty-bourgeois Philistine.

The Party cannot be judged by these persons. They are not communists, even though they temporarily carry a Party card in their pockets. By ridding itself of those who do not justify the proud name of communist, the Party becomes even stronger and more monolithic.

Admission to Party membership is granted only to individuals. Entry into the Party requires filing a personal statement, which is examined by the full meeting of a primary Party organization. Thorough knowledge of the applicant's personal qualities and detailed inquiry into and evaluation of his merits as well as defects are ensured by the policy of individual admissions.

If the Party organization is convinced that a certain individual is not qualified or not yet prepared to participate actively in the Party and satisfy the requirements of its Rules and Program, understandably it has not only the right but the duty to reject his application.

New members are admitted from among the candidates who complete the required probation period of one year. A resolution of the primary Party organization on admission to membership is considered adopted if at least two-thirds of the attendance at the meeting votes in its favor.

Persons who reach the age of eighteen can be admitted into the Party. Young people up to the age of twenty-three enter the CPSU through the *Komsomol*, whose members must present a recommendation from the district or city committee of the *Komsomol* upon entering. Only those CPSU members can make recommendations for admission whose membership is no less than five years and who know the recommended person from associating with him in production or communal affairs for no less than one year.

A communist's rights guarantee to him the possibility of active participation in Party life. The CPSU member has the right to elect or be elected to Party organs. He participates in free, matter-of-fact discussions during Party meetings and in the Party press of policy problems and practical Party activity. He has the right to criticize any communist, irrespective of position, and to insist on being present at a meeting or session where any matter concerning his personal activity or behavior is under discussion. He may request information from or make statements to any Party organ, the CPSU Central Committee included. The Party's strength lies in the communists' active participation.

Toward the Great Goal

The Communist party sees the construction of communist society as its final goal. This goal and the means to its achievement are defined in the CPSU Program.

The Program's Importance

V.I. Lenin attached exceptional importance to the Party Program. He wrote: "Without a program the Party cannot exist as an integral political organization always capable of following its line in all possible changes of events." The program of a Marxist party is formulated on the basis of scientific theory and defines tasks that arise from the requirements of social development and express the interest of the masses.

The first Party Program was adopted at the Second Congress of the Russian Social Democratic Workers' Party in 1903. V.I. Lenin, together with the newspaper *Iskra* [*The Spark*] founded by him, was occupied for an extended period of time with its preparation. The Program set before the Party and the working class the task of struggling for the dictatorship of the proletariat, which was achieved with the victory of the October Socialist Revolution and the formation of the Soviet power.

The second Party Program was adopted by the Eighth Congress of the Russian Communist party of the Bolsheviks (RCP/b/) in 1919. It was worked out with the direct participation of V.I. Lenin as leader and chairman of the Program Commission. Its draft, once thoroughly discussed, was approved by Party organizations and served as a basis of debate at the Congress.

V.I. Lenin personally reported on the Party Program to the Eighth Congress. This was the Program of a Party already holding power and controlling the first socialist state in the world. The main goal laid down by the Program—the construction of socialism—had heretofore never confronted any society or political party. This Program, like the first one, was successfully carried out by the Party and the Soviet people.

Under Communist party leadership, the Soviet people have had great success in building socialism and won an outstanding victory over fascism in the Great Patriotic War [World War II]. The immense devastation in the Soviet Union caused by the war was repaired in the shortest possible time. Our country firmly adopted the course of steadily building its power and completing the construction of socialism. New, complicated, and important tasks have dictated the need to broadly expand organizational and political activity on the part of Party and Soviet organs, and the need to develop socialist democracy as well.

The Party has demonstrated its ability to work out a policy appropriate to new conditions, control the country's life successfully, eliminate emerging difficulties, and correct errors. The Twentieth CPSU Congress, which was held on Feburary 1956, had a considerable part in this. It discussed current theoretical and practical problems, defined the task of restoring Leninist principles of collective leadership in Party and state life, and increased the Party's organizational and educational role in the life of Soviet society. As a result, a new upsurge of creativity on the part of the Party and the people became possible.

Pursuing a course toward further development of socialist democracy, the Party courageously and resolutely—in the Leninist manner—condemned the cult of Stalin's personality manifest in the glorification of one person, an attitude alien to Marxism-Leninism, in deviation from the principles of collective leadership, in senseless repression, and other violations of socialist legality.

The cult of personality hindered our country's development and damaged its international position. The USSR could have developed even more rapidly and successfully. However, even under the circumstances of the cult of personality, the Soviet people and the Party achieved great success and advanced on the path of socialism. This cult did not and could not change the nature of the socialist system and its economic and political foundation. The mass of many millions of toilers remained the decisive motive force of Soviet society's development. The Party continued to be a living, active organism, and local Party organizations carried on important work.

In the CPSU Central Committee Theses "Fiftieth Anniversary of the Great October Socialist Revolution," there is the following evaluation of the Party's subsequent activity:

The Party carried out measures to overcome consequences of the cult of personality in all areas of Party, state, and ideological activity; to observe the Leninist norms and principles of Party life. Rights were broadened: those of the union republics, provinces, and regions regarding solution of problems of economic and cultural construction; and those of directors of individual enterprises. All this resulted in the activation of the country's sociopolitical and intellectual life, and of the Party, Soviet, and economic apparatus in all their sections. The Soviet social and state systems were strengthened and more fully developed. The sociopolitical and ideological unity of workers, peasants, and intelligentsia became more solid, and the friendship of the peoples of the Soviet Union became closer as they rallied around the Leninist Party even more fervently.

As the result of improvements in our country after the Party's Twentieth Congress and increased theoretical and practical activity by the Party, it became possible to work out and adopt the new, third Program of the CPSU, which was done by the Twenty-second CPSU Congress in October 1961.

The Party Program

The Communist Party Program is formulated on the basis of Marxist-Leninist theory. In a creative way, it generalizes the historical experience of our Party and the international communist and workers' movement. The Program clearly and precisely states the Party's achievements, goals, and the tasks it will undertake in the near future.

The Program's *introductory part* gives the general characteristics of more than one hundred years of development of Marxism-Leninism, and of socialism's victory in the Soviet Union and a number of other countries in Europe and Asia. It stresses that the Party's highest aim is to build communist society, on whose banner is inscribed: "From each according to his ability and to each according to his needs."

The Program's first section sets forth the problems of the *transition from capitalism to communism*. A brief description is given of capitalism as the last exploiting system, and the historical necessity of transition from capitalism to socialism is demonstrated. The historic mission of the working class and the Communist party is also disclosed. The fundamental lessons learned on the path already traveled by the Communist party and the Soviet people are discussed, with a concise description of the Soviet Union's experience. There is a statement explaining present-day problems of the development of the world socialist system, of the international revolutionary movement of the working class, and also of the national liberation movement. The same section analyzes the crisis of world capitalism, and of bourgeois and reformist ideology.

The second, and larger, section of the Program explains what communism is and what the means are to construct it. Communism appears in the Program as an inevitable result of human society's development, governed by its own laws, the greatest achievement in the entire economic, sociopolitical, and cultural progress of humanity.

The CPSU Program is a practical guide for people in building communist society.

It states:

Faithful to proletarian internationalism, the Communist Party of the Soviet Union always follows the battle cry, "Proletarians of all countries, unite!" *The Party considers communist construction in the USSR to be the great internationalist task of the Soviet people, which is in the interest of the entire world socialist system, the international proletariat, and all humanity.*

The CPSU and the World Communist Movement

The Communist party of the Soviet Union is the directing and guiding force of Soviet society. At the same time, it is a component and detachment with equal rights in the world communist movement.

Our Party has always been loyal to the banner of proletarian internationalism hoisted by Lenin, organizer and leader of the Communist party and the Soviet state, and founder, at the same time, of the Third Communist International. He was present at the birth of individual communist parties and helped to devise the long-range policy of the world communist movement.

The Soviet communists and Soviet people have fulfilled their highest internationalist duty toward their brothers abroad by completing the construction of the first socialist society in the world and by protecting its achievements against the encroachments of world imperialist reaction. Soviet volunteers fought, weapons in hand, on the fields of Spain against the threat of fascism. By accepting the chief burden in the struggle against Hitler's Germany, and by contributing decisively to the victory over fascism, the Soviet Union assisted many European and Asian peoples to regain freedom, thus saving human civilization from downfall.

The CPSU shares freely with fraternal parties its rich experience in the struggle to bring about the socialist revolution and build socialism and communism. For its part, it carefully studies and uses all the valuable experiences, theoretical and practical, of other Marxist-Leninist parties.

Together with other fraternal parties, our Party contributes significantly toward the development of the general policy of the international communist movement, coordinates its efforts with those of all fraternal parties in a common struggle for the toilers' interest, for peace, democracy, national independence, and socialism.

In close cooperation with fraternal parties, the CPSU actively strives for strengthening the solidarity of the communist movement. An important step in this direction was the meeting of the communist and workers' parties in Moscow, in June 1969, where discussion was on the topic "The tasks of the struggle against imperialism at the present stage, and the united action of the communists and workers' parties and all the anti-imperialist forces." Documents adopted by the meeting and speeches by the delegation heads of fraternal parties presented in-depth analyses of the contemporary international situation. Threats arising from the aggressive policy of imperialism were pointed out, as were the new possibilities of the revolutionary and progressive forces. A broad program of joint action in the struggle against imperialism was offered; ways to struggle for consolidation and further development of the communist movement were shown; as were means to bring about united action by all the partisans of peace and progress among peoples.

Faithful to the Leninist tradition and to proletarian internationalism, the CPSU consistently observes the principle of equality in relations among socialist countries and communist parties. It resolutely opposes hegemony, the submission of one party to another, since this is incompatible with the very nature of the communist movement.

Fraternal parties value highly our Party's activity and role in the world revolutionary movement. In a message of greetings from the French communists to the Twenty-second CPSU Congress, Maurice Thorez said, "Your efforts as well as sacrifices represent a great contribution to the communist cause all over the world." The First Secretary of the Central Committee of the Hungarian Socialist and Worker's Party, Janos Kadar, has emphatically said many times, "We know no anti-Soviet Marxism-Leninism, anti-Soviet internationalism, anti-Soviet communism." Orestes Guioldi, a prominent leader of the Communist Party of Argentina, has remarked, "If the imperialist powers headed by the United States have so far not succeeded in drawing the world into thermonuclear war, it is, first of all, thanks to the firm and flexible policy of the Soviet Union and other socialist countries, a policy which is gaining ever-increasing support and gratitude of all peoples."

The internationalist policy of the Communist party and the Soviet state regarding all possible assistance to the heroic Vietnamese people in its effort to repel the aggression of the American imperialists has received universal support.

Widespread recognition of the merits of our Party and our people was eloquently expressed on the occasion of the celebration of the fiftieth anniversary of the Great October Socialist Revolution and the centennial of the birth of Vladimir Il'ich Lenin. Along with the members of the Central Committee and the deputies of the Supreme Soviets, representatives of the communist, workers', national liberation, and democratic movements from nearly one hundred countries of the world were present during the festive sessions. Greetings addressed to the Central Committee of the CPSU and to the Soviet government from all continents and countries arrived in an unending flow. The directing bodies of the communist and workers' parties as well as those of left-wing socialist and national-democratic parties, of labor unions, youth, cultural, and other organizations, and progressive personalities from all over the world paid tribute in their good-will messages to the Land of the Soviets, to the Communist party, and to the Soviet people for their historic accomplishments and victories in the cause of constructing communism.

Review Questions

1. What are the sources of the Party's strength?
2. What is the role of the Party in Soviet society?
3. In what way does the Party direct the activities of the *Komsomol* and assist in improving its internal operation?
4. How does our Party contribute to the development of the world communist movement?

Points to Consider and Discuss

1. Study the most important sociopolitical changes that have occurred in our country during the years of socialism and show how they have been reflected in the Party's activity and character.
2. In order to obtain a correct understanding about Party control over the economy, it is useful to be informed about the operation of an enterprise or a *kolkhoz*. Ask a Party worker or an economic specialist to give a short talk.
3. Tell which of the famous communists you would like to resemble, imitate, and take for a model.
4. Give a report on how the peoples of our country and of the whole world celebrated the centenary of Vladimir Il'ich Lenin's birth. Tell which of his works you have read, as well as any books and stories about him; tell about motion pictures or stage plays on Leninist themes you have seen.

The Epoch of Revolutionary Transition from Capitalism to Socialism

The Great October Socialist Revolution ushered in the epoch of revolutionary transition from capitalism to socialism throughout the world. This transition is taking place as a result of a grim class struggle, under the conditions of a confrontation between the forces of socialism and imperialism, the forces of progress and reaction in the international arena.

The last remaining exploiter system does not surrender without a fight. The imperialists bring into action their total available economic and military resources, the mechanism of political power and international influence, powerful means of modern propaganda—everything to prolong the existence of the capitalist system. They take advantage of any weakness in the revolutionary movement; they counterattack and attempt to reverse the law-governed progress of history.

However, such attempts are ultimately doomed to failure. Whatever difficulties they must overcome, the revolutionary forces are confidently moving forward, conquering new positions, pressing the reactionaries on all fronts. The development of world events brings countless proofs of the correctness of the ideas of Marxism-Leninism, under the banner of which the most powerful political movement of our time, the communist movement, is advancing.

The triumph of our revolutionary teaching is embodied in the activities of the three fundamental forces of the present epoch: the world socialist system, the workers' movement, and the movement of national liberation.

The World Socialist System

After the October Revolution, the victory of the socialist revolution in a number of countries of Europe and Asia following World War II is the greatest event of our century. Socialism has progressed far beyond the confines of a single country and has become a world system. Experience with this system's development is evidence that the Leninist teaching is international and applicable to all countries; it shows all peoples the correct way to build socialism.

The world socialist system has been in existence for a quarter of a century, historically an insignificant period of time, but the fundamental trends of the development of society have already clearly announced their existence. The Main Document of the Moscow International Meeting of communist and workers' parties in 1969 noted:

Socialism has opened to mankind the prospects of salvation from imperialism. The new social order based on social ownership of the means of production and ruled by the government of the toilers is capable of providing planned, crisis-free development of the economy in the interest of the people and capable of guaranteeing social and political rights to the toilers, creating conditions for true democracy, real participation of the broad popular masses in governing society, all-around development of personality, and equal rights and friendship of nations. In fact, it has been proven that socialism alone is able to solve the basic problems facing mankind.

Practical experience has fully and completely confirmed the correctness of the two most significant ideas of Marxist-Leninist teaching about the ways to establish the new world: first, the idea of uniformity of basic laws and variety of forms, both of which characterize the transition to socialism; second, the idea that socialism's victory will lead to the formation of a new type of international relations, based on internationalism and brotherly friendship among free peoples.

Variety of Forms, Uniformity of Laws

Under capitalism there is uneven development in various countries. Therefore, when they reach the stage of the socialist revolution, some have a more developed economy while others are backward; some have independence while others are under imperalist bondage. In certain countries the peasantry predominates among the toiling population, in others, the proletariat; the status of the bourgeoisie is not always identical in strength, and so forth. International conditions also vary.

It is easily understandable that when the conditions for building socialism are different at the start, the forms, methods, and tempo of socialist transformation cannot and should not be uniform. The victorious working class and its communist vanguard are facing a complex task: to apply the general principles of Marxist-Leninist teaching to the concrete conditions of their countries, and find those forms and methods of building the new society that best permit success in achieving the objectives set down. The revolutionaries are richly experienced in socialist construction completed in fraternal countries, but they cannot simply copy that experience: what is valid in one country will not always produce the results hoped for in another. Therefore, it is important that experience gained in other countries be used in a creative manner, taking into account both the peculiarities and international situation of a specific country.

Long before socialism crossed the frontiers of one country, V.I. Lenin said that history would inevitably produce a great variety of forms of transition to socialism. Lenin's expectation was visibly fulfilled after World War II, when socialism became a world system. Socialist revolutions have been achieved in countries that are highly developed industrially, agrarian, formerly semicolonial, and colonial. Hence the variety of forms and methods of socialist construction.

One of the most important factors determining the ways of transition to socialism in the majority of these countries was that revolutions were carried to victory on the crest of the mighty antifascist movement, which had united into a single popular-democratic front the broadest strata of the population (peasantry, urban petty bourgeoisie, intelligentsia, part of the patriotic middle bourgeoisie), under the leadership of the proletariat and its fighting communist vanguard.

In a number of countries this made it possible for the working class to seize power peacefully, without armed uprising and civil war. The example of this is Czechoslovakia. In February 1948 the famous demonstration of the Prague proletariat and the revolutionary will of the entire toiling population of the country forced the reactionaries to retreat, and a government headed by communists was formed.

In the course of several socialist transformations it was obviously necessary to carry on a grim struggle against counterrevolutionaries attempting to hinder the consolidation of the people's power. But the struggle did not reach the extreme of civil war because the Soviet Union prevented attacks by imperialists on the young socialist states and the local big bourgeoisie was not strong enough, lacking open support from abroad, to take up arms against the power of the toilers.

Hence the variety of forms and timetables in these socialist transformations. The representatives of the overthrown exploiter classes were only partially restricted in their political rights, while in certain locations they were not restricted at all. In those cases the bourgeois state machinery was not torn down at once but gradually.

Many agencies and organizations of the old state were not eradicated but reorganized, filled with the new class content, and incorporated into the state system of the people's democracy; services of specialists of the former time were used on a large scale, which helped to avoid dislocations in the economic organism's functioning. In a number of socialist countries political parties representing part of the peasantry, intelligentsia, and other strata of the population participate in governments headed by communists. When large landholdings were liquidated, the private land ownership of the peasants was preserved at first, to be transformed later into social ownership as, gradually, the peasants freely joined cooperatives. In certain countries the people's governments partially reimbursed the bourgeoisie for the cost of the means of production. Marx foresaw this possibility when he said that under certain conditions the proletariat might find it expedient to "pay off" the bourgeoisie.

In former colonies and dependencies the road to revolution had its own distinctive character. Wars of national liberation gave birth to socialist revolutions in China, Korea, Vietnam, and Cuba.

The fact that the ways of socialist development in one country or group of countries vary greatly does not permit the conclusion that each country creates a "national" socialism of its own. The very nature of socialism is such that there is not and cannot be a Russian or Chinese, a German or Polish socialism. The fundamental characteristics of the socialist order reflect objective requirements for human society's development, and they cannot but be uniform for all countries and peoples.

For the same reason socialist transformations, for all their diversity of forms and methods, are inevitably governed by the *general laws of transition from capitalism to socialism.*

Proletariat and toilers may buy up the means of production or they may take them over without making compensation; they may expropriate the bourgeoisie forthwith or in stages. But under all circumstances, the means of production must be transferred to social ownership. Otherwise there can be no talk of socialism. This is not a matter of choice but a law governing social development.

The dictatorship of the proletariat may assume the form of a one-party system or a multiparty system, where the power belongs to a coalition of parties led by Marxists-Leninists. But whatever the circumstances, the state control over society exercised by the working class and its political vanguard is indispensable; the political system of socialism must always ensure the participation of the broadest popular masses in state administration and development of their initiative and creative activity. In other words, it must introduce socialist democracy. This again is not a matter of choice but a law governing social development. Any deviation would inevitably lead to the perversion of the very ideals of socialism and complicate and surround with artificial difficulties the way the new society is to be constructed.

It is easy to understand how important it is to know the general laws governing the transition from capitalism to socialism if we want to avoid losing our way in the dark and if we want to build all policy on a consistently scientific foundation. The Marxist-Leninist theory, verified and enriched by the experience of the USSR's development and that of other socialist countries, makes this possible.

Socialism cannot be achieved without the proletarian revolution and establishment of the dictatorship of the proletariat in one form or another, without the alliance of the working class with the large peasant masses—the basic segment—and other strata of toilers. In addition to establishment of social ownership of the basic means of production, also required in the economic field are gradual socialist transformation of agriculture and planned development of the entire economy, which is to be oriented toward building socialism and communism as well as toward raising the living standard of the workers. A socialist revolution is also indispensable in the area of ideology and culture. A numerous intelligentsia must be formed which will be devoted to the working class, the toiling people, and the cause of socialism. National oppression must be liquidated, and relations based on equal rights and brotherhood between peoples must be established. Finally, the conquests of socialism must be defended against encroachment from foreign and internal foe; the solidarity of one country's working class with that of other countries must be strengthened in accordance with the principle of proletarian internationalism.

These are the main general laws of the movement toward socialism. They were formulated in the Declaration of the Conference of Representatives of the Communist and Workers' Parties, which took place in Moscow in 1957.

By acting in conformity with these laws and using the most diverse economic and political forms, which depend on specific situations, the peoples of countries that have entered upon the path of socialist development have brought about a radical transformation of the entire social order. In the states presently part of the world socialist system, social ownership of the means of production has been firmly established; in the overwhelming majority, cooperative forms of agriculture have been introduced. As noted in the decisions of the communist and workers' parties, certain countries have laid the foundation for the building of socialism; others are completing the construction of socialist society.

Understandably, the successful construction of socialism depends upon objective as well as subjective factors: how consistently the ideas of Marxism-Leninism are practiced, and the scientific level of the leadership directing society's development. Violations of these requirements and drift away from theoretically sound ways and methods of socialist construction that have proven themselves in practice can be very harmful and seriously impair the cause of creating the new society, or even result in its retrogression, as in the case of China.

New Type of International Relations

Socialism's expansion beyond the frontiers of one country and its transformation into a world system have brought the communist movement face to face with the problem of the character of relations among sovereign socialist states.

The initial requirements for the solution of this problem have always been clear. One of the main objectives of socialism and communism is to end forever national distrust and enmity and establish eternal peace and brotherhood of free peoples on earth. It is quite clear that the entire development of relations among socialist states must be subordinated precisely to this objective.

The point is not only that this objective corresponds to communist ideals, our conceptions of justice and goodness. For all peoples following the path of socialism, close partnership is an objective necessity. This has been brought out not only by theory but also by practice, by political reality. Having been threatened by imperialist aggression from the very beginning of their existence, the peoples of socialist countries have experienced the need to unite their forces in defense of the cause of the revolution and for the sake of success in socialist construction. In exactly the same way, it is only by full-scale development of economic ties with fraternal socialist countries that economic blockade can be resisted, the conditions of plunder dominating capitalist markets avoided, and reliable support and assistance for rapid development of the economy found. Finally, the socialist states are markedly increasing their political influence, their impact on the development of world events, by coordinating their foreign policy and functioning as a united front in the international arena.

A socioeconomic order in common, a single Marxist-Leninist ideology, and immediate political interests dictate the necessity of unity among the socialist countries. And we are not speaking here of a mere alliance of states but of establishing and expanding an essentially new type of international relations.

It is enough to recall the history of international relations to understand the innovations socialism has introduced into relations among sovereign states. Scarcely had the first states appeared when an uninterrupted struggle among them began, as the ruling exploiter classes attempted to expand the territory under their control and enslave other peoples at any price. Successive wars brought countless misfortunes, and brief respites of peace were used to prepare for new war adventures. Deception, perfidy, violence—any means were considered permissible if they helped to conquer neighbors, subjugate other states, and knock together an empire.

Brigandage in the international arena reached its peak in the period of imperialism. Economic and military power became the decisive argument in relations among the imperialist states, and even more so in their relations with weaker countries. Thus, for example, at various stages of imperialism American political figures officially described United States foreign policy as the policy of "the big stick," "dollar diplomacy," "nuclear blackmail," and "policy from the position of strength."

Following World War II, the imperialist powers created aggressive military-political blocs directed against the countries of socialism and the revolutionary movement. However, even relations based on an alliance do not remove acute contradictions existing between the allies, do not eliminate their struggle for markets and capital investment spheres.

Marx said that under the capitalist system "one state's gain is another's loss." On the basis not only of theory but also experience, today we can say that within the socialist system one state's gain is at the same time gain for all the others.

To be sure, the new type of international relations does not emerge in its final form immediately. A complex system of new economic, political, and cultural ties among socialist countries must be made to harmonize. The new type of international relations requires a comparatively long historical period to take shape, and the process is far from completed.

It is generally accepted that our country has played a great part in establishing and developing the new type of international relations. The victory of the socialist revolution in a number of countries after World War II was greatly assisted by the fact that the Soviet Union paralyzed the forces of international reaction, prevented intervention, frustrated the plans of the imperialists to suffocate the young socialist states by a blockade by helping them create their own industry.

The first postwar years witnessed the conclusion of economic agreements and treaties of alliance and mutual aid in case of aggression between the USSR and the other socialist countries in which the socialist revolution had been won. When the imperialist powers concluded the Paris Agreement providing for the rebirth of German militarism and the inclusion of the German Federal Republic in the Atlantic Pact, the socialist European states created a defensive alliance of their own, in May 1955. This was the *Warsaw Pact Organization*, which has at its disposal combined armed forces under a joint command. The joint defense measures of socialist states and, most important, the nuclear rocket might of the USSR are socialism's reliable shield, restraining the militaristic circles of the imperialist countries.

It would be naïve to assume that the unity and cohesion of the countries of the world socialist system will emerge spontaneously, automatically, so to speak. After all, the new relations among peoples need to be constructed on ground already soiled by centuries of national enmity, distrust, nationalistic prejudices. Some controversial problems in interstate relations may be inherited from capitalism. In certain cases specific national interests of individual countries may not coincide. While all these difficulties stand no comparison with the impact of fraternal cooperation among the socialist countries insofar as the extent of their influence is concerned, nevertheless they are capable of doing considerable damage to the cause of socialism, and constant, strenuous effort is needed to overcome them.

That is precisely why under present circumstances a correct Marxist-Leninist policy and ability to reconcile national interests of their countries with the common interest of the entire socialist commonwealth is tremendously important for the communist and workers' parties.

People do not think in stereotypes, and even though they may hold identical convictions, their approaches to various problems of socialist construction and interstate relations may not always fully coincide. But the point is that the unity of convictions and a common aim provide the opportunity to work out concerted solutions based on free discussion. To that end the communist and workers' parties of the socialist countries conduct mutual consultations and negotiations, discussing in a frank, comradely manner all questions of interest.

Adherence to time-tested *principles* that have been confirmed in a number of programmatic documents of the communist movement is particularly important in order to carry on normal, friendly relations among the socialist states. These principles are equality, respect for independence and national sovereignty, and mutual noninterference in internal affairs. At the same time, relations among the socialist countries are not limited to these principles. The principle of *socialist internationalism* is the basis of these relations. It is precisely the concept of internationalism that encompasses the entire enormous and multifaceted mutual assistance that increases the strength of the socialist countries tenfold. It is precisely loyalty to internationalism that guarantees the successful development and growth in power of the world socialist system.

Internationalism presumes a resolute struggle against all signs of nationalistic ideology, which is alien to the proletariat.

The petty-bourgeois environment is the breeding ground of nationalism. Alongside the working class, the peasant masses and bourgeoisie in the cities are taking part in the movement toward socialism. Under capitalism the living conditions of these social strata are the cause of the dual and contradictory character of their consciousness. This has already been discussed. (See Chapter 3, pp. 65-99.) When the egotism of a petty owner characterizes an entire nation, it turns into national egotism, that is, the inclination on the part of a nation, on the one hand, to insulate, separate, and isolate itself from the outside world within the confines of its own frontiers; and on the other, to place itself above all others, impose its own way of thinking and acting on them and establish its predominance over them. Tied in with all this is an inclination to the cult of "the strong personality" and deification of an "infallible" leader who supposedly will bring glory and power to the nation.

One of the most important tasks for the proletariat is to induce the petty-bourgeois masses to adopt the proletarian Marxist-Leninist ideology, inculcate in them an internationalist consciousness, and lead them on the road of scientific communism. V.I. Lenin never tired of stressing the importance of this task, especially within countries with an overwhelming preponderance of peasant population. The danger of the petty-bourgeois and nationalistic views is particularly serious when they appear within the ranks of a party that has already successfully carried out the socialist revolution and holds power. In this case the negative consequences not only result in distortion of the concepts and practical requirements of scientific socialism within the country but also violate the principle of socialist internationalism in the international arena. Nationalistic prejudices feed antisocialist tendencies capable of inflicting great losses on the cause of socialism.

In China grave damage to the cause and to the cohesion of the world socialist system is being done by anti-Leninist views and practical activities of the present leadership of the Chinese Communist party headed by Mao Tse-tung. By setting their own separate political course against the general policy line of the communist movement, the Maoists have unleashed a struggle against communist parties and fraternal socialist states. They are practicing a militaristic great-power policy on the international arena. Contrary to the most vital interests of the Chinese people, they have elevated anti-Sovietism to the status of state policy;

they make slanderous attacks on our country, and organize armed provocations on the Soviet-Chinese border.

The Ninth Congress of the Communist Party of China, which took place in April 1969, confirmed the establishment of personal dictatorship by Mao Tse-tung and declared Maoism to be "the summit" of Marxism-Leninism. These attempts to replace the scientific revolutionary theory by an opposing system of petty-bourgeois origin are accompanied by appeals in the Chinese press to "hoist the banner of Mao Tse-tung ideas over the entire globe."

The problem of the sources of contemporary events in China, of the causes which allowed Mao Tse-tung to impose his vicious direction on the Communist party of China, is complex. It has been analyzed in depth in a number of documents of the CPSU and other Marxist-Leninist parties.

Our Party has always made a sharp distinction between the anti-Leninist political course of the present Chinese leadership and the communists and toilers of the Chinese People's Republic. It has always recognized the vital necessity of preserving and strengthening Soviet-Chinese friendship. Our policy remains the same today. The CPSU and the Soviet government are aiming at normalization of interstate relations with the Chinese People's Republic, at preservation and development of friendship between the Soviet and Chinese peoples, and at organization of joint action in the struggle against imperialism. This also corresponds to the vital national interest of the Chinese people. It is not by means of struggle against the USSR and other socialist countries, but by means of an alliance, fraternal cooperation with them, that the national rebirth of China and its development on the road to socialism can be achieved.

At the same time, as our Party has repeatedly emphasized, it will never consent to any concessions in the matters of principle. The CPSU has upheld and always will uphold the ideas of scientific communism, and oppose the attempts of Maoists to force their vicious anti-Leninist direction on the revolutionary movement, and will naturally defend the Soviet Union from hostile activity, whatever forms it may assume.

However complicated and difficult the overcoming of the Maoist menace, the Chinese communists, working class, and toilers will find strength, no doubt, to extricate themselves from the present crisis and return to the tested Leninist principles of building socialism, to the policy of friendship and cooperation with other socialist states.

As they fight various manifestations of petty-bourgeois nationalism, Marxist-Leninist parties of the world advocate strengthening the unity of all socialist countries. On this road from time to time one must deal with the tortuous "zigzags of history." But however complex and difficult, the great cause of creating a new type of international relations will be carried to a successful conclusion, since it corresponds to the objective needs of the development of the world socialist system and to the interests of its member-countries.

The World of Socialist System of Economy

The advantage of the new type of international relations that socialism is establishing has become clear in the field of economic collaboration of socialist states.

The people of each socialist country is interested in seeing that in all other socialist countries industry and agriculture grow and the living standard of the population increases. What socialist countries achieve depends to a great degree on mutual economic assistance being rendered in a variety of forms: mutually profitable trade, credits (loans), aid in industrial enterprise construction, exchange of scientific and technical expertise.

Naturally, this assistance is extended primarily by the countries most developed economically. Many industrial plants have been built in the fraternal socialist countries with the help of the Soviet Union. The USSR has made considerable amounts of credits available, assists in training specialists, and has provided several thousand designs, blueprints, and other technical material to help accelerate production.

The more developed countries of the socialist commonwealth seek no particular gain from the aid they extend to the fraternal countries. Nor do they assume the role of philanthropists. Socialist states are not divided into "benefactors" and "dependents." The people of each country mobilize their own domestic resources, first of all, for the construction of the new society. At the same time they collaborate with all the others; when successful, they do not conceal it but try rather to share their experience and progress with other socialist peoples. Thus, multilateral relations of comradely, mutual assistance are being formed within the socialist commonwealth.

Czechoslovakia is helping the fraternal countries to develop a machine-tool industry; the GDR [German Democratic Republic] is sharing its own rich experience in the manufacture of first-class optical instruments; Poland contributes its accomplishments in manufacture of mining machinery; and so forth. The socialist countries exchange their production, including consumer goods. Soviet citizens gladly purchase Czech footwear and Polish furniture, Bulgarian cigarettes and Hungarian silk. And our watches, cameras, and other products are in great demand in the fraternal socialist countries.

The socialist countries are increasingly making use of the opportunities for economic collaboration. Those with the advantage of a large supply of coal or oil or of great experience in machine-tool manufacture are developing these branches of industry so as to provide not only for their own needs but also for exports to other fraternal countries. They, in turn, supply to the coal, oil, or machine-tool-producing countries the commodities they manufacture. Numberless advantages result: the necessity for every country to build plants to supply all its requirements is eliminated; the possibility is created for expansion of precisely those branches of industry and agriculture most favored by a given country's natural environment and accumulated experience.

Historically speaking, an *international division of labor* by territory has developed among the countries of the world. This means that individual countries specialize in production of specific types of commodities, sell them on the world market, and purchase the particular commodities they need. Clearly, of itself the international division of labor is progressive, since it leads to increased labor productivity.

However, under the conditions of capitalism, the international division of labor is deformed. The bourgeoisie turns it into a source of profit, a means of exploitation of poorly developed countries.

In the colonies and poorly developed countries, as we have already pointed out, the imperialists sought to limit the economy to production of one or two commodities. As a result, these countries became entirely dependent upon the imperialist states, being their raw-material appendages and objects of cruel plunder. If, for example, little Venezuela, where two hundred million tons of oil are being extracted, cannot sell this oil, it is threatened with ruin and starvation. And this oil is exported by American imperialists. They price the toil of the Venezuelans according to their own arbitrary decisions, and consequently, the country, which could be fabulously rich, remains wretchedly poor.

Under socialism the situation is quite different. The international division of labor is free of the ugly diversification for which capitalism has been responsible; it is being expanded and developed in depth. Socialism does away with the exploitation of some countries by others, brings equality into the international division of labor, eliminates antagonistic contradictions between countries, and gradually creates conditions for harmonious development of the economy of all the countries within the framework of the world socialist system. One may therefore conclude that in the world socialist system of economy a *new type of international division of labor* is developing that rests on a voluntary basis and on the principle of equal rights, serving the cause of common economic growth of all the countries of this system.

The international socialist division of labor is comparatively recent in origin and has not yet reached its full development. And this is understandable: after all, the world socialist system has existed only for two decades, whereas much time is needed to harmonize specialization and cooperation among countries. Much has already been accomplished, but still more remains to be done to realize the possibilities and advantages of the international socialist division of labor. The European socialist countries have created a specialized agency, the SEV (Council for Mutual Economic Aid), for the purpose of ensuring a scientific solution of the complex problems of economic cooperation.

Powerful economic aggregates are being created by the joint effort of a number of countries.

In 1963 the gigantic "Druzhba" [Friendship] oil pipeline, some five thousand kilometers long, was put into operation. It joins the Volga Region and the Ukraine with Czechoslovakia, Poland, the GDR, and Hungary. Its length considerably exceeds that of other large oil pipelines—the American "Big Inch" and the "Trans-Arabian"—built by capitalist monopolies.

A unified electric power grid called "Peace" has been set up for the European socialist countries. Thus, the trend, described by V.I. Lenin, "to create a worldwide economy regulated according to a single plan by the proletariat of all nations" is becoming an increasingly visible reality.

The development of the world socialist economic system does not in any sense signify that the socialist states separate themselves from other countries and live in their own exclusive circle, so to speak. On the contrary, their goal is mutually advantageous economic cooperation and normal trade relations with all states. Economic cooperation based on equality is not only beneficial to all but also has great political importance, because it facilitates relaxation of international tensions and consolidation of friendly relations and peace among the peoples of different countries.

The Leading Revolutionary Force

The world socialist system is the leading revolutionary force in the contemporary world.

How is this expressed?

First of all, by the *power of the socialist example.* As they create the new society where there is no place for the exploitation of man by man and of nation by nation, the peoples of the socialist countries are demonstrating, by their example, the great advantages of the socialist order. Rapid economic growth, elimination of unemployment and other social disasters inherent in the capitalist mode of production, establishment of an extensive system of social security and public education, flowering of science and culture—all these accomplishments of socialism are furthering swift expansion of the ideas of Marxism-Leninism and constitute the most obvious and effective form of propaganda for the socialist transformation of society.

The role of the socialist system in the world revolutionary process is also *to pin down the imperialist forces*, thereby creating possibilities favoring the development of the revolutionary movement. Relying on their increasing economic power and political influence, the socialist states counteract the imperialist policy of "exporting counterrevolution" and defeat the designs of imperialism's most reactionary and aggressive circles, which aim at unleashing thermonuclear world war. The rocket-nuclear potential of the Soviet Union, constructed at the cost of tremendous effort, serves to contain the militaristic impulses of the imperialist aggressors, thereby serving the cause of defending the peace.

Finally, socialist countries render every conceivable *support to the revolutionary movement* and directly assist—materially, morally, and when required, militarily (as, for example, in Vietnam)—the peoples struggling for national independence and the right freely to decide their destiny.

Revolutionary Movement of the Proletariat

Increasing Influence of Communist Parties

Aggravation of the contradictions within capitalism is leading to an upsurge in the class struggle by the proletariat. This struggle is increasingly assuming a mass character.

The wave of strikes is rolling over the capitalist world, reaching its crest now in one country, now in another. Strikes and other organized actions clearly show increased resolve on the part of the working class to struggle for its interest.

Under these circumstances, it is of the utmost importance that in the large majority of strikes the toilers bring forward not only economic but political demands. In Japan the working class and peasantry are struggling against transformation of the country into an American nuclear proving ground. In the US marches are organized in defense of peace and civil rights, against discrimination toward and oppression of Negroes; the protest movement against the aggressive war of the American imperialists in Vietnam and, recently, in Cambodia is growing and expanding. The spring of 1968 was marked by the powerful action taken by the toilers of France, where over ten million persons participated in a general strike. The proletariat and other toiling strata of the population in Latin America are becoming more active; one of the most important demands of the workers' movement is to end the domination of the North American monopolies.

Economic and political actions taken by the working class and other toiling strata of the population are a unique barometer giving proof of the toilers' growing organization and consciousness. The workers' movement is entering a new, qualitative phase; the level of its demands is rising. Along with wage increases, shorter working days, and improvement in social security and retirement benefits, the workers struggle to achieve participation in production management, conditions favoring cultural development, upgraded educational levels, and respect for the dignity of toiling people. They want to live active and rewarding lives filled with important social interest, lives requiring broadened social rights and democratic freedoms. Naturally, these trends are directed essentially against the domination of the monopolies, are shaking loose its foundations, and causing or aggravating the instability in the capitalist world. Not a year goes by without an acute sociopolitical crisis in one or another of the capitalist countries of the world. All this foreshadows a new period of class struggles that could jeopardize the very existence of capitalism in its chief citadels.

The communist parties are marching in the front ranks of the working-class struggle. Never ceasing, they unmask the reactionary policy of the ruling imperialist circles and are rallying all the progressive forces for the struggle for peace, democracy, and socialism.

Hence the unprecedented growth of the communist movement. Communist parties now exist in nearly ninety countries of the world, with a membership of nearly fifty million persons.

Anti-communist propaganda and the oppression of communist parties in a number of capitalist states create unusually difficult conditions for their activities and, naturally, impair their growth. Needless to say, a great many communist parties are compelled to work semilegally or underground. Nevertheless, communist parties in numerous capitalist countries are actually aiming at becoming mass parties within the next few years.

Successes of the communist movement are determined not merely by the increased numerical strength of the parties themselves but also by their growing prestige among the masses. Communist parties in the capitalist countries exercise considerable influence in a number of large labor unions. Their increasing political influence can also be deduced from the fact that larger numbers of voters are voting for communist candidates in elections to representative governmental bodies.

What are the goals of the communist parties in capitalist countries?

The Working Class, Leading Force in the Struggle for Peace and Democracy

For the communist parties the ultimate goal of their struggle has always been the revolutionary transformation of society from capitalist to socialist, and the construction of communism. And it will remain so. The strategy and tactics of the contemporary communist movement are aimed at achieving that ultimate goal.

Socialist revolution is not a mutiny, nor is it a coup d'état; it is a natural, law-governed social process initiated by the development and intensification of all inherent contradictions of capitalism. Revolutions are not made to order. They take place when the specific, indispensable economic and sociopolitical prerequisites are mature; when the consciousness and organization of the proletariat reaches a sufficiently high level to execute its will for revolutionary actions and its determination to lead the masses in an attack on capitalism. It is inadmissible to rush events artificially, to run ahead of them, and thereby create the danger of isolating the Party from its class, the militant vanguard from the revolutionary army. This kind of political adventurism is characteristic of anarchists and has nothing in common with the Marxist-Leninist theory.

This does not at all mean that the toilers' revolutionary vanguard is

269

condemned to passive anticipation of events. On the contrary, it has the important tasks of rallying the masses, enlarging their consciousness, and improving their organization; of spreading communist ideas. The strategy and tactics of bringing the masses closer to the revolution require the Marxist-Leninist party to be able to gather all forces patiently, even in the most difficult situations, for the approaching decisive struggle. This can be done successfully in the struggle for national independence, and for the preservation and broadening of civil rights and liberties; in the struggle against militarization of the economy, against fascism, and against war. As V.I. Lenin noted, political transformations in the truly democratic direction are readying the ground for socialist revolution, "are bringing it closer, widening its base by involving in the socialist struggle the new strata of petty bourgeoisie and half-proletarian masses." Thus, the *struggle for democracy constitutes part of the struggle for socialism.*

The primary enemies of democracy in modern capitalist society are the powerful monopolies, which pit themselves against the overwhelming majority in the nation. With each passing year protest against domination of the monopolies is spreading. New social groups are joining the movement. Big capital flouts the interests of the peasantry and the middle strata of the population in cities (small businessmen and storekeepers, craftsmen, and some office and professional employees). These strata of society are either ruined or fall into bondage created by the monopolies and banks. It is understandable that they defend their interests actively.

The numerical strength and influence of intellectual workers have been increasing rapidly in our time, as the direct result of science and culture's tumultuous development and expanded educational and public-health systems. Formerly, intellectual work in bourgeois society offered great opportunities for acquiring positions of privilege. Because of its social outlook, a large portion of the intelligentsia was close to the bourgeoisie and served its interests. Today, increasing numbers of intelligentsia join the ranks of the army of hired labor, and together with the workers they are being ruthlessly exploited by financial capital. Their interests are closely interwoven with those of the working class. The profit motive and gain considerations permeating the policy of monopolistic capital place increasingly unbearable restraints upon the creative possibilities and noble aspirations of men of science, art, culture, and education. Under the impact of the deepening spiritual crisis of bourgeois society and the attractive power of socialism, conflict between the progressive intelligentsia and the monopolies is becoming more acute. Representatives of the intelligentsia, shoulder to shoulder with the workers, are following the path of the antiimperialist struggle, and this creates broad possibilities for uniting intellectual and manual labor.

In recent years the capitalist world has encountered another menacing phenomenon. This is the "youth revolt." Young workers, students, and school-age pupils see no opportunity for themselves in the world of the all-powerful monopolies, the world in the throes of a deep crisis. They demand change. Not infrequently, the opposition actions of the young are spontaneous in character; at times they fall under the influence of anarchist and other pseudorevolutionary ideas and sentiments. Nevertheless, these actions demonstrate youth's unwillingness to tolerate the oppressive atmosphere of contemporary capitalism. This creates a basis for rapprochement between the young and the workers' movement, with its communist vanguard, capable of providing the correct way to struggle for the realization of the young generation's aspirations and hopes, the way of struggle against the supremacy of the moneybag.

As more social groups join the antimonopoly struggle, the social foundation of the power of the monopolies inevitably shrinks; conditions are created favoring the unification of all the democratic forces and trends into a political alliance directed against the reactionary domestic and aggressive foreign policy of imperialism. Communist parties actively champion this union of progressive forces and their rallying in an *antimonopoly coalition.*

The working class, playing the leading role in the democratic movement, has the ability to forestall the menace of fascism and achieve adoption of such measures as will go beyond the usual bourgeois-democratic reforms and facilitate continued struggle for the victory of the socialist revolution. Thus, as the communist and workers' parties concluded, a peaceful transition to socialism is possible by winning over the overwhelming majority of the people, by politically isolating the monopolistic bourgeoisie, and by carrying out far-reaching democratic transformations, making the socialist reconstruction of the entire system of social relations inevitable.

However, if and when the exploiter classes resort to violence against the people, it becomes necessary to consider the prospects of a nonpeaceful transition to socialism.

As they creatively develop Marxist-Leninist theory and work out the strategy and tactics of the world communist movement, the Marxist-Leninist parties are waging a decisive struggle against revisionists and dogmatists, "right" and "left" opportunists. Opportunism of the right represents a trend within the communist movement to abandon for various reasons a consistently revolutionary course, to make concessions to bourgeois ideology, and, not infrequently, to slip into reformism, i.e., compromise with the class adversary of the proletariat. Opportunism on the left finds its expression in ultrarevolutionary attitudes, indifference to any creative work, and exclusive reliance on armed violence. Although the two varieties of opportunism are apparently contradictory, they are in fact closely related in their opposition to Marxism; also, they have the same petty-bourgeois origin. V.I. Lenin wrote:

Every specific turning point in history causes changes in the forms of the petty-bourgeois hesitation—always happening close to the proletariat, always, to a certain extent, penetrating into the midst of the proletariat.
Petty-bourgeois reformism—servility to the bourgeoisie disguised by nice

democratic and "social" democratic phrases and helpless wishes—is one trend in that hesitation; the other is petty-bourgeois revolutionizing, fierce, arrogant, boastful in words but in fact an empty shell, dissipated, scattered, and harebrained. Both are unavoidable until the deepest roots of capitalism are removed.

Consistent struggle against all forms of opportunism is one of the important tasks of the fraternal parties.

In their programs, communist parties formulate immediate and long-range objectives of the struggle and timetables based on a comprehensive appraisal both of the international situation and specific conditions in every country. Since specific conditions of development in various countries differ, it is natural that the communist parties' programs for action cannot coincide on all points. However, all the communist parties of the capitalist countries agree that their most important objective is to achieve *working class unity of action.*

Unity of the Proletariat, Guarantee of Victory

The socialist and social democratic parties enjoy considerable influence among a certain segment of the working class and the other population strata in the capitalist countries. They are given votes by a considerable part of the electorate, have strong parliamentary representation, and in a number of countries head the government.

In their majority the rightist leaders of social democratic parties are heirs to the opportunistic leadership of the Second International, who had opposed Marxism by their reformist theories. At best, all these theories advocate introduction of certain reforms and do not strike at the foundations of capitalism, private ownership and exploitation of hired labor.

Once they had assumed power in a number of European countries, the rightist socialists, it would seem, had every opportunity to realize their plans for the reformist "transformation" of capitalism into socialism. Yet their activities proved the failure of reformism once again. In not a single country have the rightist socialists built socialism.

When comparing the two ways, the reformist and the revolutionary, the working class is clearly convinced that the communist way is correct. The accumulated experience of the workers' movement and vigorous criticism of opportunism by the communists are worsening the crisis of the reformist ideology. As a result, there is a cleavage within the ranks of social democracy, and its leaders' attitude is also being affected. As before, the majority of them stubbornly advocate the bankrupt dogmas of reformism, faithfully defending the interests of big capital. Others, however, show an inclination to take heed of the toilers' economic and social wishes in their struggle for peace and progress. The forces of the left within social democracy are attempting to find new vistas that would permit them to take a place in the general front of the anti-imperialist struggle by socialist and social democratic parties. Social democracy's most forward-looking leaders are beginning to realize that this prospect is possible only through rapprochement with the communist parties, which have most consistently defended working-class interests.

By advocating the unity of the workers' movement, the communists support cooperation with socialists and social democrats in order to establish a progressive democratic system today and build socialist society in the future. Communists do whatever is in their power to realize this collaboration. However, it is self-evident that progress on this road can be made only if the social democrats abandon their policy of class collaboration with the bourgeoisie and firmly uphold the position of struggle for peace, democracy, and socialism. Because of social democracy's duplicity, hesitation, and lack of consistency, the road to the unity of the workers' movement will not be easy. It will be necessary to surmount many obstacles and survive many disappointments. Communists will have to make tremendous efforts, but this is indispensable.

One may say without exaggeration that capitalism still exists chiefly because there is a split in the ranks of the proletariat. The growing and ever stronger unity of the workers' movement hastens the advent of the socialist revolution and brings the end of capitalism closer.

Liberation Movement of Peoples

Colonialism's Downfall

The national liberation movement is dealing powerful blows to the foundations of capitalist oppression.

Colonialism is a genuine disgrace to mankind, and the capitalist system under which a handful of imperialist powers enslaved the overwhelming majority of the earth's population is fully responsible for it.

The October Revolution awakened the peoples of the East and inspired them with courage to fight their oppressors. This struggle assumed an especially resolute character with the crushing defeat of fascist Germany and militarist Japan in World War II. The strongest blow to the colonial system was dealt by the victory of the great Chinese people and the peoples of Korea and Vietnam, who, after driving out their enslavers, began building socialism. India, Indonesia, Burma, and a number of other countries won their independence. One after another the countries of the colonial East achieved political independence.

Let us see how the world map has changed since the time the October Revolution broke the imperialist front and opened wide the road to freedom to all peoples:

Colonies, semicolonies, and dominions

1919	*1968*
97,800,000 sq. km. or 72 percent of the earth's total area, with 1,235,000,000 inhabitants; or 69.4 percent of the earth's total population	5,300,000 sq. km. or 3.9 percent of the earth's total area, with 37,800,000 inhabitants; or 1.1 percent of the earth's total population

The downfall of colonialism represents a major historical event, second in importance only to the formation of the world socialist system. It is one of many significant factors causing the general crisis of capitalism to become drastic.

National Liberation Revolutions

The oppressed peoples in the colonies stubbornly fought imperialism. However, the power was in the hands of the colonizers, who drowned national uprisings in blood. Victory became possible only after the world socialist system was formed and the imperialists lost their dominant positions in international affairs forever. This means that national liberation revolutions in our time are part of the single revolutionary process encompassing the world, the process in which the liberation struggle of oppressed peoples is organically interwoven with the actions of the two other basic contemporary revolutionary forces, the world socialist system and the workers' movement in the capitalist countries.

The new circumstances under which the national liberation revolution is unfolding affects its character, motive forces, and prospects. As a rule, the material and social prerequisites for the transition to socialism do not exist in the former colonies and semicolonies. That is why the national liberation revolution is not socialist in character. But it cannot be considered a bourgeois revolution either. It is an anti-imperialist and antifeudal revolution: its first demand is independence, its second, agrarian reform. Its further development depends upon the correlation and struggle of class forces within the national liberation movement.

A broad coalition of social forces usually participates in a national liberation revolution, composed of the young working class, the peasantry, the petty bourgeoisie in the cities, and the patriotically oriented strata of a nation's intelligentsia. The identity of the political leadership of such a coalition is a question of the utmost importance.

In those countries where combat-ready detachments of the proletariat already exist and communist parties capable of leading the struggle of the masses have been organized, the national liberation revolution may become a socialist revolution. Where the working class does not exist or is politically weak, leadership, under the influence of socialism, may be assumed by revolutionary democratic parties composed of radical representatives of the local intelligentsia, office workers, and military personnel. In this case, also, the revolution develops in the progressive direction, though in a more complex way.

In countries where the leadership remains in the hands of the bourgeoisie, the tasks of national liberation and of eliminating the vestiges of feudalism are dealt with halfheartedly and inconsistently. To keep the revolution within the framework of bourgeois concepts is the observable trend.

The problem of the liberation movement leadership becomes extremely acute after political independence has been achieved.

The Struggle Continues

The colonial system's downfall does not mean that colonialism has been completely eradicated. The imperialists, in fact, have not reconciled themselves to the loss of colonies. They are using new, more refined methods to continue robbing the peoples of liberated countries.

How is this being done? First of all, the imperialists attempt to place in power in the new states men devoted to them who obediently execute the colonialist's will. Where they succeed, the proclamation of independence does not bring any substantial change in the people's situation.

Since World War II the imperialists have on a broad scale resorted to the practice of enlisting the former colonies as members of aggressive blocks. Thus, they seek to maintain their hegemony. Under the pretext of "protection from communism," the United States has built military bases on the territory of these countries, flooded them with troops and "advisers," and are imposing their will.

But even if the imperialists were not successful in maintaining political domination in the former colonial countries, they continue to retain an economic position and extract huge profits from those exploited peoples. Annual profits of the Western monopolists from the exploitation of the poorly developed countries amount to twenty billion dollars.

This is why the struggle against imperialism is not yet over. Only after creating their own industry, training their own specialists, and expelling the imperialist monopolies will the recently organized states be able to free themselves from economic servitude and stop the plunder of their own natural wealth. Overcoming their economic backwardness and creating independent national economies have become crucial for liberated countries.

In the struggle to strengthen their independence, the peoples of the former colonial countries find friendly support from the USSR and the other socialist states. Our country helped India to build a huge metallurgical combine in Bhilai; the first stage of the famous Aswan Dam in United Arab Republic has been completed. With USSR assistance scores of industrial enterprises and roads, hospitals and research institutes are being constructed in India, Burma, Afghanistan, the new states of Africa, and numerous other countries. In the Patrice Lumumba Friendship of the Peoples University in Moscow there are young Indian students, Guineans, Arabs, and Somalis, young men and women from every corner of our planet. Once they have completed their training and become specialists, they take their acquired knowledge and skills to their peoples and help them fight economic and cultural backwardness.

The peoples of these countries still face not a few difficulties, and they must find solutions to complex problems.

As long as the struggle for independence lasts, the various classes and social groups march together; they share a common enemy, imperialism. But once independence has been won, the opposing nature of class interests comes to light. Conflict becomes more acute between the working class, peasantry, and other democratic strata on the one hand and, on the other, imperialism and the forces of internal reaction. The bourgeoisie seeks to exploit the independence won by the people in order to achieve its own domination. It reveals the inclination to compromise with imperialism and the feudal lords at the people's expense, and it tries to establish the capitalist order based on exploitation of the workers and peasants.

Actually, as the experience of the countries that took the capitalist road has demonstrated, capitalism is incapable of solving the problems of liberated peoples. It brings them new privations and burdens. Dissatisfaction on the part of the popular masses is answered by the internal reactionaries with ruthless repression and attacks on democratic freedoms. The reaction fans intertribal and religious conflicts and splits the anti-imperialist alliance, thus menacing the gains already achieved by the national liberation revolution.

What is the way out of the predicament in which the liberated countries find themselves? The way was shown by V.I. Lenin:

Can we recognize the correctness of the assertion that the capitalist stage of economic development is inevitable for the backward peoples who are now liberating themselves, among whom, since the war, a movement along the road of progress is now noticeable? We have answered this question in the negative.

The experience of the socialist countries shows the peoples of the former colonies and semicolonies a straight and broad road to national rebirth and social progress. But in order to reach this road and follow it resolutely, certain specific conditions are indispensable. In countries seriously lagging in socioeconomic development it is quite difficult to create these conditions. Many dangers lie in wait for the liberated peoples. Imperialism and internal reaction are doing their best to prevent the escape of the newly organized states from the capitalist system and to preserve the old order. Some liberated countries have already experienced reverses caused by counterrevolutionary forces. To paralyze reaction and prevent movement backward it is necessary to consolidate the alliance of all progressive and patriotic forces struggling to carry on to success the anti-imperialist, antifeudal, democratic revolution.

In recent years the ruling parties and political figures of a number of states that adopted the way of independent development have declared the construction of socialism to be the objective of their policy. Social transformations of varying intensity are taking place in these countries: nationalization of the means of production owned by imperialist monopolies; creation of a state sector of the economy; and agrarian reform and promotion of cooperative peasant farming. The social-development programs according to which these transformations are being carried out are not consistent in all their aspects; on many problems it is possible to confuse correct, scientific, socialist ideas with the vestiges of utopian views and, at times, even with a religious outlook.

While asserting that they proceed in their own way and create socialist society according to the historic traditions of their peoples, these states' leaders stress at the same time that they follow the example of the socialist countries in many instances and that they are profiting from the rich experience of the world socialist system.

This powerfully demonstrates the invincibility of mankind's movement toward socialism. The socialist countries do not impose their experience on the recently organized states. They render them all imaginable assistance, but they do not interfere in their affairs. Life itself will suggest to peoples which theory offers the most reliable and correct path to socialism; with greater frequency it will induce them to arm themselves with the only scientific theory, the communist teaching of Marx, Engels, and Lenin.

Fundamental Problem of the Present

We shall now try to take a general look at the overall picture of the contemporary international situation. Two social systems exist in this world, and they are developing in opposite directions. With ever-increasing clarity the world socialist system demonstrates the advantages of the new order. The world capitalist system inexorably approaches its end. Comparison of these two trends, these two directions of development, gives every reason to affirm that the confrontation of the two systems, the confrontation between the two opposite worlds, will unquestionably culminate in the victory of socialism.

However, no trends in society's development will prevail by themselves, without struggle by the peoples.

The imperialist powers strenuously arm themselves, organize military provocations, resort to interference by force in the internal affairs of other countries. They regard all this as the means of struggle against the world socialist system and against the liberation movement of peoples as well.

Thus, there is danger of a new world war. Under the existing conditions, with socialism firmly establishing itself and gaining strength while capitalism weakens and decays, this dying order threatens to take along with it to the grave hundreds of millions of lives and the inestimable wealth that the labor of many generations has created.

The question of war and peace has become the *fundamental problem of today*. "The Appeal in Defense of Peace" adopted by the international meeting of communist and workers' parties in 1969 states: "The struggle is being waged for the most important objective—the future of mankind."

Indictment of Capitalism

Three million human beings perished in all the wars of the seventeenth century; 5.5 million in those of the eighteenth century; 16 million in those of the nineteenth century; in the twentieth century the victims of World War I numbered 10 million and those of World War II, 50 million.

In the seventeenth century the chief weapon of war was the rifle; in the eighteenth and nineteenth centuries the artillery predominated, converted from a simple auxiliary weapon into the "God of War." In the two world wars the single "deity" yielded to a "trinity": artillery, tanks, and aircraft. To these has now been added the most destructive of all weapons, the nuclear weapon. And still military technology continues to develop. When Albert Einstein was asked what weapon might be used in World War III, he answered: "I don't know about World War III, but in World War IV it will be the bow and arrow."

War must not break out. This much is clear to any man of sound mind familiar with the destructive power of modern weaponry. The first atomic bomb had an explosive capacity equal to 20,000 tons of TNT. Hydrogen bombs with a capacity equivalent to 100,000,000 tons of TNT have now been made. In addition, there is lethal radiation. One of science's greatest discoveries, promising unlimited quantities of free power to mankind, is in danger of becoming a source of destruction and death. And only the inhuman capitalist system is responsible.

In August 1945, when Japan's capitulation was literally a few days away, Truman, President of the US, ordered atomic bombs dropped on the Japanese cities of Hiroshima and Nagasaki. The result was that nearly 200,000 human beings perished or were afflicted with radiation sickness, and Hiroshima was left in ashes. Mankind will never forget that black day.

Why, even in the absence of military necessity, did the ruling circles of the US decide to use the atomic bomb? Because they needed a "show of force," because they were counting on intimidating the USSR and forcing the whole world to submit to their will. With its monopoly of the atomic weapon, American imperialism began pursuing a policy of atomic blackmail. The zealous generals of the Pentagon (the US ministry of war) were developing plans for the atomic bombing of the largest industrial centers in our country. They were making ready to annihilate millions of Soviet citizens in order to crush the hated socialist system.

Under these circumstances our country was forced to produce its own nuclear weapons: the defense of the socialist conquests of the Soviet people, the independence of our fatherland were at stake. Soviet scientists brilliantly met the challenge and ended the United States monopoly in this area. This was a powerful blow to the aggressive plans of the American warmongers. The USA feverishly began to push manufacture of the hydrogen bomb, hundreds of times more powerful than the atomic bomb. But here again their calculations failed: in 1953 the USSR produced the hydrogen bomb ahead of the USA.

Even then, military circles in the USA did not become still. "Bombs," they said, "are only half the task. The main thing is to have bomber aircraft and military bases close to the frontiers of the Soviet Union. The USA will then be able to deliver a strike without fear of retaliation."

That was their strategy, monstrous in its intention. Even if the USA were able to escape a retaliatory strike, their allies in Europe and Asia on whose territory the American military bases are located certainly would not escape. Besides, even laymen clearly understand that a nuclear war would be especially deadly for countries with comparatively little territory and high population density. And the specialists have calculated that only a few hydrogen bombs are sufficient to wipe such countries as England, France, and West Germany off the face of the earth.

Despite this, the militarists on the other side of the Atlantic called for aggression against the socialist countries. What did they care about the danger threatening the peoples of Europe and Asia? They were only concerned with their own skins!

However, their strategy again failed. Intercontinental ballistic missiles and global rockets capable of hitting any point on the earth's surface with exceptional accuracy were in manufacture in the USSR.

Now the aggressors are threatened with a crushing retaliatory strike, irrespective of the oceans they may hide behind.

The Cause of Peace Is in the Peoples' Hands

By its very nature, policy "from the position of strength" is alien to socialist countries. Despite the might of its military equipment, the Soviet Union consistently fights for cessation of the arms race and promotion of a durable peace.

But the imperialist governments, who in public avow their commitment to peace, are continuing the arms race. The criminal policy of the US imperialists has more than once brought humanity to the brink of war. War or peace? This is the question that today disturbs hundreds of millions of people in every corner of our planet.

Is it possible to prevent a world war? We know, after all, that imperialism by its very nature breeds wars; this has been confirmed by the entire course of history. Its nature has not changed, even now. Consequently, as long as this system exists, the source of war danger remains.

But one must not apply a theoretical proposition without considering the specific situation and altered historical conditions. Yes, as before, imperialism continues to breed wars. However, the imperialist states do not exist in a vacuum but on this earth, where other social forces in addition to themselves exist. We must therefore find out whether these forces are capable of bridling imperialism and rendering its sting harmless. In other words, we must analyze the correlation between the forces of peace and the forces of war in the contemporary era.

The forces of peace are, first of all, the Soviet Union and the other countries of socialism, capable of delivering a crushing blow to the imperialist aggressors.

On the side of peace there is a large group of nonsocialist states that have no vested interest in unleashing war; they are in need of peace to solve the problems of their national rebirth.

Peace is being defended by the international working class's organization of the struggle by the broad popular masses against the imperialist war.

By the united efforts of the mighty socialist camp, the peace-loving nonsocialist states, the international working class, and all the forces defending the cause of peace, *world war can be prevented.* The growing superiority of the forces of socialism over those of imperialism, of the forces of peace over those of war, will make it possible, even before socialism's complete victory and even while capitalism persists in part of the world, to exclude world war from the life of society. The victory of socialism the world over will finally eliminate the social and national causes that are the origins of all wars. *The abolition of war and establishment of lasting peace on earth is the historic mission of communism.*

This balanced and well-substantiated conclusion in our Party Program gives us firm confidence in the victory of the forces of peace over those of war.

Of course, international developments do not proceed along a straight path, and the possibility of preserving the peace does not automatically result from the general correlation of forces in the world arena. In these times the decision about war and peace is being made in sharp skirmishes with imperialism unwilling to abandon its policy of military adventures and creating now and again dangerous situations in different regions of the earth. The international situation today reminds one of the sequence of tides on an ocean shore. Relaxation of tensions, achieved by the struggle of the peace forces, alternates periodically with aggravation of the international situation as a result of aggressive actions by the imperialists.

The direct military aggression of the USA in Vietnam, which has provoked the scorn of all honest people throughout the world, can serve as an example. In fulfillment of its international obligation to a fraternal socialist country, the Soviet Union renders great economic and military assistance to the Vietnamese people. On the basis of this help and the broad, worldwide movement of solidarity, the heroic people of Vietnam are inflicting defeat on the interventionists. A just political settlement of the conflict can only be achieved if the American troops withdraw from Vietnam as well as from Cambodia and Laos, and if the peoples of Indochina should be assured of their sovereign right to decide their own destiny, according to their wishes.

The communists have marched and continue to march in the front line of the struggle against the imperialist policy of aggression and war, the struggle for peace and friendship among nations. They have fought persistently for the cessation of nuclear weapon tests. This led in 1963 to the conclusion of an international agreement banning nuclear tests in three areas—on the earth's surface, in the air, and on the water. The Bucharest Declaration by the Warsaw Pact member-countries (1966) and the Documents of the Conference of the European Communist and Workers' Parties later at Karlovy Vary [Czechoslovakia] contain a concrete program of struggle for peace and security on the continent of Europe. The Marxist-Leninist parties have resolutely supported the idea of concluding an agreement on nonproliferation of nuclear weapons, which by the end of 1969 was already signed by over one hundred world states.

As long as the danger of war persists, sharp vigilance against the intrigues of the enemies of peace is indispensable. This is the main purpose of the Appeal in Defense of Peace adopted by the Moscow meeting of communist and workers' parties of 1969. Every honest person on earth must consider it his sacred duty to do all within his power to prevent the outbreak of a thermonuclear holocaust.

The Appeal in Defense of Peace states:

The struggle for peace includes peace-promoting initiatives of the socialist states, victorious battles of Vietnamese patriots in the jungles of South Vietnam, antiwar demonstrations in the cities of Europe and America, and the struggle of the Japanese people against American military bases, as well. The cause of peace is also well served by actions of the working class against the omnipotence of the monopolies, resistance by the peoples of Latin America to the dictatorship of military cliques, and anticolonial movements in Asia and Africa, as well as the fight by the Negro population of the USA for their rights. Everyone participating in this struggle—irrespective of whether he wears worker's overalls, tills the earth, or toils in a laboratory—contributes his share to the common cause of the defense of peace.

Our task, the Soviet people's task, therefore, is to work untiringly to strengthen the economic might of our country, which is the foundation of its defensive capacity; to serve with honor in the Soviet Army; and to be ready at any moment to defend the fatherland.

In its fight for peace the Soviet Union consistently pursues the policy of peaceful coexistence of states with divergent social systems. This policy, whose principles were formulated by V.I. Lenin, assumes that renunciation of war is the means of solving international disputes, that there must be strict respect for sovereignty and equality, noninterference in the affairs of other states, and development of mutually advantageous economic and cultural ties among all nations, irrespective of their socioeconomic and political systems. Experience shows that political differences between states can be fully resolved by peaceful negotiations.

Peaceful coexistence does not mean abandoning the struggle of ideas, the struggle between the communist and the bourgeois ideologies. The ideas of Marxism-Leninism have spread all over the world, since they express the vital interests of the toilers. The very truth of life is embodied in them, and there is no hiding from the truth! And it is clear to everyone that of itself the ideological struggle does not lead to military clashes, that it is fully compatible with peaceful coexistence between capitalist and socialist states. Of course, in this struggle one cannot impose on peoples alien ideas by force of arms and threats, as the imperialists frequently attempt to do.

Peaceful coexistence by no means applies to relations between the oppressed peoples and colonizers, between the exploited and exploiters; and it does not signify reconciliation of antagonistic classes. Each nation has the sacred right to fight against any kind of oppression, and if the reactionary classes resort to armed resistance, the people also have the right to resort to the force of arms.

Peaceful coexistence does not mean perpetuation of the capitalist system wherever it now exists. After they become convinced, by their own experience, of the superiority of socialism, the peoples of the capitalist countries will choose the more progressive social order.

The struggle for peace and international security, for mankind's progress toward socialism, is a protracted and tenacious struggle. Progressive forces are confronted by a crafty enemy—imperialism—which still has considerable resources at its disposal. But revolutionaries and all the partisans of progress possess a more powerful weapon—their fighting unity. The document of the International Meeting of Communist and Workers' Parties (Moscow, 1969) entitled "The Tasks of the Struggle Against Imperialism During the Present Stage and the Unity of Action of Communist and Workers' Parties, of all Anti-Imperialist Forces," contains a warm appeal for strengthening this unity: "Peoples of socialist countries, proletarians, all democratic forces in the countries of capitalism, liberated and oppressed peoples! Unite in the common struggle against imperialism and for peace, national independence, social progress, democracy, and socialism!"

Review Questions

1. What are the specific features of the new type of international relations?
2. What are the advantages and prospects of the international socialist division of labor?
3. How does the socialist system exert its influence on world development?

4. What are the immediate tasks to be solved by the revolutionary workers' movement in the capitalist countries?
5. What are the immediate tasks to be solved by the newly established states that have freed themselves from colonial dependence?
6. On what basis may we conclude that prevention of war is possible in the contemporary era?
7. What is the meaning for the Marxists of the concept of peaceful coexistence of states with divergent social systems?

Points to Consider and Discuss

1. Share what you know about the specific economic and political forms used within the social system of fraternal countries. In this context, what is the significance of the exchange of experience among the countries of socialism?
2. Invite a comrade who has taken an official trip to one of the socialist countries to participate in your discussions. After hearing his report, consider how the Soviet people fulfills its international obligation toward fraternal peoples.
3. Prove the thesis that nationalist views damage not only the interests of the commonwealth of socialist countries as a whole but also, first of all, the interest of the country whose policy reflects such attitudes.
4. Think over the following question: What is the connection between the successes of world socialism and the fact that the workers in capitalist countries in recent years have managed to achieve marked improvement in their life conditions and wrest a number of concessions from the bourgeoisie?
5. In the view of petty-bourgeois ultrarevolutionaries, thermonuclear war on a world scale is fully acceptable as a means of solving the conflict of the two systems in favor of socialism. Give them your answer.
6. Become familiar with the document prepared by the communist and workers' parties entitled "Indictment of Imperialism" (in the journal *Problems of Peace and Socialism*, 1969, No. 7, pp. 29-46). Prepare a statement on the topic: "The accusation of the peoples of the world against imperialism and the terrible threat it poses for the future of mankind."
7. How do you envision mankind's further movement toward socialism?

Conclusion

There is no need now to guess at what communist society will look like, since we have a scientific conception of it. Obviously, we cannot make judgments about every detail of this society. Solutions to many problems will be suggested by life itself and by the practical experience of communist construction. But the most important, most essential traits of the future are clear.

Let us make a broad review of what we have learned, repeating, consolidating, and summarizing our knowledge.

Communism establishes lasting global PEACE.

For the first time in its long, laden history, suffering-mankind will breath freely. There will be an end to the senseless use of the human capacity, wasted to create destructive weapons of war. Thousands of enterprises in all the world's countries now turning out deadly products will be converted to the manufacture of goods to satisfy people's various needs. Instead of fighter planes and bombers, they will turn out fast passenger airliners and powerful transport aircraft; instead of ballistic missiles, space rockets; instead of tanks, tractors; instead of artillery guns and shells, items like refrigerators and vacuum cleaners.

And what a brilliant perspective will open to science! A multitude of scientific institutions and scientists now busy with creating new types of offensive and defensive weapons (this occupies over two-thirds of all scientists at present) will switch their efforts to searching for new kinds of power and material, to designing machinery to ease man's labor and adorn his life, and to struggling for the final eradication of disease and extension of the life span.

The word "war" will be retained only to designate such humanitarian concepts as the war on disease and old age, on drought and crop failure, on natural disasters. And the word *mir* [meaning both "world" and "peace" in Russian] will be used in its single, original sense: all of society, the planet, the whole universe.

The prosperous and powerful human race will be able to direct all its forces to the conquest of the worlds of outer space. Of course, it is out of the question to forcibly impose our will on the inhabitants of other planets (and we have no doubt, and neither do you, that sooner or later a meeting of the earth's inhabitants with their "celestial neighbors" will take place). The question is, rather, to open and develop the entire universe and spread civilization.

All of you, certainly, have read in H.G. Wells's novel *The War of the Worlds* about how the Martians come to Earth and annihilate every living thing in order to subjugate our planet, and how mankind is saved from extinction only with the aid of microbes. Many American writers similarly describe future space encounters in their science-fiction novels and short stories. One writer has Earth people subjugating the inhabitants of Venus and establishing on that planet a regime of . . . colonialism. Another depicts a series of bitter clashes breaking out in the vast reaches of outer space over "spheres of influence." These writers are thinking in the categories of their capitalist circumstances.

No. This is not what the meeting of the worlds will be like. The Soviet science-fiction writer Ivan Yefremov has expressed the following thoughts in one of his novels: only beings of exceptional intelligence who have attained the pinnacle of science are capable of organizing interplanetary flights and visits to their space neighbors. And this level of development of science and technology as a result of intellectual achievement is possible only in a society organized on just and rational foundations. The emissaries of Earth (and of other planets) will be incapable of vile and cruel pursuits and of sowing violence, destruction, and death. They can have but one purpose: association of rational beings cooperating to conquer nature and glorifying reason and labor.

However, let us now return from outer space to Earth, where there is still a tremendous amount of work to do. In the words of Mayakovskiy, our planet ought to be "equipped for mirth." This is achieved by LABOR, which under communism will become the principal content of society's entire life and the principal meaning of every individual's personal life.

Let us consider this matter first of all from the point of view of the results of social labor. *A gigantic development of the productive forces, assuring an abundance of all the goods needed by man*, will be attained by society's organized efforts. Under communism, said Marx, wealth will be flowing full stream. And the streams of wealth will swell at an ever-increasing rate, thanks to the natural combination of science and production. Science has now already become a great productive force, but the goods it provides are nothing compared with what it will offer mankind in the future. More distant prospects aside, science is now on the threshold of several solutions that would revolutionize the production of material goods.

Undoubtedly the most important problem to be solved is control of thermonuclear reaction, which will assure practically inexhaustible energy supplies. Neither is it difficult to imagine the importance of learning methods of directed growth conditioning of plants and living organisms. Or of weather control, which will make it possible to prevent crop failures. Or of manufacture of synthetic proteins and many other materials nature has failed to provide.

An unusually high productivity level of social labor, due to development of science and technology and improvement of personnel—scientifically, technically, and culturally—will cause enormous growth of productive forces. In speaking of communist production, we anticipate systems of automatic self-regulating devices to perform all work, from drawing blueprints to the output of the finished product, without intervention of manual labor and with control operations only in the hands of workers.

The source of well-being and joy, *labor under communism will become the vital need of every member of society*.

A man works well and with enthusiasm for a number of different reasons: he counts on a rich reward for his labor; he recognizes an obligation to society; he is fascinated by his work, seeing in it only the chance to reveal his personal creative abilities; and, finally, work has become a habit for him, as natural and usual as the need to breathe or communicate with other persons. Combine all these motivations and you will get communist labor.

Certainly, you will object: "One can agree with each of these except the material incentive to labor. Isn't it true that V.I. Lenin called communist labor unremunerated labor for the common good? How, then, can one talk of expecting remuneration?"

Of course, a communist man would never think of demanding as reward for his shock work that things not yet available to all should immediately be placed at his disposal.[a] He will work without pay and does not measure his labor either by money, which simply will not exist, or any material value. He is interested, nevertheless, in growth of the social wealth. Only his interest is no longer egoistic, since he is not thinking of himself alone but rather of society as a whole. Thus, one of the incentives to labor under communism will be the collective material incentive to increase the social wealth and steadily improve the living conditions for every person.

But were we to limit ourselves to the assertion that the communist man is distinguished by the need to work, we should be far from telling the whole story. It is not simply a question of need to work but a *need to work according to ability*. This is the reason, precisely, why the social wealth will be constantly on the increase and society will find it possible to satisfy fully all its members' reasonable needs.

Realization of the main principle of communism, "From each according to his ability, to each according to his need," will mean that complete EQUALITY has been established in society.

Let us consider to what extent the principle of satisfaction according to need corresponds to the idea of equality.

Under socialism people receive equal pay for equal work, and this reflects the justice of the socialist distribution principle. But persons differ in their abilities, and the composition of their families is not identical. Some, therefore, earn more and live better than others. Introduction of the communist distribution principle eliminates this distinction, overcoming to a degree the injustice of nature itself, which endows persons with unequal ability for work and creativity.

From the point of view of formal law, this is a violation of equality, inasmuch as communist society satisfies everyone fully, regardless of the quantity and quality of his labor. But this formal law is not suitable for communism, which rejects it and introduces a higher justice, the truly humanitarian ideal of equality: let everyone give to society all he can and society will generously satisfy all his reasonable needs.

---

[a]Take an orchestra or choir, for comparison. If it consists of true artists and music-lovers, they will not play or sing halfheartedly just because a special effort does not bring better remuneration.

Communist equality is also expressed in the *elimination of socioeconomic, cultural, and everyday life distinctions between urban and rural areas*. Farm labor will be converted into a form of industrial labor, meaning that there will be no more difference between industrial and agricultural labor than exists between labor in different branches of industry; in due time, in agriculture as in industry, equally favorable opportunities for *integration of intellectual and manual labor in people's productive activity* will develop.

Vestiges of inequality in the social position of women will also finally be eradicated. The question here is primarily to liberate women from burdensome household tasks (preparing meals, doing laundry, sewing, etc.) and ease their difficulties connected with child-rearing, especially with the care of infants.

Finally, the inequality of the sexes, because woman is not physically as strong as man, will on the whole be overcome under communism. After all, with mechanization and automation of production, the advantage of physical strength will be experienced less and less. And the time is not far off when women will be able to work in any branch of the economy on an equal footing with men. In short, when speaking of work, it will no longer be either meaningful or correct to use the age-old terms of the "weaker" and the "stronger" sex. The former "weaker" sex will yield in nothing to the "stronger" sex, once equipped with knowledge and operating the powerful technical machinery of communism.

The institution of a single, communist ownership of the means of production and elimination of class distinctions will lead to the creation of *classless society*. And this is the ultimate ideal of equality—any other interpretation of equality is meaningless: people will always differ in ability and tastes. Justice does not consist in trying to level them but rather in creating for each person taken individually and for all of them together the best conditions for creative living. That is why the formation of classless society is the best conceivable ultimate of equality. When this ultimate will have been attained, the word "equality" will no longer have its present stirring meaning.

Hand in hand with equality goes LIBERTY, because only free men can be equal and only equal men free.

The socialist revolution frees the toilers from exploitation. Society's entire subsequent development is in the direction of creating conditions that will enable *every person to develop freely and use his creative abilities in his work*. Therein lies the communist ideal of liberty.

Real life under socialism has fully confirmed V.I. Lenin's words that the talents of the people represent an untapped spring. Now we can boldly proclaim that the spring has been brought to the earth's surface and adorns our world with marvelous fruits. But the real flowering of popular creativity still lies ahead. Under communism this spring of talent will turn into a deep river, because the richer our lives and the higher the level of popular education, the greater are the possibilities for creative work reflecting the people's abilities extensively and diversely.

Under communism especially favorable conditions for free creative work are connected with the *elimination of the former division of labor*, which used to enslave man. Under capitalism the worker is tied down for life to one labor operation. Often he does not even know where the part he manufactures will be used. Monotony and uniformity, daily repetition of identical motions, drain the man of all his strength and waste his intellectual power.

Under the conditions of socialist production the worker understands the social significance of his labor. He visualizes behind the part he produces the machines that will help the *kolkhoz* members grow a rich harvest or the construction workers erect new dwellings. This awareness inspires his labor and encourages him to consider how he may fulfill his assignment better and faster. The worker in our country, furthermore, is not tied to a single operation: opportunities to raise his cultural and technical level, to accumulate knowledge and experience, are wide open, enabling him to transfer to other more complex production sectors.

The adverse consequences of the former division of labor will, however, be overcome finally under communism, where all the monotonous labor operations will be performed by automatic production lines and man will work at designing, regulating, and controlling the machines. Every kind of labor therefore will acquire a creative character. Broad education together with improved cultural outlook will enable people not merely to live for the sake of their own basic specialization but also to develop and use their other abilities in a practical way. In other words, the man of communism is a *fully developed man, possessing spiritual wealth, moral integrity, and physical perfection.*

Life expectancy will be greatly prolonged (scientists talk about one hundred fifty years; and the most optimistic among them, even two hundred years), thanks to the exceptionally favorable material and cultural conditions of existence, medicine, and many other sciences.

Society as a whole, as well as individual persons, will profit from this increase of the life span. At present a man devotes from ten to twenty years of his life to study, so that only from twenty-five to forty years remain for work and creative endeavors. When a man has reached full maturity, when he has acquired experience and knowledge, his physical forces begin to fail. How many marvelous ideas are never realized, how much incalculable wealth of intellect are we deprived of, because nature has been so stingy in setting man's life span. It is not difficult to imagine how much social progress will be accelerated when centenarians will still be in the full bloom of their physical forces.

Having surveyed in the most cursory way the prospects for comprehensive development of the individual personality, we begin to understand the magnitude of the liberty communism will establish. Under capitalism the working people dream of freedom from poverty, exploitation, and lawlessness. Socialism has given us this freedom, and now with our own hands we are constructing the society in which freedom will find its highest expression, will be embodied in the flowering of the human personality.

Another element inherent in free development of the human personality is participation by everyone in the management of society, and a high degree of conscious discipline will assure coordination, efficiency, and precision in the function of all organizations managing society's affairs. Connected with this is the question of the moral understanding of freedom. Even now one often meets persons for whom liberty means the opportunity to do as they please, who ignore the established order or the interests of others. But if everyone begins behaving arbitrarily, not liberty but anarchy will reign in society.

No. Liberty in society does not in the least signify freedom from society; personal freedom does not at all mean arbitrariness. True freedom consists in coordinating one's ideas and deeds with those of his collective and with those of our entire society. When personal interest and social interest merge in the consciousness of men, they will have *no other concept of freedom than that of opportunity to act for the good of society*. This understanding of freedom, natural to the conscious builders of communism, will finally triumph in communist society.

Where liberty and equality reign, BROTHERHOOD of all the toilers, of all the peoples, will inevitably prevail.

How beautiful the word "brother" is. When we speak of fraternal relations, we want to emphasize that we mean not just comradely, not simply friendly, but even more beautiful and exalted personal relations.

It would, obviously, be empty and useless to sort out everything neatly and try to draw an exact line between what is comradeship and friendship, on the one hand, and what brotherliness. That is not the point. The fact is that the notion of brotherhood reflects those genuinely humane relations among persons, that deep confidence of man in man, without which communism is inconceivable.

These relations are expressed in a general way by collectivism, the collaboration and mutual assistance among people. In a collective, as you know, people always depend on one another; and the common success not infrequently depends on the actions of each one. The words "You can depend on that man" have long been taken to be the highest praise, just as during the war years there was no stronger expression of confidence than the words "I'll go with that man on reconnaisance."

Collectivism, which arose from the practice of social ownership under the conditions of the transition to communism, will continue to develop, become enriched with new content, and acquire forms heretofore unknown.

One cannot forge ahead towards communism as an individual, in isolation. Communism can only be constructed by united efforts, and those in the front ranks must consider it their primary duty to assist others who lag behind for any reason. This is the idea that our Party never ceases to promote and that finds great sympathy among the Soviet people. Soviet citizens who are progressive and entire collectives act in this way when they render assistance to those falling behind.

All these and others that you yourself can offer are examples of the fact that we need not take guesses as to exactly how communist brotherhood will find expression. It is our precious possession already, and we must guard, spread, and strengthen it in every conceivable way.

The collectivist consciousness instilled into the Soviet people by the Party is vividly reflected in our people's readiness to share its achievements with the toilers of the countries of the world socialist system and with the peoples of Asia, Africa, and Latin America who have entered upon or are now entering upon the path of independent development. Wherever they go, whether as engineers and workers in the Bhilai Combine in India, construction workers at the Aswan Dam in the UAR, roadbuilders in Afghanistan, geologists in Pakistan, or physicians in Ethiopia, the Soviet people carry the torch of collectivism and devote their strength and knowledge to the noble goals of progress and friendship among peoples.

And although we are fervent patriots of our own great fatherland, we shall always remain consistent internationalists. We cannot pave the way to brotherly relations between the individual persons and peoples in our own country and then, stopping for breath with self-satisfaction, ignore the rest of the world and let it fend for itself.

And when socialism and communism shall have won the final victory all over our planet, the most wonderful dreams and longings of the world's peoples will be fulfilled, of which Robert Burns wrote with inspired faith:

> *For a' that and a' that*
> *It's comin' yet for a' that*
> *That man to man the world o'er*
> *Shall brothers be for a' that.*

We no longer predict the advent of this golden age of history now but talk about it with perfect certainty given to us by the Marxist-Leninist science and social practice. Already in the USSR the frontiers between republics have lost their former significance, and when we travel from one end to the other of our limitless country, who gives a thought to counting how many borders he crossed? Gradually, even national distinctions will be erased, and only names will remain as reminders of the past. United into one family of brothers, mankind will reach the peak of its power and realize the most daring plans to conquer nature.

The constructive labor of free and equal fraternal peoples in the conditions of lasting peace, is this not the HAPPINESS *that communism will bring to the peoples of the world?*

It would be difficult, perhaps, to find anywhere on earth two persons who give the same answer to the question of what they understand by happiness. For one the whole joy of life consists in the possibility of devoting himself to his favorite occupation without being distracted by the small problems of everyday existence. A second cannot imagine happiness without being involved in social activity. A third will talk about comfortable living, a chance to eat well and wear beautiful clothes. A fourth will surely mention sports. Many will put love, the joys of marriage and parenthood, first, depending on age and temperament. Any one of these different kinds of happiness, and many more, will become accessible to everyone in full measure. Or rather, all of them taken together.

No one, of course, can issue a coupon guaranteeing happiness. Human destinies take different routes. It seems that no one will ever succeed in banishing such age-old causes of mental anguish and such conflicts as the dissatisfaction of the creative mind or disappointed hope, jealousy, and un-requited affection. In short, there will be plenty of work for writers, those engineers of the human soul. Life will go on producing subjects not only for vaudeville and comedy but also for drama and tragedy. Nor will the sharp-edged weapon of satire ever get rusty: as long as mankind marches forward, it will leave its shortcomings behind it with a laugh.

And it will always march forward. And surely nothing can give people greater happiness than the consciousness that they are part of this movement, that they are in step with their times. Whatever we may concede to future generations, we will not yield to them in what is most important of all—the capacity to enjoy happiness.

Poets have pictured happiness as a bluebird slipping away at the very moment we are ready to grasp it by the wings. We have a firm grip on happiness. It exists in our labor, in the nobility of our goal, and in our urge to struggle for its earliest possible realization. And then new frontiers, new perspectives will again appear.

Now we must part. One can be confident that after you have turned over the last page of this textbook, you will continue without tiring to broaden your political outlook and avidly draw knowledge from books and the rich treasure chest of practical life.

And above all, of course, you will try to apply the knowledge you have acquired in your work. To this our heroic times and the Communist party summon you.